HQ 1064 .U5 L29 1983

Lammers, William W.

Public policy and the aging

Fairleigh Dickinson University Library
Teaneck, New Jersey

D1456832

Public Policy and the Aging

875999

Issues in Public Policy

Series Editor
Dorothy B. James
American University

Public Policy and the Aging

William W. Lammers

Andrus Gerontology Center
University of Southern California

Fairleigh Dickinson
University Library

Teaneck, New Jersey

CQ Press, a division of
Congressional Quarterly Inc.
1414 22nd Street N.W., Washington, D.C. 20037

Cover Photos:
American Association of Retired Persons

Copyright © 1983, Congressional Quarterly Inc.

All rights reserved. No part of this publication may be
reproduced or transmitted in any form or by any means,
electronic or mechanical, including a photocopy, recording,
or any information storage and retrieval system, without
permission in writing from the publisher.

Printed in the United States of America

Library of Congress Cataloging in Publication Data

Lammers, William W.

Public policy and the aging.

Bibliography: p.
Includes index.
1. Aged — Government policy — United States.
I. Title.
HQ1064.U5L29   1983   362.6'0973   82-22138
ISBN 0-87187-246-3

Q
264
.5
29
'83

In Memory of Minnie Hoefer
A Charming and Spirited Centenarian
(1878 - 1981)

FOREWORD

During the protest movements of the 1960s and early 1970s, Americans were bombarded by media images of a "youth-quake," the "now" generation, the "me" generation, and slogans such as "never trust anyone over 30." The years have passed. Quietly, behind the public facade of a culture that seemed composed primarily of jean-clad, long-haired, carefree youths, a demographic revolution was taking place — the aging of America. Today the reality of American life is greater longevity and, after the post-World War II baby boom, a declining birthrate. The age cohort of the 1960s "flower children" is fast becoming "middle-aged." Now well over 30, its members loom as a significant future addition to the already growing rolls of the elderly. Thus, the current aging of American society is only the beginning of a trend that will become an increasing focus of the policy-making process well into the next century.

Important lessons have been learned from the protest movements of two decades ago. The techniques of group organization and influencing the decision-making process, practiced by the anti-Vietnam, environmental, women's rights, and black power activists of the 1960s and 1970s, have been absorbed by the burgeoning "gray power" movement of the 1980s. The growing significance and political impact of the aging coincides, however, with an unfortunate period in the nation's economic life. While the severe rates of inflation of the 1970s or the depression of the early 1980s may not continue, they are reflective of a general decrease in resources that is likely to face Americans in the future. In making determinations about public policy, presidents such as Franklin Delano Roosevelt or Lyndon Baines Johnson did not have to worry about redividing the public pie. They had the luxury of focusing on how to expand it. More recent policy makers and those of the future face the prospect of dividing a shrinking pastry. Consequently, increasing demands by the aged will have to come at the cost of decreasing support for some other groups or interests in our society.

Public Policy and the Aging by William W. Lammers of the Andrus Gerontology Center at the University of Southern California provides valuable insights into this volatile political situation. His book is particularly informative concerning the remarkable diversity of the aging. The great variation in their geographic location, economic and social circumstances, and physical health has important implications for their voting behavior and interest group participation. It also greatly influences how they will be affected by existing programs and possible changes in policy. In his portrayal of five elderly individuals, in his analysis of the changing age structure of the American population, and throughout the book, the author carefully avoids stereotyping the aging or lumping them together as a homogeneous group (an easy and common error for policy analysts, decision makers, and citizens generally).

The major programs especially affecting the aging are extensively analyzed for their development, current status, and the alternatives that are under consideration. The careful assessment of policy areas as complex as Social Security, retirement and pensions, Medicare and Medicaid, long-term health care, social services, and housing demonstrate both the scope of the author's scholarship and the range of aging-related public policies. In all of these areas, the aging face critical difficulties, and existing programs are being scrutinized more closely than ever before to see whether they address their objectives adequately and respond to the changing circumstances of the aging. Lammers' analysis of key policy issues is enriched by a consideration of some of the relevant issues that are emerging such as shifts in federal and state government roles, the tension between means and incomes tests in existing and future programs, the special problems of older women, the hospice movement, safer environments, the aging as consumers, and the consequences of inflation.

Public Policy and the Aging makes a major contribution to our understanding of the extent and complexity of the problems facing the elderly today. The author has effectively met the challenge of integrating this richly faceted material and conveying it in a coherent and readable manner. In so doing, he has greatly enhanced our understanding of the aging, their concerns and problems, and the prospects of developing policy on their behalf.

Dorothy B. James

PREFACE

The growing size of the aging population in the United States and the pressing economic problems of the 1980s make the development of sound public policies for the aging an increasingly difficult challenge. This book is an attempt to clarify, for academic and professional audiences and those with a general interest in aging policies, the political issues and policy alternatives involved in that challenge.

It is my extreme good fortune to have had excellent support in writing this book. My research partner in the study of state politics, David Klingman, who is now teaching at George Washington University, has been a constant source of insight to me in many areas of aging-related policy analysis. Many of my colleagues at the Andrus Gerontology Center have been generous in contributing both their ideas — often from their own recent publications — and their support. I particularly want to thank Sally Coberly, Eileen Crimmins, Neal Cutler, Richard Davis, Thomas Gillaspy (now the demographer for Minnesota), Stuart Greathouse, Stephen McConnell (currently serving as a staff member of the House Select Committee on Aging), David Mangen, Robert Myrtle, Pauline Robinson, Raymond Steinberg, Fernando Torres-Gil, and Judy Treas. James Birren, the executive director of the Andrus Center, deserves a special note of thanks for his efforts in developing the Center's intellectual environment. To my colleagues and others whose works have made this book possible, I cannot begin to express my appreciation.

I also am indebted to the Administration on Aging and the National Institute on Aging, which have contributed to my understanding of major policy issues as a result of my involvement with specific research projects.

Public Policy and the Aging

Marjorie Grace and Joann Slead deserve praise for their ability to create clean copy from my initial drafts. In the review process, Robert B. Hudson at Fordham University was unusually generous with his time and suggestions. The careful assistance provided at Congressional Quarterly by Barbara R. de Boinville in the preparation of the manuscript has been very helpful. Finally, I wish to express my appreciation to my editors, Joanne Daniels and Dorothy James, for their advice and encouragement.

My family has been highly supportive in the face of the inevitable stresses that authorship creates. My daughters Linda and Caroline have been remarkably understanding about Dad's schedule. To my wife Mary I want to express my loving appreciation of her willingness to gracefully shoulder additional responsibilities. My parents Claude and Lorraine deserve thanks for their longstanding encouragement of my scholarly activities and their continuing reminder of the opportunities for community service that exist for Americans of all ages.

The book is dedicated to my wife's grandmother, Minnie Hoefer. Through her remarkable life, she was a marvelous example of the extent to which one can remain "young" regardless of age. In future years, as more people have the privilege of knowing individuals such as Minnie, the myth that aging produces an inevitable decline in the requisites of a good and full life may well disappear from the American scene.

William W. Lammers

CONTENTS

FIGURES AND TABLES

I

THE AGING IN AMERICA

The aging are destined to become a larger and more influential segment of American society. The falling birthrate beginning in the early 1960s, coupled with increases in life expectancy, makes this demographic shift inevitable. The number of older persons with the personal resources and political skills needed to participate in the political process is growing, and elected officials are becoming increasingly sensitive to their voting strength. This suggests the likelihood of greater political influence for the aging. The mixture of policies that will emerge in response to those political and demographic changes will have important implications not only for present and future aged populations but also for the very nature of American society.[1]

The specific directions that future policies will take are less apparent than the growing numbers and greater political influence of older persons. It is easy to find predictions of a system of Social Security benefits gradually collapsing in the face of skyrocketing claims, younger age groups becoming more resentful of the constraints that the aging place on opportunities for housing and jobs, and a society growing stagnant due to a resistance to change on the part of increasingly large older populations in many states and communities. Theories of modernization have depicted the role of the aging in somber terms. For Cowgill and Holmes (1972), the aging in the United States and in other highly industrialized nations increasingly face negative influences, including loss of prestige, reduced opportunity for gainful employment, and declining family contact in a mobile society.

---

[1] The terms "aging," "aged," "elderly," and "older persons" are used interchangeably to refer to persons who are approximately age 65 or older. While we are all "aging" in different ways, the term has been used increasingly in recent years to identify older persons because of its emphasis on the continual process of change among persons of advanced years.

1

Yet hopeful developments are also emerging. The same demographic trends that have increased the aging as a percent of the total population are somewhat belatedly giving them a more important role in a changing labor force. At the same time, some of their personal resources, which make the present and future aging populations increasingly apt to participate politically, also make them more apt to engage in a variety of rewarding personal activities. The segment of the aging population sometimes categorized as the "young-old" (ages 65 to 74) shows a potential not only for reversing the earlier emphasis on a likely disengagement of older persons from society but also for significant assistance in caring for the frail elderly.

Several key questions thus confront those interested in the politics and policies of aging in America. Why has the United States, when compared with other industrial nations, been a distinct laggard in developing income maintenance and health insurance programs? What factors have produced the surge in aging policy commitments since the mid-1960s? Are the emerging aging-based interest groups really effective, and what impact are they likely to have on policy development? What will be the effect of demographic changes on aging policies in the future?

In examining specific policy issues, perhaps the most common question involves the adequacy — and financial burdens — of Social Security. Understandably, younger persons are concerned about the effects on their careers of laws reducing or eliminating mandatory retirement at specified ages for older workers. From both humanitarian and cost effectiveness perspectives, the possible strengthening of social services and home-health care as an alternative to the ever increasing use of nursing homes deserves careful attention. Finally, given the growing importance in recent years of such issues as inflation, housing, and crime, it has become more apparent that new policy issues will demand attention. To begin addressing key questions, it is essential to review major characteristics of the aging population.

DIVERSITY AMONG THE AGING

Despite age similarities, the range of differences within America's older population in such critical areas as health, income, education, and ability and willingness to engage in meaningful activities is at least as great as the overall differences that exist within American society on each of these dimensions. While it is true that the problems of health and income generally become more pronounced in one's senior years, the aging in our society always have had varied life conditions, and those conditions are likely to become increasingly diverse in the 1980s. Rather than existing as an easily definable group with obvious needs, the aging include many subgroups and possess widely differing needs. Thus to focus only on the frail elderly, the impoverished, and those in nursing homes is a serious misperception. Yet to think only of widows in big houses and wealthy couples taking ocean cruises also fails to recognize the range of existing conditions.

The diversity reflected in the nation's older population has contributed to misperceptions not only by younger segments of American society but also by the aging themselves. For example, some readers may assume that the percentage increase in the number of older persons in the U.S. population in the next two decades will surpass the increases of the recent past, that older persons have been retiring at later ages in the past decade, and that a substantial percent of the nation's aging live below the inflation-adjusted (but governmentally defined) poverty line. Yet each of these propositions is false. Proportional increases in the older population will be smaller than in the 1950s and 1960s until the baby boom retires in the next century, the average age of retirement has been going down (at least until about 1980), and major reductions in the proportion of the aging population living in poverty did occur between 1965 and 1980. Major patterns and trends deserve close attention.

Every Ninth American

As of the 1980 census, 25.5 million persons in the United States were age 65 or older, which represents some 11.3 percent of the total population or one-ninth of all Americans. The size of the aging population is roughly equivalent to the number of persons in the state of California. In comparison with other groups in American society, the size of the aging population is also roughly comparable (with some overlap) to the number who are categorized as developmentally disabled and to the number of black Americans.

The seemingly straightforward numbers involved in demographic portraits of the aging require examination from several perspectives to convey an accurate picture of the most likely future developments in aging policy. It is essential to remember in any projection that changes in

3

life expectancy can alter significantly the number of older persons in the population and that both life expectancy and future birthrates will have a major impact on the percent of the aging in the entire population in future years. Furthermore, to understand the policy implications of demographic distributions it is necessary to view them in terms of percentage increases and absolute numbers and in terms of a variety of subcategories.

It is helpful at the outset to place the seeming "graying of America" in a comparative perspective. Historically, the combination of high birthrates and youthful immigration kept the percentage of older persons in America substantially below the percentage of older persons in Western Europe. As of 1900, for example, the comparative figures were United States, 4 percent; United Kingdom, 5 percent; and France, 8 percent. Similarly, as of the 1930s, the U.S. figure was still only 6 percent whereas the figures for the United Kingdom and France were 8 and 10 percent, respectively. Perhaps more surprising to American readers, in the wake of the discussion of the rapid growth in America's aging population, is a more recent comparison. The U.S. figure of 10 percent as of 1970 compares with figures of 13 percent in France, 14 percent in both West Germany and the United Kingdom, and 15 percent in Sweden. While the phenomena of an aging population increasingly in excess of 10 percent is new for the United States, it is definitely not an unprecedented development in other advanced industrial nations (Lammers and Nyomarkay 1980).

The Size of the Aging Population. Table 1-1 presents the numerical and percentage increases in the total aging population in the United States from 1900 to 1980. Population projections for the next four decades also are shown. Policies for the aging, both past and future, need to be considered in light of these figures.

The number of persons age 65 and over has increased by at least one-third in each decade from the 1930s through the 1960s. Significantly, however, while the number of persons being added to the aging category in the next several decades will still be substantial, the percentage increases will be much smaller. Furthermore, the projected net increase in the older population between the years 1990 and 2010 will be relatively small. Largely because of the low birthrate during the depression and World War II, the same number of net additions are

4

Table 1-1   The Total Aging Population in the United States

Year	Number of Persons Age 65 and Over (Thousands)	Percent of Total Population ᵃ	Percent of Increase from Preceding Decade
1900	3,099	4.1	—
1910	3,986	4.3	28.6
1920	4,929	4.7	23.7
1930	6,705	5.4	36.0
1940	9,031	6.8	34.7
1950	12,397	8.2	37.3
1960	16,675	9.2	34.5
1970	20,087	9.8	20.4
1980	25,544	11.3	27.1
Projections:			
1990	29,824	12.2	16.7
2000	31,822	12.2	6.7
2010	34,837	12.7	9.5
2020	45,102	15.5	29.5

ᵃ Projections are from Series II of the *Current Population Reports*, which assumes that women average 2.1 births at the end of the child-bearing years.

SOURCE: U.S. Department of Commerce, Bureau of the Census, *Current Population Reports*, Series P-23, No. 59, "Demographic Aspects of Aging and the Older Population in the United States" (May 1976); Series P-25, No. 704, "Projections on the Population of the United States: 1977 to 2050" (July 1977). The 1980 figures are from the *Statistical Abstract of the United States, 1981.*

projected in the decade between 1980 and 1990 as are likely to occur in the two decades between 1990 and 2010.

In terms of the overall proportion of older persons in American society, it is the retirement of the post-World War II baby boom that stands to substantially alter basic age relationships. Between 2010 and 2020, a net increase of approximately nine million persons is projected — an increase that is as large as the entire aging population in the United States as of 1940. This also may constitute as much as 18 percent of the population. By way of comparison, the percentage of Florida's population age 65 and over reached 17.3 percent as of 1980 (Statistical Abstract 1981, 29). Viewed more directly, the size of the aging population is estimated to be some 45 million persons, which constitutes a population about the size of the present total populations of California and New York combined.

In contemplating these figures, it is important to recognize that they could be altered very easily. Major demographers, such as Easterlin (1976), have projected a sizable increase in the birthrate in the 1980s. According to Easterlin's interesting cyclical theory, individuals who do not experience the crowding and competition of a crowded birth cohort are apt to have larger families than those who do. Whereas the baby boom birth cohort has tended to have a relatively low fertility rate, those born in the period of the "baby bust" beginning in the early 1960s will, in this view, tend to have larger families. Although Easterlin's projections may not incorporate sufficiently the potential impact of changing roles for women in America, his work contains an important reminder that the proportion of older persons in the United States in the next century will be substantially influenced by birthrate developments in the next two decades. Birthrate projections are particularly important in light of the growing concern over the seeming overabundance of older Americans in the coming years. Indeed, indications of an increasing birthrate, which would have been viewed negatively from a limited natural resource perspective a few years ago, today are being hailed as "good news" by some involved in developing public policy for the aging.

The importance of the birthrate in the next years becomes dramatically apparent if one considers the differences in *dependency ratios* that may result. Dependency ratios are based upon the proportion of the nonworking age population to the working age population. Thus, in a hypothetical society of 100 million persons with 20 million below age 18 and 20 million age 65 or above, the dependency ratio would be 2-to-3 (or 40 million to 60 million). In looking at possible future dependency ratios, the average age of death as well as the impact of the birthrate must be considered. Levels of female participation in the labor force and levels of overall unemployment also are important.

Long-range dependency ratio projections have inherent limitations. Nevertheless, they have yielded some striking findings. Comparatively encouraging results emerge from such careful works as the recent assessment by Sheppard and Rix (1977). They conclude that between 1975 and 2010 the working age population will increase by about 38 percent while the dependent population will increase by only 19 percent. This is projected on the basis of a 50 percent increase in the age of the 65

6

and over population but only by a 8 percent increase in the younger segment of the population. As a result, the dependency ratio is projected to decrease until about 2010 and then to increase again, but not steadily or at a particularly rapid rate.

Today there is growing concern over "the graying of America." But is this concern justified? The demographic relationships reviewed thus far might seem to indicate it is not. We now have smaller percentages of older persons than most European countries (some of which have accommodated those age distributions surprisingly well), the absolute increases in the future are predicted to be slowing down, and, at least in terms of dependency ratios, the situation even in the next century would not seem to be particularly difficult. However, two additional factors are emerging that complicate the picture.

The "Aging" of the Aging Population. First, the proportion of the population 65 and over that is also 75 or more years of age is increasing. This somber aspect of the demographic assessment is already well established (General Accounting Office 1982, 4-5). The composition of the aging population is itself growing older as a result of two factors: the present older population has been living longer and the number of newcomers to the age 65 and over category has not experienced a comparable increase. Whereas those age 75 and over comprised 29 percent of all the individuals age 65 and over in 1930 (and 31 percent in 1950), they comprised 37 percent by 1979. At the same time, the population group age 85 and over grew more rapidly than any other group in the 1970s (Leaf 1982, 486).

By the turn of the century, those 75 and over may comprise 45 percent of the aging population — a population in which a full 25 percent is at least 80 years of age. This segment of the aging population is disproportionately composed of women. In 1978, for example, there were 178 women for every 100 men in the population 75 and over, and in the 85 and over category the ratio was a highly disproportionate 224 to 100. The related categories of individuals of advanced age and of elderly women have major policy implications, since needs for income maintenance and health care go up sharply for individuals older than 75 and for persons living alone (which disproportionately includes elderly widows).

Increases in Life Expectancy. Second, the fairly steady increases in the life expectancy of the aging will increase more rapidly in the next

7

decades. In terms of life expectancy at birth, the U.S. figure as of 1977 was 73.2 years, with a major sex difference of 76.5 to 68.7 between women and men. Since changes in these figures primarily have reflected sharp reductions in infant mortality in recent decades, the more relevant changes are in the life expectancy of those who reach age 65 at different points in time. The figures for years of remaining life expectancy at ¼ge 65 have been increasing as follows: 1959, 14.4; 1970, 15.2; and 1977, 16.3. In other words, the person who reached age 65 in 1980 also could expect to live past his or her eightieth birthday. While the figure of a one-year increase per decade may not seem to be very large, it constitutes about a 7 percent increase in the life expectancy of the aging population — an increase in expectancy that comes at the end of the life span and thus at a time in which the need for supportive public policies is apt to be the greatest.

An increasingly substantial body of literature — presented in sources such as Rosenfeld (1976), Sheppard and Rix (1977), Fries (1980), and Crimmins (1981) — points to the likelihood of future mortality changes that significantly, and possibly even radically, expand the average length of human life. The potential forces for change are numerous. In terms of man's environment, the nature of the workplace has reduced the number of individuals who are physically worn out by their fifties and sixties. Medical advances have reduced the number of deaths from cardiovascular illnesses as well as from a variety of other illnesses affecting individuals of all ages. The emphasis today on preventive medicine and on personal health care and physical fitness will affect the aging population in the future. Since cancer has become an increasingly common cause of death among the aging, any significant advances in cancer research will have a substantial effect on the average age of death in the United States. On the basis of an extensive review of changes in the impact of major diseases on mortality between 1940 and 1977, Crimmins (1981, 251) concludes:

> This is the first time in history that mortality declines have been dominated by decreases in diseases of old age or degenerative diseases. Because this is so, we may be beginning a new era of mortality decline, which, if it continues, will lead to large increases in life expectancy at older ages.

Dramatic breakthroughs are also a possibility in other areas. During the past decade, the greater attention given to the aging process itself

8

caused an increasing number of researchers to predict substantial improvement in our ability to control aspects of the aging process and thus to stem the physical decline traditionally associated with advanced age. Recent breakthroughs in medical knowledge of DNA (which has a major impact on the chemistry of the aging process) is beginning to suggest the possibility of direct manipulation of the aging process (Strehler 1974; Sheppard and Rix 1977). In addition, organ transplants may become more common. In the not too distant future it may be possible to prevent deaths now caused by deficiencies in certain organs of the body.

A 1980 analysis by Fries uses the concept of a normal life span to reach a somewhat different conclusion. In an interpretation paralleling that of Crimmins, Fries sees fewer people suffering and dying from chronic diseases in future years. He also foresees, however, a larger number of individuals living a "normal" life span of about 85 years. From a variety of perspectives, then, there is a basis for concluding that the average age of death in the United States will continue to increase and possibly at a rate greater than in the recent past. If this is the case, the demographic projections based upon modest increases in the average age of death clearly will be too low, and the dependency ratios in the future will be nudged toward higher levels than has been anticipated.

It is important to conclude this consideration of life expectancies by underscoring the underlying health issue. There are a variety of indications that our concept of what constitutes normal deterioration will be modified in the future. There may be significance beyond the sports pages, for example, in the achievements of baseball pitchers now well into their forties or in an Olympic caliber discus thrower able to improve on his performance at age 45. As Fries suggests, individuals at seemingly advanced ages may be able to enjoy good health, and they also may be able to perform physical tasks at ages now considered quite improbable. Yet conversely, the prospect of individuals being kept alive who possess limited physical and mental capacities is sobering. Future successes in health research and changes in health care, along with future birthrates, can dramatically affect not only the size of the aging population in the years ahead but the quality of life for millions of older persons.

Select Characteristics

The financial status, ethnic group membership, education level, geographic distribution, and housing patterns of the 25 million older persons in the United States today differ widely. Each of these character-istics of the aging population will be discussed in turn.

Financial Status. Historically, the aging in the United States have found themselves in difficult financial circumstances. Recent historical research by Fischer (1978) has underscored the extent to which major segments of the aging population have existed with meager finances since the first years of the nation's history. The number of persons existing in destitute conditions, however, appears to have increased in the decades since the Civil War. The use of families to help support the aging began to decline. Personal savings were virtually nonexistent, and yet there was little in the way of public assistance.

The first primary sources of public assistance for the aging came with the growth of pensions for Civil War veterans and the development of lo-cal government facilities giving minimal support to the destitute. Surpris-ingly, the pension system worked fairly well, while the local government relief systems invariably were limited and poorly operated. By 1900, two-thirds of the older population were receiving Civil War pensions, and at points in the late 1800s these pensions comprised as much as 40 percent of the federal budget (Fischer 1978, 70). The Confederate states also operated separate systems for their veterans and widows — a policy that has provided modest assistance to a few individuals for many decades.

As the proportion of the aging population that was eligible for Civil War pensions began to decline after the turn of the century, more of the elderly who did not have other means of support were thrust upon local government facilities. The labels used for those institutions, such as "poor houses" and "poor farms," suggest the reluctance with which this nig-gardly assistance was provided. According to Stevens and Stevens (1974, 5), "Such assistance was typically given grudgingly by the towns and counties, and there continued to be more than vestiges of the attitude that pauperism was a form of social disease and degeneracy: the poor were a population which floats between the alms houses, the jail, and the slums."

The impact of the depression also had a negative impact on income sources for the aging. Social Security was established in 1935, but the first payments from the contribution-based system were not made until 1940, and the early benefits, while often extremely helpful, were still very modest. At the same time, bank failings in the 1930s had an extremely harsh impact on an older population that had made, in many instances, at least some effort to save for the needs to be encountered in old age. One of the consequences of the enactment of Social Security, with its benefit eligibility set at age 65, was that more and more employers began to require their employees to retire at that age. Finally, the population movements of American society, particularly to the cities but also between regions, meant that an increasingly small percentage of the aging were able to live in three generation families.

Given the problems of income support for the aging in the early and middle decades of this century, it is perhaps not surprising that as of 1959 some 35 percent of the aging fell under the governmentally defined poverty level in comparison with 22 percent for the entire population.[2] Even more dismal were the figures of 49 percent in poverty for aged persons living in families headed by a female head of household, and 65 percent in poverty among nonwhite persons living in families with a female head (Schulz 1980, chapter 2).

Measured against the baseline of the 1950s, the financial status of the aging has improved greatly in recent years. As of 1977, the number of older persons in the inflation-adjusted poverty category stood at 14 percent — only slightly above the 12 percent figure for the entire population. Considerable progress also was recorded in 1977 in the category of female-headed households, with a drop of 25 percentage points and a resulting 24 percent level. The figure for female nonwhite aging households also had declined, although it still stood at a disturbing 47 percent. The figures were not as encouraging, however, for the number of older persons in the "near poor" category.

Individual and public efforts of the past few years have pulled a substantial number of persons above the poverty line. Yet the increase to 15.1 percent below the poverty level income for 1979 ($4,394 for a nonfarm couple) left some 3.5 million persons with very low incomes (Statistical Abstract 1981, 445). There also tends to be a concentration of persons whose income level is not far above that rather minimally defined level. As of 1977, for example, most elderly persons with individual incomes received less than $6,000 per year, and median

---

[2] The poverty level measure was developed in the early 1960s on the basis of an assessment of the amount of money needed annually to purchase food for a minimum adequate diet. That figure is multiplied by three to determine the poverty income level, with separate indexes for different family sizes and farm and nonfarm residents. According to many analyses, the resulting income levels are substantially below that of an appropriate minimum standard (Schulz 1980, 34-42). The poverty level for a two-person nonfarm family headed by an individual age 65 or over was $1,761 annually in 1959, $4,394 in 1979.

incomes for families with an aging head of household were at a level almost $7,000 less than the figure of $16,000 being reported for all families in the United States (Schulz 1980, 16). Despite the existence of such advantages (when compared with other age levels) as greater assistance with health costs through Medicare, the tax free status of Social Security benefits, and the absence of work-related expenses, the figures on individual and family income reveal continuing problems surrounding the adequacy of income for substantial segments of the aging population.

Various analyses of the financial assets of the aging based on Social Security Administration surveys have repeatedly shown an overall pattern of modest assets for the aging. These figures will be increasing in the face of increases in housing values. Moreover, some real dollar increase in the assets of the aging in the next decades is likely due to the better earning patterns that those who are retiring in the future will have enjoyed. Individuals with earning patterns that reflect the rapid economic growth of the 1960s and exclude the 1930s are apt to have somewhat greater economic assets than those who retired in earlier years. It is also important to note that a small percentage of the aging are extremely wealthy. Nonetheless, when one looks at the present asset levels of the overall aging population, the results are not encouraging for those who would like to see major additional self-financing of personal income needs on behalf of the aging.

In a recent review of the Social Security Administration's survey data, Friedman and Sjogren (1981, 130) summarize the asset issue as follows:

> One way of illustrating how little assets most older Americans have is to translate the value of these assets into annuity income. As noted, married men had more assets than other groups: their median amount of assets was approximately $20,000. If a man age 66 (whose wife's age is 64) converted all his assets into a lifetime income-producing annuity contract, then the annual income from this annuity would be only $1,900 (assuming that the amount is reduced by one-third after one spouse dies). If the husband's age is 70 and the wife's age is 68, the annual income would be approximately $2,100. If only assets other than equity in a home are converted into an annuity contract, the annual income would be only about one-third of these amounts.

Clearly, the overall financial status of the aging has improved in recent years. Nonetheless, the number of persons with incomes only slightly above the poverty line, coupled with the devastating impact of inflation and medical costs on the financial well-being of the aging, promises continuing tension over income maintenance policies.

Ethnic Group Membership. Many of the aging today are foreign born as a consequence of the large migration to the United States from Europe in the years between the turn of the century and World War I. As a result of that migration, the aging population today includes pockets of individuals, from a variety of European countries, who are now located in such seemingly unlikely places as small towns in Iowa and Texas as well as in sections of the older industrial cities.

The proportion of blacks among the aging is distinctly smaller than in the population as a whole — an unfortunate consequence of a significantly lower life expectancy. Thus as of 1980, the percent of those age 65 and over among blacks was approximately 7.6 percent as compared with a figure of 11.7 percent who were age 65 and over in the rest of the population. It is useful to note, in this regard, that the likely expansion in the life expectancy of the black population may be another factor contributing to the growing size of the older population in future years. Despite their proportionately smaller size, blacks, along with Hispanics and native Americans, are apt to be disproportionately in need of significant income and health support.

Education Level. The aging are now in a position of rapid change in terms of education attainment. Education through the high school level was uncommon in the United States until after World War I. As a consequence, in 1970 the aging had completed only 8.7 median years of school, compared with 12 years for the general population (Deming and Cutler 1983, 64-65). Because of the rapid expansion in schooling opportunities that began in the 1920s and continued with a rush after World War II, each new wave of older persons in the next years will have had the advantage of longer opportunities for formal education than was the case for those who preceded them into the ranks of the aging. Since those with less education also have tended in each birth cohort to have shorter life expectancies, the ranks of the aging will increasingly reflect substantial amounts of educational experience.

Geographic Distribution. In recent years the aging population has been concentrated in a few states. The state by state distribution in the early decades of this century, however, showed both substantial uniformity and low concentrations of older persons (Wiseman 1979, 29). Only the New England states reported a somewhat higher concentration, as did, to a lesser extent, eastern, midwestern, and Pacific states. It is primarily since World War II that the major shifts in levels of concentration have occurred. Thus as of the late 1970s, almost 25 percent of the aging population was located in three states: New York, California, and Florida. Eight states (these three plus Pennsylvania, Illinois, Ohio, Michigan, and Texas) accounted for more than 10 million, or approximately 45 percent, of the aging population.

Table 1-2 on pages 16 and 17 presents, by state, the U.S. population age 65 and over in 1980. It also shows what percentage of each state's total population this figure represents. The concentrations of aging populations among the states displayed in the table have been produced by two distinct migratory patterns. The most publically noted has been the migration of older persons to the Sun Belt. Not only Florida but states such as Arkansas, Texas, and New Mexico have attracted droves of retired persons in recent years. Condominium complexes in Florida, retirement communities in the Southwest, and, more recently, the development of mobile trailer homes in a variety of rural settings have all been characterized by their picnics, bridge clubs, and social networks among individuals who trace common roots (and often even common friendships) to specific communities in the older industrial areas of the East and Midwest.

Concentrations of older persons in some states also have occurred as a result of migration — but a migration of the young, not the old. The inclusion of Iowa, Missouri, Nebraska, South Dakota, Kansas, and Oklahoma among the 10 states with the largest concentrations of older persons in their populations is an important testament to the migration by younger persons, generally in search of greater job opportunities. As a result, some of the rural counties in states such as Iowa and Missouri are among the areas that have had particularly large concentrations of older persons in recent years.

The types of communities in which the elderly are increasingly located include, most predominantly, the older sections of the nation's central cities. There is also a disproportionate concentration in rural nonfarm environments. Moreover, a flight from central cities to smaller communities within one's home state is becoming more common (Minnesota Planning Agency 1980). Retired residents of cities such as Minneapolis, Chicago, and Detroit, for example, are finding that within-state moves can reduce their costs of living while minimizing distances from family and friends. It is also important to emphasize that some of the older suburbs of the nation are going through a natural aging process in their populations. The suburbs are a fast-growing but still more lightly concentrated area for the aging than the central cities. With the inevitable passage of time, some of the nation's World War II veterans, who helped pioneer the move to suburbia, are now beginning to live in communities with higher concentrations of senior citizens.

Housing Patterns. What are the living arrangements of the aging? For a substantial majority the answer is: in a single family dwelling, and often with one's spouse. As of the 1970 census, 72 percent of the aging lived in owned homes compared with 63 percent for the general population. Not surprisingly, these homes tended to be older homes, with nearly half of the older residents having lived in the same house for at least 20 years. Some 48 percent of the elderly in 1970 lived with their husbands or wives. An additional 20 percent were living with other relatives; about half of the elderly in this category were in households headed by their children.

Nonetheless, the category of older persons living alone has grown substantially. In 1970, some 26 percent were living alone compared with 18 percent in 1953 (Dunlop 1979, 34). As of 1980, there were additional indications that increasing numbers of the aging were tending to live alone. The number of one-person households increased in actual numbers and as a percent of the aging population for both renters and home-owners. At the same time, the percent of older renters living with at least one other person declined slightly (U.S. Census, Annual Housing Survey 1980, 6). In contrast to the practice of taking in borders, which was common early in this century among individual homeowners, fewer than 1 percent of the elderly share a house or apartment with nonrelatives.

In recent years, approximately 5 percent of the aging population or a total of well over one million persons have lived in nursing homes. About one person in every 200 was an occupant of a nursing home as of 1980, as the total for all age groups reached some 1.3 million persons (Statistical Abstract 1981, 115). The use rates are substantially higher for women than for men, for whites than for nonwhites, and for those over 75 years of age (Dunlop 1979, 15). According to the Master Survey of Health Facilities (1976) conducted by the National Center for Health Statistics, the average nursing home resident was 81 years of age. Increases in the

Table 1-2   U.S. Population Age 65 and Over, 1980

State	Total (Thousands)	Age 65 and Over (Thousands)	Age 65 and Over as a Percent of State Total
Florida	9,740	1,685	17.3
Arkansas	2,286	312	13.6
Rhode Island	947	127	13.4
Iowa	2,913	387	13.3
Missouri	4,917	648	13.2
South Dakota	690	91	13.2
Nebraska	1,570	206	13.1
Kansas	2,363	306	12.9
Pennsylvania	11,867	1,531	12.9
Massachusetts	5,737	727	12.7
Maine	1,125	141	12.5
Oklahoma	3,025	376	12.4
New York	17,557	2,161	12.3
North Dakota	653	80	12.3
West Virginia	1,950	238	12.2
Wisconsin	4,705	564	12.0
Minnesota	4,077	480	11.8
Connecticut	3,108	365	11.7
New Jersey	7,364	860	11.7
Mississippi	2,521	289	11.5
Oregon	2,633	303	11.5
Vermont	511	58	11.4
Alabama	3,890	440	11.3
Arizona	2,718	307	11.3
Tennessee	4,591	518	11.3
Kentucky	3,661	410	11.2
New Hampshire	921	103	11.2

Table 1-2 (Cont.)

State	Total (Thousands)	Age 65 and Over (Thousands)	Age 65 and Over as a Percent of State Total
Illinois	11,418	1,261	11.0
Montana	787	85	10.8
Ohio	10,797	1,169	10.8
Indiana	5,490	585	10.7
Washington	4,130	431	10.4
California	23,669	2,415	10.2
North Carolina	5,874	602	10.2
Idaho	944	94	10.0
Delaware	595	59	9.9
Michigan	9,258	912	9.9
Louisiana	4,204	404	9.6
Texas	14,228	1,371	9.6
Georgia	5,464	517	9.5
Maryland	4,216	396	9.4
Virginia	5,346	505	9.4
South Carolina	3,119	287	9.2
New Mexico	1,300	116	8.9
Colorado	2,889	247	8.5
Nevada	799	66	8.3
Hawaii	965	76	7.9
Wyoming	471	37	7.9
Utah	1,461	109	7.5
Alaska	400	12	3.0

SOURCE: U.S. Department of Health and Human Services, Office of Human Development Services, *The Elderly Population: Estimates by County, 1980.*

number of the aging who are 80 years of age or older and who live alone are projected. Because both these categories affect nursing home admittance, these projections clearly pose a major challenge to policymakers in the field of aging.

Summary

In reviewing the present and prospective demographic aspects of the aging population, six key points stand out:

(1) The growth in numbers will continue for the next two decades but the percentage increase will be lower than in recent decades.

(2) The major increase will come as the "baby boom" begins to retire in the second decade of the next century.

(3) The number of persons in the above 80 category will increase in the next 20 years. These persons will comprise an increasingly large proportion of all persons age 65 and over.

(4) The economic well-being of the aging has improved tremendously in recent years, but a substantial number of elderly persons still are not far above the poverty level.

(5) The aging are becoming increasingly concentrated in a few states.

(6) About 5 percent of the aging population, some 1.3 million persons, presently reside in nursing homes.

FIVE PORTRAITS

The diversity of the aging also can be seen through a consideration of specific life situations. Interpretations of life at advanced ages can be found in autobiographies and the accounts of ordinary citizens in particular situations. (A useful collection of these materials has been compiled by Lyell, 1980.) The following sketches seek to dramatize the life situations that specific individuals face and the policy questions that their conditions present.

John MacDonald

John MacDonald has always been glad that he decided to enter accounting as a career. When he looks back on his life, he is content. He enjoyed many friendships, financial security, and the pleasures of seeing his family raised with few problems. Although life seemed to pass too quickly, it was a life full of success and a sense of personal growth. Now, at age 63, he is relieved that he doesn't have to retire in two years —

thanks to the federal legislation passed in 1978 that abolished mandatory retirement at 65.

John does have fears, however, about the future. Although he has golfed a bit, and his wife keeps talking about new travel activities, he simply can't imagine what life will be like once he can no longer go to the office. His job has been virtually his whole life, and it is hard for him to contemplate the absence of office friendships and the loss of the satisfaction that comes from successfully resolving difficult problems at work. His wife has encouraged him to enroll in a retirement planning program his company started, but he has resisted because it would force him to confront the ultimate necessity of planning for retirement.

In recent years John also has become increasingly concerned about the impact of inflation on his plans for financial security in retirement. Because his company's pension plan is not indexed, he can count on only the Social Security component of his future income to keep pace with inflation. In addition, the investments in the stock market that he made so carefully have not been keeping pace with inflation, which has been a blow to both his financial planning and his pride in his ability to handle his financial affairs. As John meets some of his friends at church who have retired in recent years, he is saddened by the financial problems some of them are having and their too-frequent loss of enthusiasm for future activities in life. For John MacDonald, life now involves increasingly restless nights and the unhappy realization that his worries not only have added inches to his waistline but also have made him periodically irritable with his wife and friends. The uncertainty of life in retirement makes John MacDonald more anxious with each passing day.

Nancy Golden

The second of our aging Americans, Nancy Golden, is a widow, age 73, living in a pleasant home in an older section of Philadelphia. Nancy and her husband raised their family in that city, and she is glad that one of her married sons still lives in the same metropolitan area. She also feels extremely fortunate that her health has remained fairly satisfactory despite sporadic problems with arthritis. Yet in the four years since her husband's death she has had to struggle with loneliness, and she has begun to view the future with increasing concern. Her husband's pension does not seem to go as far as it once did, and her Social Security benefits as a widow are quite limited.

The most immediate issue for Nancy involves the question of whether or not she should sell the family home. The house with its four bedrooms is clearly too big, and upkeep and energy costs have become a big problem. She senses philosophically, too, that it would be nice for a younger family to be able to enjoy a home of that size. Yet where should she move? Leaving town would mean giving up a close circle of old friends as well as some of her cherished family contacts. Furthermore, in an age of inflation, selling the family home to move to an apartment would eliminate her most familiar hedge against inflation.

Nancy realizes that her health will inevitably begin to deteriorate. As she thinks about the future, this is her overriding concern. Can she realistically envision moving in with either of her sons, especially since her daughters-in-law both seem to be so busy in their efforts to combine working careers and child-raising responsibilities? Most of all, she wonders if she will find herself in a few years cooped up in one of the nursing homes she continues to visit as part of her service club's volunteer program. Those visits, she notices, have become emotionally more difficult for her each year. Visiting used to give her good feelings and re- mind her how fortunate she had been in life. But now, as her own future becomes more uncertain, she looks at the frail persons she visits with growing anxiety and asks, "What will my future hold?"

Sam and Gloria Paulucci

The problems associated with aging are more immediate for Sam and Gloria Paulucci. Twelve years ago, when Sam was forced to retire early because of a retrenchment program at the General Battery Corporation in Cleveland, Ohio, they decided to move from their small home in that city. Although Sam was then only two years from the typical retirement age of 62 in his industry, he felt that his uncertain health made it unwise for him to try to find other work. The Pauluccis are now part of the large retirement population in Florida. Using the equity from their Cleveland home and most of their small savings, they purchased a modest house in a retirement community near St. Petersburg.

At their present ages of 72 and 69, Sam and Gloria are in trouble. Be- cause he worked for several different companies, Sam is without any pension benefits despite the contributions he had been making to a variety of plans in different companies. It was small comfort to Sam to learn at a recent lodge meeting that legislation passed in 1974 had reduced that inequity for present workers in his situation. The most immediate problem, however, is Gloria's rapidly deteriorating health. A hip she broke last year healed improperly, and now she has more and more difficulty walking. She also has a kidney ailment. Sam has been having increased difficulty caring for Gloria, and yet they both realize that if she enters a nursing home, his Social Security payments will drop, making it impossible for them to maintain their home. Because both their children have had economic problems in recent years, they are reluctant to approach them for help. But where else can they turn?

Karen Watson

Karen Watson always has struggled to make ends meet. After her marriage broke up, she faced the difficult task of raising four youngsters on her salary as a secretary. Although the children are now raised, health problems have forced her to stop working at age 63. She looks with envy at some of her friends who were able to buy even small homes, since she has no assets other than a few personal possessions, and her only income is from Social Security. She would like to move because of burglaries and purse snatchings in her neighborhood, but she knows that a more expensive apartment is out of the question. Few apartments that she could afford are for rent in her city, and she fears that it is only a matter of time before her present apartment is converted to a condominium.

The biggest immediate worry for Karen also involves health problems — in particular health costs. Because her Social Security benefits place her above her state's eligibility level for health assistance on the basis of need, she finds that she must rely exclusively on her Medicare benefits. In the last several years, these benefits have not been enough to cover her actual medical costs. She is particularly resentful because she knows that if she had worked less regularly in her lifetime, she would have been eligible for a pension based upon need. Then she would have received more substantial assistance with her health costs.

There are also pleasures in Karen's life. Her children bring the grandchildren for evening visits, which she loves, and she has taken pleasure in her regular church attendance. Yet since she has no car, the increasing costliness and inadequacy of public transportation makes those activities more difficult. Idly, Karen wonders what it would be like to have more money.

Louise Arnold

Louise Arnold has been in Oakwood Hills Convalescent Home for four years. Now 87 years old, she finds that her present existence strains the basic affirmation of life which has always sustained her through the years. Some days it is hard for her to look on the bright side of things. Still, her life is not without its rewards. She treasures her memories of family, friends, and community activities, and she is proud of what she was able to see and learn about the world despite the limitations of a sixth grade education. The nursing home staff appreciates the knitting that she does for them, and it helps her keep busy and maintain a sense of purpose in life. She knows that Oakwood Hills is a clean and well-kept nursing home and that the staff tries to provide special programs, and for this she is thankful.

Nursing home life has nonetheless been difficult for Louise. Although her children and grandchildren write fairly often, most of them are located too far away to visit. Almost all of her friends have passed away or are too frail to be able to visit. The hours seem to pass so slowly now. Television helps on occasion, but it is getting more difficult to hear even with the special amplifier. She also gets depressed and bored with the people around her. So many of them seem to have nothing to say, and there are so few opportunities for real friendships. Although she knows that her family really could not have cared for her at home, she can't help periodic feelings of resentment when she reflects on that awful day almost four years ago when they brought her to Oakwood Hills. Those thoughts quickly fade on this day, however. Her son is going to be able to come for a game of double solitaire in the evening. She often wonders if people realize the difference even a few minutes of conversation and the feel of a caring hand can make for the residents at Oakwood Hills.

Policy Implications

Each of these five portraits raises important issues regarding public policy and the aging. Despite the widely differing conditions of the respective individuals, each of them could be aided by changes in our existing policies for the aging. For John MacDonald, the answer to his fear of retirement might be found in a job-sharing plan in which he would continue to work, but only on the peak days of each month. Such a plan would help smooth out his company's workload and help to relieve his own financial pressures. A job-sharing plan would allow John and his wife to plan interesting activities together without the often tedious retirement routine of suddenly having only shared activities to engage in and talk about. One suspects, too, that if John's company had started a retirement planning program earlier, he just might have been able to develop more interests outside of work and to be less apprehensive about the future stages of his life. Similarly, if John's company had followed the example of a few leaders in retirement planning and systematically organized and supported former employees in finding interesting volunteer jobs in their community, John might contemplate life after retirement with expectancy rather than dread.

In the case of Nancy Golden, a number of emerging public policies could be helpful. If a wider range of alternative housing options was available, then she might be more apt to sell the family home. Alternatively, the use in her case of a reverse annual mortgage would provide additional annual income and lessen her fears about inflation. In the long run, the question of possible residence with one of her sons raises questions of policy incentives. In other words, would it make more sense for one of her daughters-in-law to reduce her outside work commitment in exchange for public compensation (perhaps in the form of tax deductions) for the care being rendered? Alternatively, will there be a program in her community that seeks to help individuals in her situation pair up for joint living arrangements to reduce housing costs and alleviate some of the sense of loneliness? Finally, as Nancy grows older, will there be such services as visiting nurses to forestall the need for admission to a nursing home?

The Pauluccis present a classic case of the serious problem facing married couples on a limited income when one partner requires institutional care. Besides dramatizing the inadequacy of current benefit levels for persons in their situation, the Paulucci case points up the need for supportive services if one spouse is going to be able to give substantial care to the other. The Pauluccis also are an important reminder of the unresolved issues surrounding the movement to reform private pension plans.

Policies exist in some states that would greatly improve Karen Watson's situation. In the more progressive states, eligibility for medical assistance on the basis of need is calculated to allow those with incomes above the maximum eligibility levels to deduct their initial medical expenses in calculating their eligibility for additional medical assistance.

Yet with the curtailment of Medicaid eligibility that began in 1981 along with cuts in federal spending, the chances that she would reside in a state with the broader eligibility requirements have decreased. Karen's situation is also a reminder that a variety of policy issues, from crime to public transportation systems, often have a very strong impact on the aging. Karen's case indeed stands as one of many in which it is most inappropriate to take a narrow definition of policies that affect the elderly.

The Louise Arnold case represents both a success story and a sad reminder that so much more could be done for those who require full nursing home care. Oakwood Hills is obviously one of the better homes, reflecting the very real improvement in the typical nursing home in the last few years. Yet her daily life could be made more rewarding. Better segregation of residents in terms of relative levels of alertness might make it easier for her to make friends, and an adjacent day-care center might provide opportunities for enjoyable contact with those in other age groups. Beyond the question of specific public policy choices lies the critical, but difficult to control, question of family and community contact for those who reside in nursing homes. Life could be better for Louise — as well as for the many nursing home residents who are in far worse situations than hers.

The challenge of public policy and the aging in the United States thus touches many policy areas and individuals with many different needs. A variety of policy ideas on the horizon today would significantly alter the lives of each of the individuals we have discussed, from John MacDonald and his fear of retirement to Louise Arnold and her necessary residence in Oakwood Hills. To address those issues, it is essential to consider both the political process that has produced our existing policies for the aging and the range of specific policy ideas that has emerged in recent years.

II

POLICY DEVELOPMENT

After a very slow start, the level of policy development for the aging has grown dramatically in recent years. Not until 1940 were regular Social Security benefits awarded under the Social Security Act of 1935.[1] The first recipient, a retired law clerk by the name of Ida Fuller, received a monthly check for the modest sum of $22. As of the late 1950s, the United States — still without a health program covering its older population — was a distinct laggard in aging policy development when compared with other nations. Then, after two decades of expansion beginning in the 1960s, spending for the aging dramatically increased. As of 1982, that spending level was substantially beyond $200 billion and approaching 30 percent of all federal spending according to some observers (Samuelson 1982). The nation had indeed come a long way since the first Social Security check was issued in 1940.

The development of aging policy in the United States is examined in this chapter in three sections. First, alternative sources of policy development are discussed. Second, with the aid of that basic developmental framework, the early policy responses in the United States in the 1930s, 1940s, and 1950s are reviewed. Third, an overview of the nation's expanding commitment to the aging in the last two decades and in the early 1980s is presented as an introduction to the policy areas considered in subsequent chapters.

What forces shape public policy for the aging? This question preoccupies interest group members and their lobbyists, whose job it is to

---

[1]References in the book to Social Security benefits pertain to the major contributory-based benefits paid to older persons and those going to survivors. Social Security benefits on the basis of trust fund designations will be referred to as Old Age and Survivors Insurance (OASI). Disability payments are considered separately as are the benefits paid on the basis of economic need through the Old Age Assistance program (OAA) and its successor, the Supplemental Security Income program (SSI).

determine the strategies that will be effective with members of Congress or state legislators. Policy planners also must consider a variety of related questions. For example, is the growing number of elderly persons likely to increase the demand for nursing home facilities? Both older persons and those looking toward their own old age must make personal decisions on the basis of what is likely to happen in aging policy in the years ahead. For most Americans this involves in particular an assessment of future levels of Social Security benefits and their impact on personal financial planning.

SOURCES OF POLICY DEVELOPMENT:
A DEVELOPMENTAL FRAMEWORK

Attentativeness to the sources of policy development can help to achieve several related objectives. First, a developmental framework provides a basis for examining specific policies without ignoring major factors that may have contributed to their development. Second, a developmental framework provides a basis for tentative forecasting of issues and potential policy responses. Third, it helps reveal how political influences are most likely to affect policy development.

Figure 2-1 outlines the major factors that need to be considered in a developmental framework. This model is similar to those presented and discussed in Hofferbert (1974) and Dye and Gray (1980). In the field of aging policy, attention also needs to be given to private sector programs and the characteristics of the older population. The following discussion briefly identifies the sources of policy development that have guided the case study analyses in this book.

Systemic Factors

The systemic factors influencing policy development for the aging include not only the characteristics of the aging population itself but also general levels of socio-economic development, societal attitudes, and private sector activities.

Socio-economic Characteristics. In terms of general levels of socio-economic development, the related factors of *urbanization* and *personal income levels* have been emphasized most often, not only for aging-related studies but for most policy analysis studies (Hofferbert 1974). With urban populations growing, basic changes have been occurring in the conditions of the aging population in the United States. The number of elderly persons who rely upon families for support has declined, and more older persons are living alone in cities. Both changes are having important policy impacts. Greater urbanization also is apt to produce greater bureacratization of social roles. For example, formal nursing home visitation programs may develop in the place of fewer spontaneous visits by church groups or neighbors.

As personal income levels increase, public sector activity is apt to expand. There will be more revenue to be taxed for new programs, and the greater complexity of life in wealthier (and generally more urban) areas will increase the need for public sector programs. On a personal level, changes in income, either upward or downward, also may be associated with increased political activity. For example, a downward shift in social status often is cited to explain the rise in the 1930s of the Townsend Clubs for the elderly, a phenomenon discussed later in this

Figure 2-1 Policy Formation and the Aging

Systemic Factors	Political Participants and Roles	Policy Characteristics	Policy Outcomes
Socio-economic Characteristics	**Participants**	Cost	Social Security
Income Levels	Voters	Impact	Retirements Laws
Urbanization	Interest Groups	Visibility	Pension Regulation
Economic Conditions	Executives		
	Bureaucracies		Medicare and
The Aging Population	Legislatures		Medicaid
Size and Composition			Older Americans
Income Levels	**Roles**		Act
Living Arrangements	Issue Raising		Social Service and
Health Status	Policy Design		Home Care
	Support Building		Programs
Societal Attitudes	Bargaining		
Views of Aging	Implementation		Housing Assistance
Views of the Public			
Sector			Consumer
			Protection
Private Sector Effort			Other Aging-
Pensions			Related
Retirement Policies			Policies
Health Insurance			
Charitable Programs			

chapter. Conversely, a substantial increase in income may cause a change in expectations and a desire for further increases, much like the thirst for modernization in some developing nations.

Economic conditions are also potential sources of policy change. Levels of economic growth, unemployment, or inflation can affect the development of policies. For example, the responsiveness of state legislatures to social service programs for the aging often is influenced by economic activity, particularly as it affects tax yields (Lammers and Klingman 1982). Whether a state's budget is tight or flexible will help determine what policies it implements. A climate of confidence in economic growth and a lack of concern with unemployment in 1977 and 1978 may have contributed to the enactment of age discrimination legislation during the Carter administration (Walker and Lazer 1978). Clearly, short-run changes in economic conditions deserve consideration along with the more general aspects of economic and social development.

Conditions of the Aging Population. The conditions of the aging population, conditions that tend to emerge out of the general lines of socio-economic development, also are significant. Consider first the *size and composition* of the aging population. The low percentage of the aging in the U.S. population in the twenties and thirties can be viewed as a possible explanation for the slow American start on aging programs. In his crossnational comparison, Wilensky (1975, 22-27) attaches considerable importance to the size of a nation's older population in explaining levels of Social Security program development. Similarly, predictions that national population concentrations increasingly will resemble Florida's present levels lead some observers to anticipate a growth in policy commitments in the next few years (Cutler 1977).

Income levels comprise a second major factor influencing policy development although views vary regarding the extent to which the presence of persons with inadequate incomes prompts changes in policy (Harbert 1976; Lammers and Klingman 1982). *Living arrangements* comprise a third, and perhaps insufficiently recognized, characteristic. The decline in the number of three-generation families, and the corresponding increase in the number of persons living alone, appears to be a significant force leading to additional use of nursing homes. Living arrangements also influence political behavior. Condominium complexes or housing projects, where there are high concentrations of elderly persons, are likely targets for politicians seeking supporters and potential areas for "get out the vote" campaigns. Finally, *health status* must be considered. If the health of those between the ages of 65 and 74 improves significantly, greater interest in opportunities for work options beyond age 65 can be expected. Another possible consequence would be more political activity on the part of persons who are able to undertake interest group roles.

Societal Attitudes. The impact of societal attitudes is important in two respects. First, it is essential to consider attitudes toward public sector programs in general. Public skepticism toward an expansion in governmental roles often has been seen as an important factor contributing to the slow movement toward a national Social Security system. Obviously, a key issue in the 1980s surrounds the extent to which that skepticism may be intensifying in the face of higher program costs in some areas and a stagnant economy.

The second key attitudinal dimension surrounds public views of the aging as appropriate recipients of governmental assistance. On a number of policy issues, including housing programs and forms of income assistance, the public tends to regard the aging as more deserving of assistance than those who are categorized simply as welfare recipients. In a 1977 survey summarized by Ladd (1977, 213-226), Americans were asked their views concerning programs they would like to see expanded or cut. Their responses are illustrative of the importance of attitudes in this area. Aid for the elderly produced the highest level of affirmative response of any of the policy areas being mentioned, with 67 percent favoring higher levels of support. Conversely, the question of "helping the poor with welfare programs" produced the lowest response of any item in the survey. Public attitudes toward the aging and toward the aging in comparison with other groups seeking assistance clearly stand as an important component for consideration in assessments of policy development.

Private Sector Effort. The nature of private sector programs also influences the level of public commitment. The price and quality of health insurance that is available through private plans, for example, will have an impact on the development of public sector programs. Private pensions and retirement arrangements also constitute an important aspect of the total setting in which public sector plans will be developed. The huge financial stakes that health and life insurance companies have in protecting the scope of private sector programs often leads, in turn, to intense political activity.

Finally, it is important to consider the magnitude of private charitable efforts. Potentially, these may serve either as substitutes for public action or as models of what can be done, models which may prompt greater interest in publically supported programs. Private sector activities thus join societal attitudes, socio-economic conditions, and the life situations of the aging as factors shaping political activity and the resulting public policies.

Political Participants and Roles

The nature and extent to which political factors influence policy development has long been the subject of lively debate among students of public policy. Several studies in the 1960s broke new ground by stressing the effects of socio-economic conditions on policy development (Dawson and Robinson 1963; Dye 1966). Since socio-economic factors often are easier to measure than political behavior, however, it also can be argued that these studies inappropriately focused upon the irrelevance of political influences. As Hofferbert (1974) correctly emphasizes, both politics *and* economics can play an important role in the development of public policy.

Many discussions of policy development suffer from a limited attentiveness to the contributions of key participants. In studies of state politics, too much emphasis has been placed on the possible impact of formal structural arrangements and not enough on the actual patterns of influence (Uslaner and Weber 1977). Studies of national politics, in turn, have not always emphasized sufficiently the interrelated manner in which the presidency and Congress contribute to policy development. Greater attention needs to be paid to the instances in which presidents and members of Congress play important and often collaborative roles in the creation of new policies.

Figure 2-1 on page 27 presents the full range of political participants in policy formation for the aging: *voters, interest groups, executives, bureaucracies, and legislatures.* With some exceptions, such as the recent adjudication of issues surrounding the employment rights of older workers who charge job discrimination, the courts have not been a major participant in the development of policies for the aging. Regarding structural relationships, the issue that emerges most often in discussions of public policy and the aging is the impact of federalism on policy development. Some see the federal system acting as a constraint on potential federal action (Riker 1964), while others view the states as promoters of policy innovation that then can be built upon to create new federal policies (Sharkansky 1972).

In considering the nature of political action on aging-related issues, it is useful to think in terms of five basic roles: *issue raising, policy design, support building, bargaining, and implementation.* The importance of analyzing policy development along these lines has been demonstrated by Cronin (1980) and Rosenbaum (1981).

Issue-raising activities are such specific actions as the documentation of problems promoted in the media, attendance at hearings, and the development of position papers by interest groups. The selection of a policy design — President Franklin D. Roosevelt's emphasis on a particular approach for the Social Security system, for example — is often an extremely important factor in shaping the nature of the ultimate policy response. Building political support can involve appeals to the electorate and attempts to develop support within the legislature. The fourth role, bargaining and the use of specific political resources, includes such actions as presidents making promises to key state legislatures to secure needed votes, interest groups lobbying legislators, and members of Congress making it known to recalcitrant colleagues that they will have to pay for their opposition with loss of support when their pet bill reaches the floor. Program implementation and oversight involves attempts by such groups as legislative committees and the president's Office of Management and Budget to ensure that programs, once passed, are developed as intended. Although these five roles are not always distinct in actual practice, they are helpful in examining how political action contributes to policy development.

Policy Characteristics

For more than a decade, students of policy formation, following the leads of Lowi (1969) and Salisbury (1970), have stressed that different characteristics of public policy need to be considered in assessing the nature of policymaking activity. In terms of aging-related policies, it is helpful to consider three basic characteristics: *cost, impact, and visibility.*

The levels of cost of Medicare and home-care programs, for example, are vastly different. Thus they would be expected to produce different patterns of political activity. The second characteristic, policy impact, must be examined in two respects. First is the extent to which a given policy seeks to redistribute benefits and costs among social classes. For example, a Social Security proposal to increase minimum benefits will produce a different political response than a proposal to modify benefits for more affluent segments of the older population. Second is the extent to which a given policy will alter the economic well-being of key interests. Rather than simply looking at the extent to which recent policies have increased expenditures for medical care, for example, it is also important to consider the extent to which differing policy approaches may have had a differing impact on the likely fee levels — and thus profit margins — for doctors and hospitals. The development in 1965 of Medicare, with its lack of effective cost controls, is a good example of this issue.

The visibility of program cost and impact also requires consideration in assessing policy development. Social Security benefits developed without as much cost visibility as would have occurred if those benefits had been funded with general governmental revenues. Conversely, in developments within a given policy area, visible benefits may be an advantage. Thus readily visible social service programs, such as nutrition sites, where hot meals are served to groups of older persons, may have advantages over individual care programs, which can be publicized less readily. Visibility, along with cost and impact, is an important dimension in the assessment of policy outcomes for the aging.

Policy Outcomes

As Figure 2-1 indicates, major aging-related policies have emerged in recent years such as Social Security and Medicare and Medicaid, to name a few. These policies are briefly reviewed in the final section of this chapter and become the focal point for discussion in the middle chapters of this book. Obviously, in an analysis of policy development it is important to consider the evaluative issues that particular policies present. For now, it is sufficient to emphasize the extensive linkages in any framework seeking to explain policy development. The impact of those policies becomes the "feedback," which alters the conditions of the aging population. This "feedback" also becomes one of the forces influencing future political activity and policy development. Similarly, important interactions occur within specific components of the model. For example, a new policy being implemented by an interest group may help expand its advocacy role.

The framework presented in Figure 2-1 serves as a useful introduction to the early development of aging policy in the United States. The forces producing the belated American response to the problems of the aging will now be considered.

EARLY RESPONSES

When the delegates to the 1961 White House Conference on Aging met to review existing policies and propose new initiatives they had good reason to feel that their nation had given short shrift to the problems of the aging. A system of Social Security benefits was not established in the United States until 1935 — much later than in other countries with a comparable level of socio-economic development. In 1961 health costs still were not covered for the aging (or any other group) as a matter of right, and the expanding nursing home industry was receiving very little effective regulation. Social services for the aging existed only to a limited extent even in the most progressive states.

Although the United States made some gains in the development of public housing during President Roosevelt's second term (1937-1941), by the 1950s little was being done — in contrast to the extensive public housing initiatives being taken in Europe. Socio-economic conditions, the size and composition of the aging population, the cost and visibility of aging-related programs, societal attitudes, and other factors presented in the developmental framework help explain why the United States did not act sooner and do more for its older population.

The Slow Start

The first decades of this century found the United States well behind a long list of nations in its policy commitments for the aging. Many other countries, including Argentina, Australia, and New Zealand as well as more expected European leaders in the field, were busy establishing pension arrangements for the aging prior to World War I. In the United States, however, the only direct pension efforts involved state level assistance for those in severe need and the system of Civil War pensions, which declined rapidly after 1910.

During the 1920s, action at the state level was very slow and the number of persons receiving pensions extremely small. By 1929, only eight states had pension programs. A movement toward state pensions in the early 1930s prompted about half of the states to take some action. Nevertheless, only a few individuals were aided in most states, and payments were skimpy. Even by 1934, only 180,000 persons were receiving pensions, and the average monthly payment was less than $15.

Systemic Factors. One explanation for America's slow start can be found in the size of its aging population. In the 1930s the United States had a lower proportion of older persons than many — but not all — nations that were adopting social security systems. Canada, for example, had a fairly comparable demographic structure, and yet it established an initial system in 1927 for older persons with the greatest economic need. The status of the aging population is difficult to systematically compare among different countries in this period, and the United States may have perpetuated somewhat greater use of family support systems than did some of the countries that moved more rapidly to develop social security systems. Yet in its general levels of socio-economic development, with their likely influence on the position of the aging, the United States was rapidly moving toward a level of industrialization and urbanization that was associated with stronger policy efforts in Western Europe.

The economic situation of the aging became increasingly harsh in the first decades of this century. With the rise of urbanization, labor force participation gradually declined. In 1890 about two-thirds of all men age 65 and over were in the labor force; by 1930 that proportion had declined to slightly less than one-half. As many as 2.7 million, or some 40 percent of the nation's six million older persons, were economically dependent in 1930 (Holtzman 1963, 22).

Private pension systems were woefully inadequate. The railroad industry in its youthful days of rapid growth and easy profits had been a pioneer in private pension development, but these early models did not become widespread. Existing pension plans became increasingly inadequate in the face of inflation during and after World War I. As Greenough and King (1976, 28-67) point out, employee pensions made a small contribution to income support for the aging in the years prior to the enactment of Social Security. Similarly, while many unions started plans, they were generally poorly funded. The onslaught of the depression produced a virtually complete collapse of the union pension plans. Only after World War II, when the shortage of skilled workers prompted employers to do more for their employees, did private plans begin to make a substantial contribution to income support for the aging. Ironically, the very absence of private sector plans can be viewed as a cause of delay in establishing a pension system since a contributory plan was more unique in the United States than in countries with expensive experiences with private pensions (Rimlinger 1971).

Societal attitudes in America also retarded policy responses to the dramatic social needs that were emerging by the 1930s. Kaim-Caudle (1973, 184) reviewed the development of pension systems in 10 nations. According to this scholar, the United States was being influenced by

> . . .unbounded confidence in the efficacy of individual effort in all spheres of activity. There was a belief, unshaken by evidence to the contrary, that such effort could adequately protect prudent and deserving citizens against all the contingencies of life; the corollary of that view — that the underserving should only receive public support after a searching inquiry into their means, under conditions which do not encourage unnecessary application — was held equally firmly.

Societal attitudes and the lack of an underlying necessity to act, which stemmed from the lower proportion of older persons in the population, emerge as the most significant systemic factors contributing to the sluggish response in the United States.

Political Influences. U.S. political structures and early political actions (or their absence) also had important policy consequences. Prior to the 1930s old age pensions remained largely a nonissue in national politics. The absence of a strong "left" party at the national level reduced potential competition over possible pension plans (Wilensky 1975, 65-67). Individual presidents, including Theodore Roosevelt, expressed some interest in the issue of public pensions for the aging. Yet neither major political party gave the issue sustained attention. While U.S. pension advocates caught the attention of political leaders in a few urban states, they were not able to make pension reform a hotly competitive issue among political parties.

The potential impact of political competition is illustrated by the early experience in Germany. Bismarck, the Prussian chancellor of the

German Empire from 1871 to 1890, feared the rise of socialists. As a result, he was intent upon thwarting a possible issue for his opponents, and thus he promoted the establishment of public pensions for workers who reached the age of 65 (Schottland 1970, 12-14). Without a strong party of the left in the United States, similar political pressures were not created.

The federal system also may have had some impact. As Wilensky (1975) found in his crossnational comparison, federal systems contributed somewhat to the forces resisting the development of social security systems initially and their expansion later on. (Germany, an apparent exception, began its old age pensions in an era in which the chancellor had extensive power.) It seems doubtful, however, given societal attitudes and the positions of political parties in America during the first decades of this century, that the federal system had a particularly decisive role in either aiding or delaying the development of Social Security in this country.

The federal system should be credited, however, for facilitating some initial experimenting prior to passage of the Social Security Act of 1935. Pension plans that developed in a few urban, industrial states (Massachusetts, New York, Ohio, and Pennsylvania, for example) provided some guidance concerning possible lines of program development — as well as assistance to a small proportion of the dependent group in the aging population. These plans also helped sustain political interest in the issue. Thus in a careful analysis of reform efforts, Chambers (1963) concludes that the state experiences created an important base from which the pension movement could build during the 1930s.

Other political factors were at least as important for their absence as for their presence. There were not, as Pratt (1976) has emphasized, interest group leaders for the aging who were very effective in translating their concerns into action by the rank and file. Early reform efforts often included a strong academic tie to major universities; mass-based organizations were notably absent.

The most prominent social security advocate in the 1920s was Abraham Epstein. He became a well-known spokesman after working initially with Isaac Rubinow, an early advocate in New York. The focus of Epstein's research was social security systems in Europe. As a result of the European comparisons he made, early reform efforts often were well informed and included careful presentations of specific legislative proposals. In the 1920s Epstein also had some success in developing state political organizations in Massachusetts, New York, Pennsylvania, and Ohio. Yet Epstein's very emphasis on European comparisons and the prominence of immigrants in early interest groups made it difficult to translate the pension ideas of other countries into a popular, "home-grown" pension movement in the United States.

Perhaps as an indication of the importance of groups with strong local ties, a fraternal order — The Eagles — began to take on an active lobby role in the late 1920s. The disinterested, and at points directly hostile, po-sition of labor unions also contributed to the lack of effective interest group activity. In part because of their concern with pensions as a potential issue in contract negotiations, union leaders did not provide the effective lobbying for social security programs that was common in Europe. It was not until 1929 that the American Federation of Labor took a strong stand in favor of an old age pension system.

Would stronger interest groups have made a difference? Heclo's extensive study of pension developments in Great Britain and Sweden gives interest groups some credit for the enactment of initial legisla-tion, but very little credit for subsequent development. He writes (1974, 155-156):

> In both nations, popularly organized pressure was an important initial impetus behind the first pensions but proved an ephemeral force for long-term policy development. At no time did organizations of the aged or pensioners themselves play any prominent part.

On the basis of the experiences in Great Britain and Sweden, it seems plausible that if interest group activity in the United States had been stronger, some legislation might have been initiated at an earlier date. Yet the limited long-term impact that Heclo found in these cases of two early adopters of social security systems raises lingering doubts regarding the extent to which interest groups might have contributed to more substantial early development of old age pensions in this country.

Two other political factors must be considered. The low visibility and weakness of pension proponents in the United States may have given interest group opponents, such as the commercial insurance industry, more political influence than in other countries (Kaim-Caudle 1973). American presidents, prior to Franklin Roosevelt, did not give sus-tained attention to pension issues, and few popular pension champions held elective state office. In addition to limited interest group activity, this contributed to the lack of continuing interest in pensions for the elderly.

Overall it is not surprising that old age politics and policies remained on the fringe of the American political process until the 1930s. As we have seen, societal attitudes worked against reform, and a political party system with a major voice for social legislation was lacking. The slow start also can be attributed, in part, to the federal system and to the power of established interest groups.

The Emergence of Social Security

The present size of programs under the Social Security Act makes it easy to overstate the scope of the initial legislation. Given the absence of federal programs in the early 1930s, the victory in 1935 was a major political triumph. Yet the scope of the initial system was modest by the standards of what other nations were doing in the 1930s.

The system established in 1935 was based, first of all, upon earned rights rather than universal eligibility for all older persons. The concepts of universal benefits and federal pensions based upon economic need (regardless of previous contributions) were both rejected. Eligibility for participation in the system was very limited at the outset; only 60 percent of the labor force was eligible initially to earn future benefits on the basis of the 1935 law. This policy design was based upon the probably correct view that a plan built around individual participation and an "earned" benefit was the only plan that could be sold to the American public.

Second, the system was based upon a payment formula to keep the initial costs small. Payments did not begin until 1940. (Payments to the states to encourage their expansion of the means-tested system of old age pensions, known as Old Age Assistance (OAA), did expand more quickly.) Third, no funds from general tax revenues were to be used to finance the system. (Roosevelt's insistence upon this provided the basis for future debates over the possible use of money derived from general tax sources to finance Social Security benefits.) Fourth, only in the area of contribution-based Social Security benefits — now Old Age and Survivors Insurance and Disability Insurance (OASDI) — did the act establish uniform national policies. For other programs in the Social Security Act, including assistance to needy older persons through Old Age Assistance, the states were given responsibility for final decisions. Matching funds in the Old Age Assistance program gave incentives to the states to expand their programs, but the size of the monthly payments was to be decided in the state capitals.

The limitations of initial programs within the Social Security Act were sufficiently substantial to elicit a variety of negative responses. Early reformers such as Abraham Epstein were bitterly disappointed, and the Townsend Clubs continued to push their proposals. Some historians looking at the 1930s also have criticized the act. A major Roosevelt historian, William Leuchtenberg, described the Social Security Act of 1935 as "an astonishingly inept and conservative piece of legislation" (Leuchtenberg 1963, 131). Nonetheless, that first step in 1935 made an important contribution to the development of more extensive programs. An analysis of the forces behind that decision follows.

Systemic Factors. Several crucial factors in the early thirties contributed to the emergence of the Social Security Act. First, an overwhelming number of observers (including many leaders of private pension programs) felt that the private sector efforts that had been pushed repeatedly by President Herbert Hoover were inadequate to meet the income needs of the several million impoverished elderly persons.

Second, the economic situation for the aging deteriorated markedly as the depression worsened. Dr. Robert Townsend, a physician in Long Beach, California, and the founder of the most extensive pension organization to emerge in the 1930s, serves as a fitting example. In his own life he reflected the downward mobility experienced by so many older persons in the 1930s. At the time he introduced his bold new pension proposals (at age 66), he had recently lost a county job as an assistant health officer. Holtzman (1963, 58) describes Townsend's prospects for the future, prospects which were almost as bleak as those for thousands of other older persons. He did have some savings, but they were inadequate to sustain retirement. Yet he saw no hope of starting a new private medical practice. Townsend's personal experience in many ways resembled the experience of many older persons in the early 1930s. Individuals who had assumed that poverty was a condition that only affected those who did not plan carefully — and perhaps were lacking in virtue — found themselves very unexpectedly in dire financial straits.

The depression dislodged many essentially middle-class people both from the financial security they had always enjoyed and from their belief that those who sought assistance were somehow unfit individuals. Within the general population, it is not clear whether a similar shift in attitudes occurred. Some historians, such as Leuchtenberg (1963), have argued that after a brief abandonment of the values of individual initiative and an aversion for public action, the public reverted to its earlier attitudes by the late 1930s. However, early surveys of Social Security showed substantial acceptance of the program despite considerable confusion about how it actually operated. The first Gallup polls on the subject, taken in 1936, showed two-thirds of the voters indicating support for Social Security. Significantly, approval ratings climbed steadily in the early years — reaching 96 percent by 1944 (Schiltz 1970). The attitudes that emerged during Roosevelt's first term were an important factor making some form of old age assistance a likely prospect.

Economic conditions and program costs also influenced policy making. There is little indication that a reduction in the number of persons seeking jobs was a major motive of those promoting the Social Security Act. Nonetheless, the prospect of individuals beginning to retire more readily at age 65 was certainly congruent with the desire to reduce the massive unemployment of the early 1930s. The program cost factor emerged in the context of comparisons between pensions and greater reliance upon the town and country poorhouses. Surveys by the U.S. Bureau of Labor Statistics in 1930 showed that the average cost per old age pensioner throughout the country was just over $14 per month. A few years earlier, they had estimated the average maintenance cost per inmate in a poorhouse to be almost $28 a month, not counting capital costs. Thus in a debate strikingly reminiscent of the contemporary controversy over the costs of nursing home care versus social services for independent living, proponents of pensions in the early 1930s were able to argue that pensions were cheaper. As Rimlinger observes (1971, 211): "It was fortunate for the needy aged that a more human treatment was also more economical."

Political Influences. Lobby groups representing major businesses were divided on the social security issue. Many waffled in the early stages and only declared themselves pro or con once the bill reached Congress. The U.S. Chamber of Congress backed the plan; the National Association of Manufacturers fought it. The American Medical Association ended up in support, although it initially opposed a social security system, fearing that it would lead to legislation providing for public assistance and ultimately federal control of health care practices.

Discussions of the role of interest groups in the development of aging policy often center on the Townsend Movement. Beginning in early 1934, Dr. Townsend began forming clubs of older persons who wished to promote his new pension scheme. The Townsend Clubs, which began in California, quickly grew into a national movement, with particularly strong support in the West. According to Holtzman (1963, 47), the response was so spontaneous that two years after the initial club was chartered in 1934, there were 7,000 clubs throughout the United States with a membership of approximately 1.5 million aged persons. These clubs provided a dramatic rallying point for many older persons struggling with their economic problems, and members also could enjoy the social aspects of expensive club activities.

The Townsend Plan called for a massive new pension approach. All retired individuals age 60 and over were to receive $200 per month and all couples a pension of $400. A national sales tax of 2 percent was to fund the plan. The recipients would be required to spend the money within 30 days. The $200 figure (a large sum by most standards in the 1930s) was justified on the grounds that spending that amount of money would generate a job for another worker and thus contribute to a related objective of the the the plan's supporters — reducing unemployment among younger workers. It is also quite clear, however, that Dr. Townsend and his colleagues in the organization recognized that a figure of that magnitude was not likely to find them upstaged by other advocates with more ambitious goals.

The most influential role attributed to the Townsend Movement is the one given by its most thorough student. Holzman (1963, 207) writes:

> Agitation for the Townsend Plan greatly accelerated the time schedule for the appearance of a national old-age security program. In crystallizing overwhelming public clamor for action, the Townsend Movement afforded that program tremendous popular support, the political overtones of which neither the President nor Congress could ignore.

Several other observers, including two key architects of the 1935 law, give the Townsend Movement substantially less credit. Witte (1962) argues that the intensity of the movement behind an unattainable goal actually made passage of the Social Security Act more difficult. Similarly,

41

Altmeyer (1968) does not ascribe much influence to this aging-based interest group. In a more recent assessment by a political scientist, Pratt (1976, 23) concludes: "[T]he Townsend Forces did not figure prominently in the events leading up to the enactment of Social Security." He emphasizes Roosevelt's "hands-off" position toward Townsend, along with the importance of the actions that were already under way.

Several factors limit the amount of credit that should be given to the Townsend Movement. The chronology of developments is important. Roosevelt established his Committee on Economic Security and gave his major message calling for a social security program on June 6, 1934, just as the Townsend Clubs were beginning to form. Furthermore, a variety of strong pieces of legislation already were gaining legislative support even prior to Roosevelt's actions. The Townsend Movement did help "crystallize," in Holtzman's terms, the public clamor for action, but that clamor already was showing substantial momentum when the clubs were formed. It is also important to note that the leaders of the movement were not instrumental in advancing policy ideas that would be incorporated in subsequent legislation. Finally, the extent to which the extensive lobbying in 1935 by the Townsend Clubs changed the position of members of Congress is difficult to determine. They certainly appear to have given additional momentum to the social security issue and thus deserve some credit for building political support behind the view that "something had to be done." Yet as issue raisers, they appeared quite late, and a number of other socio-economic and political factors helped make that advocacy successful in 1935.

In addressing the role of interest groups in this period, it is essential to recognize that the leaders who had been active in the 1920s were largely ignored by the Roosevelt administration. In staffing his committee to draft a new program, Roosevelt turned not to Abraham Epstein, who was a supporter of a more comprehensive system, but to Edwin Witte and Arthur Altmeyer, individuals who had technical backgrounds in helping to shape the generally progressive social welfare programs in Wisconsin. At the bill signing ceremony at the White House in 1935, the forerunners in the 1920s pension movement were conspicuously absent.

The political behavior dimension also shows a set of important actions and decisions by Roosevelt — and in a context in which electoral concerns weighed heavily. As governor of New York, Roosevelt actively promoted an expansion of the state's pension system; as president, he seemed receptive, from the early days of his administration, to the importance of some package of social insurance.

By 1934 and 1935, electoral politics more than interest group activity guided executive policy making. Despite what now seems to have been an invincible position, Roosevelt was understandably worried about the political left in 1934. A variety of potential opponents, from Huey Long in Louisiana to popular Farmer-Labor Party Leader Floyd B. Olson in Minnesota, already were attracting major political support, in part because of their backing for major old age pension schemes. A poll taken by the Democratic National Committee prior to the passage of the Social Security Act indicated that Long had a chance of sweeping enough votes from the Democrats to result in the election of a Republican president in 1936. A combination of personal policy interests and electoral concerns thus prompted Roosevelt to use a fireside chat to discuss his proposed legislation. These motivations also contributed to his use of press conferences as a vehicle for maintaining interest in his social security proposals and, as the legislation reached the Congress, for intervening with key legislators to prevent a modification of his initial plan. Cornwell's (1964) account of these initiatives by Roosevelt ranks them as an outstanding instance of presidential leadership of public opinion.

Along with important aspects of political leadership, the emergence of the Social Security Act was aided by reduced conflict between the president and Congress during FDR's first term. Majorities in both houses of Congress were anxious to move on a variety of domestic policy issues. Congress did not "rubber-stamp" Roosevelt's proposals in his first term, and it made it increasingly difficult for him to gain his legislative objectives after 1936. Nonetheless, the combination of a climate of urgency, the president's own popularity, and Democratic majorities in both houses of Congress meant that the deadlock that would thwart such proposals as Kennedy's Medicare package in 1961 did not emerge for FDR. Moreover, Roosevelt was successful, through his Committee on Economic Security, in recruiting a group of technical advisers who were able to provide important analyses of alternatives and help in molding the specific legislative language. In contrast to the periodic uses of advisory committees to help a president delay action, this committee functioned efficaciously in developing legislative proposals. Although Roosevelt personally interceded at points in steering those committee actions, he was clearly aided by the group of experts at his disposal.

Multiple factors thus contributed to the easy passage of the Social Security Act in August 1935. The growing economic problems of the aging (problems that were largely ignored although already substantial in the early decades of the twentieth century) ultimately were translated into changes in attitudes — in part by the aged population itself. In the competitive political environment of the early 1930s, pension proposals quickly gained political attractiveness for elected officials. Lobbying efforts helped to intensify that interest, although it is important not to overstate their direct impact. President Roosevelt proved to be a skilled political leader on this question, while at the same time steering policy choices toward a fairly cautious initial piece of legislation. In its policy responses for the aging, the United States would continue to be less generous than many nations with comparable resources. Yet the Social Security Act represented a critical first step in 1935. The act provided the basis for an expansion that doubtlessly would have startled many early supporters.

EXPANDING COMMITMENTS

The pattern of expansion since those New Deal era decisions has been one of continuing but often undramatic increases until about 1960 followed by two decades of rapid increases in a variety of policy areas. By the early 1980s, expenditures for the aging had become increasingly costly and increasingly controversial. Before turning our attention in subsequent chapters to a systematic consideration of the forces behind the United States's expanding commitments to the aging, it is useful to chronicle the basic dimensions of that growth.

The First 25 Years

After passage of the Social Security Act in 1935, some programs expanded gradually, but the amount of national attention being given to policies for the aging declined substantially. Soon after 1935, states began to participate in the new federal Old Age Assistance program that assisted them with the costs of monthly payments to the elderly with greatest economic need. Frequently, there was a keen interest in political credit claiming on the part of state political leaders. In an important expansion, the Social Security Act was amended in 1939 to provide for payments to dependents and survivors. The amendment of the act in 1939 also speeded up initial payments and consolidated the four-year-old Social Security Administration in an effort to improve the overall coordination of the program.

After 1940 the number of Social Security recipients gradually increased. The Social Security payroll tax covering all aspects of the program also began to grow, reaching some 4 percent of federal government revenue by 1949. Nonetheless, major segments of the population still were not covered, and the state administered program of Old Age Assistance also was being held to a very modest level of maximum benefits. Although President Harry S. Truman proposed some expansion, his actions did not reflect an intense interest in policies for the aging. Pratt (1976, 35) characterized the Washington environment during Truman's first term (1945-1949) as lacking a real sense of urgency anywhere in the legislative process.

Truman's surprise reelection in 1948 produced two policy initiatives with major implications for the aging. He was successful in gaining an expansion in Social Security benefits but unsuccessful in his advocacy of national health insurance. As a result of congressional decisions in August 1950, the Social Security tax was increased one-half percent to 1.5 percent, and eligibility was extended to approximately 10 million additional workers. The first program for medical assistance also was created in 1950; an amendment to the Social Security Act provided financial help to states that chose to pay some health care costs for those needy older persons who were eligible to receive Old Age Assistance. That 1950 decision laid the groundwork for the establishment of Medicaid 15 years later.

During his second term (1949-1953), Truman persistently promoted a system of national health insurance for all Americans, but his efforts were firmly resisted. Using the loaded term "socialized medicine," the American Medical Association launched a tenacious lobby effort that involved record levels of expenditures and new advances in public relations approaches to the lobby process. The advertising firm of Whitaker and Baxter distributed more than 55 million pieces of literature describing the AMA position and spent over $1.5 million in the process. The extensive account by Poen (1979) of these legislative battles gives that lobby effort major credit in generating the stalemate that ultimately resulted. After the nation's attention turned to the Korean War, the national health program continued to be promoted, but its chance of passage in Congress was practically nil.

During the 1950s Social Security coverage and benefits expanded, and public interest in the problems of the aging gradually increased. With surprising ease, coverage under Social Security was expanded again in 1954. Only a few Republican legislators resisted (under the leadership of Sen. Carl Curtis of Nebraska), and President Dwight D. Eisenhower supported the plan which had substantially emerged from within the Social Security Administration. Coverage was extended to farmers, self-employed persons (such as some architects and accountants), and to some state and local government employees. The tax also was raised to 2 percent. With these decisions, the size of the system began to grow. In 1949, Social Security taxes represented 4 percent of federal revenue; in 1963, 10 percent.

States began to take action in the mid- and late 1950s. In about half of the states, advisory commissions were formed, often within the governor's office, to promote public and private programs for the aging. Among the most active states were Massachusetts, Ohio, Michigan, Wisconsin, Minnesota, and California. Although the programs were often very minor, they focused some attention on aging policy questions. In California, the emergence of old age political lobby groups that had begun under the Townsend Movement grew into an extensive statewide organization through the efforts of an effective new promoter, George McLain. His senior citizen clubs were well organized throughout the state and can be credited, according to Putnam (1970), with shaping the higher levels of pensions and health assistance in California as compared with other states.

Congress also took more interest in aging-related policy questions by the late 1950s. The Senate Special Committee on Aging was established in 1961, largely as a result of a series of important hearings chaired by Sen. Pat McNamara of Michigan on nursing home use. Although the newly formed Special Committee on Aging did not have the status to report legislation directly, it provided a focal point for legislators and laymen who were concerned with aspects of policy for the aging. Ideas that would later emerge in the early 1960s for expanding health care for the aging also began to surface in Congress. Even the concept of a White House Conference on Aging, which was held for the first time in November

1961, originated with the effort of Democratic Rep. Aime Forand from Rhode Island, who was developing an interest in aging issues as a senior member of the House Ways and Means Committee.

The Era of Expansion

In the early and mid-1960s, policy commitments for the aging emerged with new intensity. Although President John F. Kennedy did not win passage of a medical care bill for the aging in 1961, four years later Medicare, Medicaid, and the Older Americans Act all passed Congress. With its substantial coverage of both hospital and doctor costs, the 1965 medical care legislation represented a major victory for the aging. In addition, Medicaid expanded health care for the aging to those who were eligible for Old Age Assistance. Ultimately, Medicaid would become the major program for public financing of nursing home costs for the aging.

Passage of the Older Americans Act in 1965 was a major victory for proponents of more extensive policy efforts for the aging. The act established the Administration on Aging. Thus, supporters of social services for the elderly could look for the first time to an agency specifically responsible for developing new programs. The new administration had very small funding levels but was seen as a vehicle around which state efforts in providing services for the aging could be focused. In a manner resembling other efforts at promoting local participation and delivery of services in the early days of Johnson's Great Society, the Older Americans Act was an important first step in the quest for more adequate services for the aging. Perhaps in part because of the rapid shift in the nation's attention toward issues surrounding Vietnam and the problems of minorities, both aging issues in general and the specific programs being envisioned with the passage of the Older Americans Act drew rapidly decreasing attention in the late 1960s.

Ironically, the frustrations felt by the delegates to the 1971 White House Conference on Aging came as the nation was again on the verge of major new commitments. In 1972 Social Security benefits were expanded 20 percent, and the system of indexing for inflation — with its increasingly major impact throughout the decade — was established. In 1973 the Older Americans Act was strengthened and additional funding provided. At the same time, Congress acted to more substantially federalize the system of Old Age Assistance (OAA), with the creation of the Supplemental Security Income program (SSI). Greater opportunity for social services also was created (for the aging as well as for other groups) with further modifications in sections of the Social Security Act. After a decade-long fight, new steps were taken in 1974 to protect the pensions of participants in private programs. The House also responded by creating its own Select Committee on Aging in 1974. In 1977 benefit levels under Social Security increased again, as did Social Security taxes. Then, in 1978, to the surprise of many, Congress acted to virtually eliminate mandatory retirement prior to age 70.

Clearly, the magnitude of the U.S. policy commitment for the aging was changing dramatically. Estimates of the proportion of the entire federal budget being allocated to older persons in 1977 range from a high of one-third (Samuelson 1978) to the more conservative figure of one-fourth — a percentage which advocates for the aging have been willing to accept (U.S. House Select Committee on Aging 1981). The important differences in estimates occurred because of differing assessments of program impacts where not all of the clientele data is available on an age-specific basis. The larger estimates have included pensions in the military services, for example, which are going in many instances to individuals younger than 65.

Major expenditures have evolved in the areas of income maintenances, particularly for Social Security plus medical care. By 1981, the Social Security Administration was distributing benefits to approximately 36 million persons; almost 20 million were retired workers. (The other primary categories of beneficiaries are the disabled, widows, and the children of disabled or deceased beneficiaries.) The cost of Social Security benefits (OASDI) in 1981 was $136.9 billion for all programs; benefits to retired persons alone reached more than $90 billion. Major income maintenance expenditures also were being made in other areas, including more than $4 billion for veterans' benefits, more than $5 billion for railroad retirement system payments, and more than $13 billion for military retirement. In addition, the Supplemental Security Income program (which replaced Old Age Assistance in 1974) was costing more than $6 billion for all of its recipients, and some 1.5 of those 4 million persons were eligible because of their age (and low income).

Health cost allocations also were growing. In terms of total expenditures by individuals and the federal government, health care costs in 1977 were at the level of $1,745 per older person; those expenditures comprised some 29 percent of all health expenditures in the nation. The federal expenditures involved in the two components of Medicare (doctor and hospital costs) came to more than $36 billion. Some analysts projected that these costs would reach almost $50 billion by 1985. In terms of major areas of expenditure, the combined state and federal allocations for long-term care came to almost $10 billion (General Accounting Office 1982). Although precise figures are more difficult to compile in the area of home health care programs, federal assistance for those activities had reached approximately $2 billion by 1980.

Programs in other areas were generally less costly, but in some instances growing quite rapidly in the 1970s. The budget for the Administration on Aging was small by most Washington comparisons, but in 1981 it had grown to more than $700 million. Housing programs for low income aging and the handicapped continued to receive significant funding from the Department of Housing and Urban Development. Allocations in such areas as transportation, senior job creating activities, and Food Stamps also increased. While these individual funding levels were relatively small in many instances, the combined total for all aging programs nonetheless came to a large proportion of the federal budget.

Events in the early 1980s dramatized the critical issues surrounding public policies for the aging. Despite their costliness, aging programs are viewed by some as distressingly inadequate (Binstock 1978, 1979; Estes 1979). According to Binstock (1978, 1840), funding for nutrition programs was meeting only a tiny fraction of the existing need for an adequate diet. Yet it was precisely in the areas of social services and housing that extremely heavy budget cuts were being promoted by the Reagan administration. The magnitude of uncertainty surrounding all policies for the aging in the 1980s serves to underscore the importance of taking a careful look at how the policies developed and how they can be improved to make them more satisfactory for the aging and for all Americans.

III

ELECTORAL AND
INTEREST GROUP BEHAVIOR

Greater controversy has surrounded the politics of aging in the past decade than in any period since the 1930s. As the size, political sophistication, and lobbying activities of interest groups have increased in recent years so has their role in those controversies. The aging, in turn, have been voting in larger numbers and have held politicians more accountable for their stands on aging-related issues such as changes in the age of eligibility for Social Security benefits. The sudden emergence in 1981 of a broad-based coalition group, Save Our Security (SOS), coupled with President Ronald Reagan's hasty retreat on his initial proposals (including the reduction of benefits for those retiring between age 62 and 65), were two indications of the aging's growing importance in electoral politics.

Recent developments have intensified a long-standing debate over the influence that aging-based interest groups and the aging as voters actually possess. Some writers see the aging and their lobbyists as an influential — and increasingly potent — political force (Pratt 1976; Cutler 1977). Others, however, note the absence of block voting on the part of the aging (Binstock 1972, 1979) and the lack of cohesion and forceful action by aging-based interest groups (Estes 1979). Both points of view are explored in this chapter, which considers the electoral behavior of the aging and the changing characteristics of aging-based interest groups. Other interest groups involved in the current controversies surrounding public policy and the aging also are discussed.

ELECTORAL BEHAVIOR

Recent research has fundamentally altered established views concerning how older Americans vote and why. According to the conventional wisdom of a decade ago, it was believed that persons became more conservative and less politically active as they got older because of a life cycle change. More recent assessments of the aging's political behavior, however, see other factors influencing the way they vote. In short, the change in voting patterns is no longer viewed as an inevitable consequence of an individual's advancing age.

Several factors produce general political orientations among the aging during a certain period of time. First, let us consider education. The aging in the first decades of this century had lower levels of education than those who were born in later decades. Consequently, the seeming decline in voting participation that was noted in the 1950s may be attributed in part to the tendency for individuals of any age group to participate less extensively if they have had less education. Second, those born at a particular time (a birth cohort), such as persons born in the 1920s, will have different attitudes than those born when there was less crowding for schools and jobs (Easterlin 1976). Third, major historical periods, such as the depression of the 1930s, may alter voting behavior among age groups. While the relative impact of these three factors is not easy to unravel, the absence of support in recent analyses for interpretations associating conservatism and nonparticipation with the last years of the normal life cycle has important implications for electoral politics.

Participation Levels

One salient age-related aspect of electoral participation does emerge, but for the young and not the old. Electoral participation for those age 18 to 20 has been particularly low, and the 18 to 29 age group also has been significantly below the participation levels of the older age groups. In the 1980 presidential election, 65.1 percent of those 65 and over voted; only 35.7 percent in the 18 to 20 age group cast ballots (Statistical Abstract 1981, 499). Within the older population, only in the age 75 and over age group does voting participation begin to decline. Yet even in the age 75 and over category, participation does not decline to the levels of the youngest voters. Because of the tendency for persons age 65 to 74 to vote very extensively, the aging are apt to cast a larger percent of the vote than their percentage of the voting age population would suggest. In 1976, for example, those 65 and over cast 16 percent of the total vote although they only constituted 15 percent of the eligible electorate. A similar pattern has been observed in some legislative races.

Voting participation by the aging may increase. Historically, non-voting has been associated with a lack of education, and the aging have had disproportionately high numbers of individuals with low education levels, especially through the 1950s. Because of the increase in education levels in the United States in the 1920s, however, the older populations of the future will not be handicapped by those low levels of schooling.

Verba and Nie (1972) have carefully documented the importance of this relationship. In a major study of electoral participation, they found little evidence of a life cycle tendency to retreat from political activity and stay at home on election day. When levels of voting prior to the 1970s were corrected for differences in levels of education, the voting levels of those 65 and over differed negligibly from the levels in other age groups. While other variables may become important in the 1980s, higher education levels and the pattern of continued electoral activity late in life point to high levels of voting by the nation's aging population in the years ahead.

Attitudes and Party Preferences

Voting behavior was studied extensively for the first time after World War II. Some of those early studies indicated that the old were more conservative in their attitudes and more apt to support the Republican party than the young. Crittenden (1962) argued that the strong Republican support by the aging was the result of increased conservatism in old age. Glenn (1974) and Cutler (1977) disagreed. Their extensive work stressed birth cohort effects on attitudes and party preferences. According to Glenn and Cutler, the conservatism and Republican voting tendencies of the aging were largely a result of early experiences for that particular cohort of older persons. Differences in the way the older and younger segments of the electorate vote were attributed by them less to life cycle trends toward conservatism than to differences in experiences that shape social attitudes and identification, or lack of identification, with a political party.

The older generation, as of the 1940s and 1950s, experienced their initial political socialization prior to the New Deal, whereas younger voters were less apt to identify with the Republican party or favor more limited social welfare programs. Evidence regarding the absence of conservative attitudes associated with life cycle trends has been gleaned from several surveys. Even during the New Deal, Gallup Poll data as

53

analyzed by Hinshaw (1944) and presented in Cutler (1977, 1020) revealed little tendency toward a more conservative position on various domestic issues. Research by Campbell and Strate (1980) traced responses on opinion polls conducted from 1964 to 1976 by the Survey Research Center-Center for Political Studies at the University of Michigan. These scholars found few indications of a systematic tendency toward conservatism on the part of the aging. In his assessment of the aging as voters, Cutler (1977, 1022) concludes:

> . . . [T]his discussion demonstrates that despite the popular image of older people as being the most conservative age group politically, there is little evidence of an age-related political conservatism on the basic domestic issue concerning the role of the federal government in the areas of economics and social welfare. As a result of such factors as the group-benefits orientations and differences between generational cohorts, we should not uncritically expect older members of the electorate in the future to be conservative on the issue of making increasing demands upon the federal government for the allocation of scarce resources.

On the basis of this interpretation, such group benefits as expanded Social Security payments would seem likely candidates for substantial support from older voters. The record certainly does not show that a natural shift toward conservatism in old age takes place, thus reducing the desire for governmental assistance that individuals might have had earlier in life.

Recent assessments of the electoral behavior of the aging also show that party preferences, like societal attitudes, are not necessarily the result of life cycle tendencies. Consider identification with and support of the Republican party between 1952 and 1976. A comparison of support for Republican presidential candidates among those 65 and over, compared with those in the 30 to 64 age group, shows a mixed response. The percentage of Republican support from the 30 to 64 age group differed from an even split as follows: 1952, +6; 1956, −4; 1960, +10; 1964, +14; 1968, +4; 1972, +1; and 1976, +2. In 1980, 54 percent of voters 65 and over supported Ronald Reagan, 40 percent supported Jimmy Carter, and 4 percent supported John Anderson (Campbell and Strate 1980). Carter thus did almost as well with the aging as with other groups, but Reagan did slightly better because of Anderson's reduced support. In every presidential election between 1952 and 1976 (with the exception of 1956), the Republican candidate did better among the older voters than the Democratic candidate. However, these differences were pronounced only in the Kennedy-Nixon race in 1960 and the Johnson-Goldwater race in 1964. Cutler (1969) has stressed the electoral importance of the pre-New Deal political experiences of the older Nixon and Goldwater voters.

Although it is difficult to distinguish life cycle tendencies, cohort experiences, and period effects — as Foner (1972), Cutler and Bengtson (1974), and Glenn (1974) point out — two points are fairly clear. First, a systematic life cycle change toward conservative parties and conservative policy positions does not occur. Second, a life cycle pattern in attitudes will not systematically retard interest in public sector assistance on the part of the aging. On a third key issue, the extent of sanctioning responses in the voting booth, the literature is less conclusive. That issue deserves specific attention.

Sanctioning and Recruitment Efforts

Are specific election contests influenced by voters' sanctioning of candidates who are judged to be unsupportive of aging-related interests? This is one of the continuing areas of uncertainty in assessments of electoral influence on the part of the aging. A related question concerns the extent to which candidates who are likely to be supportive are recruited for specific election contests. Although the evidence is limited, seldom are incumbents defeated, or new legislators or executives selected, on the basis of their stands on aging-related issues. According to Binstock (1979), the multiplicity of views held by the aging on a host of issues seriously reduces the potential for block voting for or against particular candidates.

One interesting example of the elderly playing an important role in a congressional campaign occurred in Oregon in 1980. In the Democratic primary, Ron Wyden unseated six-year incumbent Rep. Robert Duncan. Wyden, while still in his late twenties, had gained considerable attention in the Portland, Oregon, area as a leader of the local Gray Panthers. That attention, along with appeals to the older voter, were viewed by Barone and Ujifusa (1982) as important factors in Wyden's primary victory and in his subsequent victory over his Republican opponent in the general election.

In considering the evolving impact of electoral influence, it is necessary to consider three basic points. First, while the evidence of sanctioning is limited, there is indirect evidence that a fear of sanctions by the aging influences legislative voting. Thus, members of Congress may vote for Medicare or Social Security benefit increases on the assumption that there could be a voter sanction. Indeed, Social Security benefits have tended to increase in presidential election years (Tufte 1978, 28-35). Similarly, prior to the 1982 congressional elections, both Congress and the Reagan administration were wary of tackling the question of changes in Social Security benefits. Politicians often are reluctant to vote against the expressed interests of older voters regardless of the extent to which a likely voter sanction can be demonstrated.

Second, the prospects for sanctioning behavior have increased in recent years due to the more widespread interest group mailings of legislative voting records. The existence of voting score cards for incumbents obviously does not ensure that they will be read or followed by the members of an interest group. Nonetheless, interest groups in an increasing number of states are now making that information available during legislative sessions and elections.

Third, the greater interest in Social Security issues in the 1980s may lead to increased tendencies to vote for or against candidates on the basis of their position on this issue. Social Security has become a hot potato that legislators juggle at their peril. Sen. Pete Wilson (R-Calif.), who ran a successful campaign in 1982, suggested exploring a voluntary system of income maintenance for persons under the age of 45. This controversial proposal sparked considerable opposition from his Democratic opponent, Gov. Jerry Brown, who aired a series of TV campaign ads in which he sought to attract voters by assuring them that he would continue Social Security benefits. More generally, conditions are ripe for greater electoral activity on aging issues. While evidence is scanty for sanctioning behavior and block voting, the risk of being categorized as unreliable on aging-related issues is likely to be greater for candidates in the 1980s than in previous decades.

Other Age Groups

Assessments of electoral roles in aging politics should not focus solely on the elderly. The attitudes of persons younger than 65 definitely affect the nature of policy responses. Young people actually expressed greater enthusiasm for changes in mandatory retirement provisions than did those in the age 65 and over category. Attention also must be given to the attitudes and political behavior of persons in the 55 to 64 age category who are contemplating their own old age and to middle-aged persons who are concerned with policies affecting the care of their elderly parents. It is interesting to note that the American Association of Retired Persons (AARP) and other mass member based groups begin encouraging membership at age 55. A variety of observers of aging politics have begun to suggest that those who are looking forward to retirement in a short time are particularly interested in the manner in which public policies will affect those opportunities. Bruner (1978, 277-278) emphasizes the increasing influence of those anticipating retirement:

> The new, age-related political drive may come more from the aging cohort "anticipating retirement" — the "older middle-aged" population, from 45 to 65. This 45-65 year-old age group already has a share of political influence disproportionate to its numbers in society, by virtue of its higher level of political participation, experience, and social and economic position. Over the next two decades, its relative proportion to the total population will be increasing, and its views on new problems in the politics of aging will be taking shape.

The vehemence of the reaction in 1981 to proposed changes in the age of eligibility for Social Security benefits may well reflect the increased political clout of the "soon to be retired." The changing behavior of voters below as well as above age 65 must be considered in assessing the impact of electoral politics on policy development for the aging.

Summary

Three central conclusions emerge from our review of the aging as voters. First, persons age 65 and over vote in large numbers and that level of participation is likely to increase. Second, attitudes toward policies do not reflect a life cycle tendency toward greater conservatism. This provides a potential political basis for an expansion of governmental programs for the aging. Third, there is as yet little evidence to support extensive block voting or specific sanctioning activity on the part of the aging, despite the fact that legislators are becoming increasingly apprehensive about that possibility. The evolving nature of the electoral role of the aging also is being shaped by interest group activity.

INTEREST GROUPS

Several different types of interest groups influence policy development for the aging. Obviously, mass member groups are important, but studies of interest groups and policy making for the aging have focused on them too heavily and paid insufficient attention to other groups. Thus, in the discussion which follows, public sector providers and professionals are considered as well as consumer groups and labor and religious organizations — potential allies in making policy for the aging. The main characteristics of private sector provider lobbies (such as those representing doctors and hospitals) and the role of other interest groups that sometimes become involved in specific controversies (such as the U.S. Chamber of Commerce and the Farm Bureau) also are described.

Mass Member Groups

The number and size of mass member interest groups have increased in recent years (Pratt 1974 and 1980). With more than 13 million members in 1980, the AARP is by far the largest aging-based mass member group.[1] Many of its members, like members of other mass member groups, have been attracted by nonpolitical rewards such as offers of a monthly magazine and insurance coverage. (One aspect of that insurance interest was altered in 1981 when the long-standing ties between the Colonial Penn Group, Inc., and AARP ended.) Because of its size, the AARP has been able to develop numerous policy-related functions. A full-time lobby operation is maintained in Washington, D.C., and lobby groups (known as joint legislative committees) have been formed in all of the states. AARP analyses and positions have become increasingly important in the development of public policy initiatives. Because of its size, the AARP has been attracting more attention from other Washington interest groups as well as from legislators and executive branch officials. It has become particularly interested in health care policy. In its view, general revenues, rather than Social Security taxes, should be used for some programs, including portions of Medicare.

The second largest mass member group, the National Council of Senior Citizens (NCSC), emerged out of the Seniors for Kennedy Clubs in

---

[1] Prior to 1982 the official name was the National Retired Teachers Association-American Association of Retired Persons (NRTA-AARP). The NRTA component was made a division within the AARP, and the longer official title was then dropped.

the 1960 presidential campaign. There were strong ties initially with labor unions in a number of states and that tie is still substantial. Organizational strength in the states differs widely with the strongest groups in the more highly industrial (and unionized) states. The NCSC has a more union-oriented and less middle-class membership than the AARP. It has been far less interested than the AARP in eliminating mandatory retirement and more concerned with protecting the Social Security benefits of those with low lifetime earnings. The NCSC has a major interest in national health insurance. In comparison with the AARP's desire for a generally bipartisan stance in terms of electoral politics, the NCSC consistently has taken a pro-Democratic party position.

On some issues, other mass member groups are influential, but they generally have smaller memberships and often a more narrowly defined policy focus. For several decades the National Association of Retired Federal Employees (NARFE) has defined its role narrowly: to protect pension rights for retired federal employees. On the other hand, the goals of the Gray Panthers, a group that began in 1970 under the leadership of senior citizen Maggie Kuhn, are extremely broad: to promote substantial social change, greater intergenerational understanding, and less emphasis on programs designed exclusively for the aging.

In the 1970s, groups devoted to the interests of specific segments of the aging population also were formed, such as the National Association for Spanish-Speaking Elderly (NASSE) and the National Center on Black Aged. Both groups grew out of the 1971 White House Conference on Aging. These groups have concentrated their activities in Washington, D.C., with particular emphasis on an expansion in social services through the Older Americans Act. Their lobbying activities were helpful in promoting amendments to the act in 1978 that increased services for those in greatest need. Limited success has been achieved, however, in building broad-based organizations that could lobby on a variety of issues.

The development of mass-based interest groups at the state level has been a recent phenomenon. Both the Townsend Movement and the health care battles of the 1960s were focused at the national level, with few groups (or programs) emerging in most states. California, with its strong pension movement in the 1950s, was a notable exception to a general pattern of limited interest group activity. As of the 1960s, the extent of aging-based interest group activity in the state capitals was extremely limited.

Developments at the state level, however, have begun to change that pattern of inactivity. First, the state organizations within major national groups have become more involved. The AARP, for example, has fairly active lobby groups in most states and some activities in all of the states. These groups have taken positions on crime protection, funeral industry regulation, generic drug provisions, Medicaid provisions, nursing home regulation, property tax reform, levels of Supplemental Security Income (SSI) payments, and other issues. The NCSC always had its strongest support in the more unionized states, but in recent years it has worked to extend its network of state organizations.

Second, more legislatures are inviting elderly persons to come and participate for a few days in practice legislative sessions. Missouri in 1973 was the first state to conduct such a program in its state capitol. By 1981, 13 states had what has come to be called "Silver Haired Legislatures." These sessions help legislators become more aware of policy interests among the aging, and they also help older persons expand their skills for influencing legislative decisions. Perhaps the most noteworthy use of a Silver Haired Legislature occurred in Florida (Matura 1981). Participants were selected carefully by older voters in local elections, and the annual legislative session in Tallahassee lasted a week. On the basis of interviews with members of the Florida legislature as well as an analysis of the bills that actually passed, the Florida SHL was given fairly high marks as a vehicle for increasing participation and for influencing decision making at the state level.

In some states the aging are beginning to establish their own organizations. Minnesota and Washington provide interesting examples (Lammers and Klingman 1982, 12-24). Begun in Minneapolis-St. Paul (as the Metropolitan Senior Federation), the Minnesota Senior Federation emerged in the early 1970s as an important lobby for the aging. It received funding from religious organizations in the Twin Cities. Labor organizations statewide also gave it financial support and lobbying assistance. The Minnesota Senior Federation has been active on a number of issues including nursing home reform, property tax relief, Medicaid benefits, SSI payment levels, and the expansion of social services programs. Separate offices and a permanent, full-time staff have allowed the organization to develop more extensive activities than most aging-based interest groups.

In 1976, Norm Schut, an experienced state lobbyist and organizational leader, helped created in Washington an effective aging-based interest group called the Senior Lobby. It has conducted numerous conferences and surveys to determine member preferences on potential policy initiatives. A number of those conferences have included training sessions at key locations in the state to increase members' skill in approaching and lobbying elected representatives. The resulting *Manual of Washington State's Approach to Senior Citizen Advocacy* (Department of Social and Health Services, Bureau of the Aging 1979) testifies to the thoroughness of those activities. A number of groups with interests in the problems of the aging are represented on the Senior Lobby's board of directors. As a result of these extensive organizational activities, the ability of the Senior Lobby to focus legislative attention on senior issues and to expand Washington's overall commitment to the aging emerged in a number of press assessments of Washington politics as of the late 1970s (Lammers and Klingman 1982, 13).

As the experiences in individual states suggest, mass member interest group activities are changing quickly and dramatically. They may change even more rapidly in the 1980s as a consequence of changes in levels of federal funding for social services and Medicaid. The Reagan administration's cutbacks at the federal level and proposed delegation of more authority and autonomy to the states undoubtedly will affect the activities of state mass member interest groups. As of the late 1970s, many of them often had difficulty sustaining effective organizations. The comparative analysis by Dobson and Karns (1979) paints a sobering picture. Advocacy groups for the aging were frequently viewed by the legislators themselves as having a limited impact. Thus while advocacy activities are growing in many states, in comparison with their virtual nonexistence prior to the 1970s, few states have extensive and effective mass-based organizations among the aging.

Public Sector Providers and Professionals

Major lobbying efforts have taken place by those who have been employed to provide services for the aging. Historically, health and social services professionals have been important voices among the very few groups of advocates for the aging. Advocacy by those providing services has intensified with the growing scope of federal and state programs in recent years. The National Council on Aging in 1950 was the first professional group to emerge with a specific focus on policies affecting the aging. Today it does substantial research and participates in policy promotion activities within the network of aging-related activities in Washington, D.C.

Since the passage of the Older Americans Act in 1965, there have been not one but two organizations that were formed around more specific provider interests: the National Association of State Units on Aging (NASUA), which represents the State Units on Aging, and the National Association of Area Administrations on Aging (NAAAA), which represents the more recently formed Area Administrations on Aging. (In terms of emphasis, NASUA focuses on the state level, and NAAAA is primarily concerned with local responses to federal programs.) The growing interest in improving home care also has generated substantial interest group activity. The Visiting Nurses Association and the Home Caring Association have made an important contribution in this area. The National Association of Social Workers also is interested in aging-related programs. Its lobbying activities were particularly effective a few years ago.

Major organizations also have emerged in recent years to foster research and training in gerontology. A national organization, The Gerontological Society, helps to promote a wide range of research activities through its conferences. The Western Gerontological Society, with a stronger representation from public sector providers, conducts research and training-oriented activities. These organizations have grown recently as government research support and public programs for the aging have expanded. Support and nurturing of policy ideas, rather than direct lobbying, generally emerges from these organizational endeavors.

Not infrequently, public provider groups are viewed with skepticism. In a review of the lobbying activities for Nixon's Family Assistance Plan, Moynihan (1973) criticized the roles of professional social worker organizations. More recently, Estes (1979) has argued that the service providers have not only developed a self-interest in a variety of programs but also have contributed to an overemphasis on the aging as being in need of services. In her view, this takes attention away from a necessary focus on possible increases in financial assistance policies and fosters an inappropriate stereotype of the aging in America. While the provider groups are not always viewed favorably by those with sympathies for the aging, they are nonetheless an important segment of the overall policy-making process.

Private Sector Providers

Groups representing those who provide services in the private sector also occupy a critical position in many policy decisions affecting the aging. Although private sector providers often oppose expansions in public programs, their efforts shape the particular forms of public response. While the American Medical Association (AMA) seemingly "lost" in the 1964 and 1965 health care fights over Medicare and Medicaid, it did play an influential role in developing those programs. Its advocacy of a "reasonable cost" rather than a fixed fee basis for Medicare and Medicaid was of major importance in shaping the form of public assistance that was provided — and in contributing to the subsequent escalation in health costs.

Two other major health-related groups are the American Association of Homes for the Aging (AAHA), which represents nonprofit nursing homes, and the American Health Care Association (AHCA), which represents the larger, and more rapidly growing category of privately owned, for-profit nursing homes. State organizations, usually with similar names, are maintained throughout the country. Although the AAHA sometimes takes positions similar to those advanced by for-profit nursing homes, it is the AHCA's lobbying activity that has been particularly influential in some states and, at points, in Washington, D.C. Various components of the nursing home industry, the medical profession, and the Life Insurance Association of America (particularly on Social Security benefit issues) play very crucial roles in policy controversies affecting the aging. Because memberships are not generally large, political action often has included major media campaigns, large campaign contributions, and the cultivation of key legislators to act as quiet supporters in killing or modifying legislative initiatives that are viewed as detrimental. These strategies for the nursing home industry take on major importance in our discussion of long-term care policies in Chapter 7.

Other Groups

Controversies over policies for the aging include other interest groups as well. In California, lobbying by groups representing the disabled has been an important asset to the aging in their pursuit of higher Supplemental Security Income benefit levels. The extent to which potential allies are recruited into coalitions is often a critical issue in the quest for influence by aging-based interest groups. Measures that have large costs, or which may substantially increase costs in the future, are likely to stimulate interest among business groups. Potential allies and business groups with histories of frequent involvement deserve specific discussion.

Many groups can become allies of advocates for the aging. In the Medicare battle in the early 1960s, for example, labor was a major participant. Consumer groups, spawned in part by Ralph Nader's efforts, have been allies, particularly on issues that are not exclusively age-related such as funeral home regulation and generic drug legislation. Student groups were involved in nursing home reform efforts, particularly in the early 1970s. Religious denominations, organized into a wide variety of federations and joint committees, also have influenced the development of public policy for the aging. More recently, state and national women's organizations have taken an interest in the problems of older women. Advocates for the blind and disabled also have worked together for expanded benefits, particularly where their policy concerns were combined in a program (such as Supplemental Security Income) which has components for each group.

Finally, American veterans may become an important ally. Although they have not been especially active on aging issues, greater involvement seems likely. Recent Veterans Administration programs may become useful models for services to other older persons, and the growing number of retirement age World War II veterans seems likely to create greater interest in a wide range of aging policy issues. In short, the role of allies is important in examining past political decisions as well as in looking toward future political action.

Aging-related issues with widespread consequences for American society have generated considerable interest among many interest groups. When large expenditures are involved, major business groups and groups from sectors of the economy that are not directly affected by the proposed legislation often become involved. These controversies have been classified by Lowi (1969) as redistributive policy-making efforts since they have potentially far-reaching consequences for a variety of groups and social classes. The Medicare controversy in the early 1960s provides an example of both redistributive policy making and the range of groups that can become involved. In his account of the controversy over Medicare, Marmor (1970) points to the opposition of the U.S. Chamber of Commerce, the National Association of Manufacturers, and the Farm Bureau as well as to the vocal support of the Farm Union. Pension reform issues and the mandatory retirement controversy also have drawn major voices from a variety of economic interests, including the AFL-CIO, specific unions, and the U.S. Chamber of Congress. Some aging-related issues do not attract a wide range of economic interests. However, when major new policy directions are considered and/or when new programs costs are projected to be high, the range of group involvement is apt to widen.

Summary

A wide variety of interest groups, including public and private sector providers as well as mass member organizations, influence aging policy in the United States. The interest of some groups in aging policy is general. The U.S. Chamber of Commerce, the National Association of Manufacturers, and the AFL-CIO will play strong roles in private sector pension reform but be little involved with such questions as home care and nutrition programs. Other groups, as we have seen, are more narrowly focused. Private sector providers such as the AMA, public sector groups such as NASUA, aging-based groups such as AARP and NCSC, and a number of labor and consumer affairs coalitions may have critical roles on issues ranging from nursing home reform to expanded support for home care programs. Whether one's interest is in calculating the best lobbying strategies for a particular bill or in assessing interest group influence, it is essential to consider a full range of potential participants. Given the pattern of interest group activity described in this chapter and the likelihood of increased electoral participation by the aging, the following developments are likely.

FUTURE DEVELOPMENTS

Increased Participation

Levels of political participation on the part of the aging probably will increase. The number of elderly persons who vote already is high when compared with the number of persons from other age groups who go to the polls. Moreover, in the next few years the number of individuals in the older population who possess the individual attributes associated with participation is likely to increase (Verba and Nie 1972; Peterson et al. 1976; Cutler 1977).

Interest group activity reflects a similar although less clear-cut trend. In the past decade, participation in aging-based interest groups has increased. This is reflected in the number of aging-based organizations and in the dramatic membership increases for the AARP and other groups (Pratt 1976, 208-218).

The growth in aging-based interest groups has been explained from various perspectives. Some emphasize the impact of changes in the personal attributes associated with group participation. As Verba and Nie (1972) have stressed, individuals who have the attributes associated with group participation as well as voting participation are likely to increase in number. Insofar as it is possible to generalize about individuals from state level characteristics, there also is evident supporting views stressing likely future growth in group membership. AARP membership is high in states that have high income and education levels in their population (Klingman and Lammers 1980, 18-20). Existing studies that relate individual level attributes to participation are not sufficiently extensive, however, to sort out the extent to which more specific motives and incentives may underlie the participation levels that have been observed in those initial studies.

Direct Incentives

A second perspective on group membership draws from the analysis of incentives by Olson (1970). According to his formulation, individuals join a group on the basis of the group's ability to give them one or more incentives for membership. Olson places particular emphasis on the tendency for interest groups in all policy areas to develop direct incentives.

The advantage of these incentives for group growth is that while individuals who belong will receive a specific inducement for joining, those who decline membership will be denied that benefit. Aging-based interest groups have attempted to build their memberships by using a variety of direct incentives, including insurance plans, group travel plans, discounts on generic drugs, and magazine subscriptions. In some instances, discounts with merchants and health service vendors also have been offered.

There is certainly nothing inherently wrong with the use of direct incentives. Indeed, in Olson's analysis, it becomes virtually essential for organizations either to require membership (as with many labor unions) or to develop direct incentives for membership. The key issue surrounds the extent to which groups that are built upon direct incentives can function in a political environment. For example, individuals are apt to get more information through newsletters than would otherwise be the case, and they may become interested in policy goals even if that was not their initial motivation. Furthermore, the sheer number of members may give an organization a politically significant voice which it might not otherwise have possessed. Nonetheless, individuals who belong to a group primarily for one of the direct benefits may be quite removed from the policy positions and appeals for support coming from central offices. A lack of influence on members is particularly apt to occur when an individual's partisan voting cues suggest a candidate choice differing from the interest group's recommendation.

Conclusion

Increasing numbers of persons may join aging-based interest groups on the basis of a specific desire to influence policy outcomes. Yet the classic problem, as Olson notes, is that individuals can enjoy the benefits of legislative gains if others "pay their dues" and lobby while they avoid the commitment and expenditure which that entails. Clearly, one of the critical questions in the 1980s will be the extent to which some combination of an increase in the attributes associated with group involvement and an increase in memberships based upon a desire to influence policy will lead to the emergence of aging-based organizations with greater political influence.

Basic questions thus emerge regarding the impact of aging-based electoral and interest group activity. In this chapter we have discussed the major growth in interest group activity and in efforts to mobilize the older voter. Those voters, at the same time, constitute a growing portion of both the eligible and the voting electorate. Before examining the impact of these forces in specific policy areas, we will consider the roles of the immediate participants in the policy process: executives, bureaucracies, and legislatures.

IV

EXECUTIVES, BUREAUCRACIES, AND LEGISLATURES

It is becoming increasingly difficult for public officials, regardless of their personal desires, to avoid involvement with aging-related policy issues. Presidents find themselves confronted with difficult press conference questions, and their campaign managers steer them to retirement communities and meetings with aging-based interest groups as election day draws near. Legislative candidates find that the intricacies of Medicare, Medicaid, and Social Security benefits — once largely ignored — need to be mastered in their preparations for position papers and campaign debates. Administrative officials, particularly from the Social Security Administration, find requests for media appearances beginning to mount — and not always for settings that are likely to produce friendly questions.

The increase in the amount of activity that key policy makers have been undertaking raises basic questions about their policy roles. Chapters 5 through 8 address these questions in the context of specific policy issues. First, however, it is necessary to review the basic patterns and characteristics surrounding executive, bureaucratic, and legislative behavior. This chapter thus begins by considering the changing patterns of behavior that have been occurring in recent years and then discusses the approach that will be used in examining policy-making roles in subsequent chapters.

CHIEF EXECUTIVES

The search for sources of policy development in American politics often has turned to the role of presidents as policy leaders. Similarly, those championing major advances in state policy commitments for the aging often hope that the election of a governor with a personal interest in aging issues will be a catalyst for new policy initiatives. To some extent this view has emerged as a result of the frequent emphasis on President Franklin Roosevelt's role in the passage of the Social Security Act in 1935. More generally, the view that presidential leadership permeates major policy initiatives has been a persistent theme, particularly in the 1950s and 1960s, in leading interpretations of presidential politics (Neustadt 1960). General changes in levels of presidential interest, accompanied by a major shift in the number of participants involved with aging-related policies in today's institutionalized presidency, emerge as central characteristics of presidential involvement.

Presidential Interest in the Aging

Perhaps the most surprising characteristic of presidential involvement in aging issues is the limited interest that was manifested until the 1960s. A review of official addresses, remarks, and public activities of presidents between 1929 and 1980 reveals that presidents virtually ignored aging policy issues between 1935, when the Social Security Act was passed, and 1961, the first year of John Kennedy's presidency when health insurance issues were hotly debated.

In a review of presidential addresses, remarks, and public activities between 1929 and 1980 conducted by this author, there was virtually a total absence of presidential attention to aging issues between the passage of the Social Security Act in 1935 and the emergence of health insurance issues in the early 1960s.[1] No major addresses on aging policy issues were delivered from 1938 until 1961, and messages to Congress with specific reference to the aging were rare. Bill-signing ceremonies for new aging-related legislation, White House receptions for leaders of aging-based interest groups, and appearances around the country before groups of older persons also were very infrequent. Often a year or two would pass without any public action in which a president singled out the aging for specific attention. Presidential actions supporting new policy steps in the areas of health care and housing did involve possible policy changes that could aid the elderly along with other clientele groups. Nonetheless, in

---

[1]The discussion of changes in presidents' public activities relating to the aging is based upon the coding category in Lammers (1981, 6-7). The specific categories were major addresses, messages to Congress, routine statements, veto statements, bill-signing ceremonies for legislation focused on the elderly, White House functions (such as receptions and gatherings of interest group leaders) involving spokesmen for the aging, and appearances before audiences of older persons around the country (such as residents of a retirement home or meetings of retired workers).

terms of activities involving issues and groups specifically defined as aging-related, the record between 1938 and 1960 is virtually devoid of presidential activity.

In the 1960s the record of presidential involvement markedly increased, especially on health care issues, and in the following decade much greater attention was given to aging-based interest groups and activities. Presidents John Kennedy (1961-1963) and Lyndon B. Johnson (1963-1969), in comparison with their predecessors in office — Harry S. Truman (1945-1953) and Dwight D. Eisenhower (1953-1961) — showed dramatic increases in levels of activity on aging policy issues in such categories as routine statements, White House activities, and (especially for Johnson) the staging of major bill-signing ceremonies. The dominant policy issue was health care, but other issues such as social services program development also were important. Richard M. Nixon's public record as president reflects a continuation of the activity levels under Kennedy and Johnson; his strongest involvement in aging-related activities occurred in the middle of his first term (1969-1973), when he appeared to take a concerted interest in increasing his level of support among older voters in his bid for reelection.

Gerald Ford showed a substantial interest in the aging, with an especially large number of appearances before groups of older persons in 1976 as part of his widespread primary and general election campaign. Jimmy Carter's record resembled Ford's in the emphasis on appearances before aging-based interest groups and in the use of the White House for gatherings of aging-based interest group leaders, but he gave a limited number of routine statements and messages or addresses to Congress. Carter demonstrated his interest in cultivating the aging as a source of political support by organizing a town hall-style meeting with members of the American Association of Retired Persons (AARP), visiting a nutrition program site in the Watts area of Los Angeles, and holding a variety of receptions for key leaders of aging-based interest groups.

Of course, public appearance patterns constitute only a portion of the total activity a president may undertake to promote policy development in a given area. Cabinet officials and key aides may be dispensed throughout the nation's capital and the country to build support for new policy initiatives, and advisory commissions may be nurtured to broaden support for a preferred alternative. Interest group leaders and agency

71

officials may privately pursue important bargaining roles. The role of staffers and advisers also constitute an important dimension of the total impact the institution of the presidency has on policy development.

Nonetheless, the public record of presidential behavior makes apparent two conclusions. First, presidents engaged in little activity on aging issues prior to the 1960s. Second, the increase in public activity, particularly in the 1970s, is more indicative of an interest in possible increases in electoral support by older voters than in expanded roles in the design and advocacy of specific new policies. Appeals to older voters with gestures of interest such as recognition of interest group leaders and appearances at general meetings of the aging have increased dramatically. Yet presidential actions in specific bargaining and support building activities have not shown a comparable increase. In the area of aging, just as in their more general responses (Cronin 1980, 75-115), presidents have been giving increased attention to the wooing of voters through public relations activities.

The Institutionalized Presidency

Staff assistants and officials within the Executive Office of the President play major roles in shaping public policy; this is an inevitable consequence of the limitations on a president's time. Since the early 1970s, the White House staff has numbered around 500 persons — a much larger contingent than the pre-World War II staff of approximately 175 (Heclo 1977, 36). This increase reflects presidential desires for personal information channels and the greater need for aides to handle relationships with Congress, the press, and major constituencies. The Executive Office of the President (one component of which is the White House staff) often has been larger than 3,000 persons and included such key policy-making and policy-advising components as the Office of Management and Budget and the Council of Economic Advisers. This growth in the Executive Office and its established policy-making activities has been referred to as the "institutionalized presidency."

Several roles and organizations influence aging policy formation from within the contemporary presidency. The most specialized role has been played by advisers to the president on aging issues. The role of special adviser to the president for aging evolved into a seemingly established position in the 1960s and 1970s but was abandoned by President Ronald

Reagan when he took office. The most well-known presidential adviser on aging issues was labor leader Nelson Cruikshank, who completed a lifetime of involvement on such legislative battles as Medicare and Social Security benefit increases by serving as Carter's presidential adviser on aging.

A secondary but periodically important role has been played by the Federal Council on Aging (FCoA), established in 1965 as a 15-member advisory group to assist presidents in formulating policy for the aging. Presidents Johnson, Nixon, and Ford occasionally used this organization to help cultivate support among the aging, but it has not been a central voice in policy development. In 1981, the Reagan administration drastically cut the FCoA budget and virtually eliminated its staff support. Visibility, more than policy formation activities, have earmarked the Federal Council on Aging. Permanent staff aides in the domestic area, sometimes organized as part of a Domestic Council, are more apt than the FCoA to have a strong and continuing role in shaping presidential policy initiatives.

Another voice in the development of aging policy has been the White House Conference on Aging. Kennedy was quite supportive of the White House Conference in 1961, while Nixon and Reagan were more concerned with the potential costs of likely proposals. As a result, both Nixon and Reagan worked behind the scenes in the 1971 and 1981 conferences to try to moderate some of the proposals. While not always welcomed by presidents, proposals that have emerged from White House Conferences on Aging have intensified interest in some policies, such as Medicare in 1961 and Social Security benefit increases and reforms in 1971.

In recent years, presidents increasingly have relied on special commissions in the field of aging and in other areas. These commissions often can exert an independent voice in policy development (Wolanin 1976). They also can become one of the vehicles through which a president and his aides work to develop support for changing a policy or seek to delay action. In the 1960s, commissions investigated private pensions, and in 1977 the National Commission on Social Security was established. In addition, every four years the Advisory Commission on Social Security, a commission within the Social Security Administration, reports to the president and Congress. The increased use of commissions reflects the growth of presidential concern with both policy development and the electoral importance of the older population.

In August 1981 President Reagan created a new presidential commission to study Social Security. Five members were appointed by him, five members by the Senate leadership, and five members by the House leadership. The commission was asked to report on its findings by January 1, 1983. Whatever the president's intentions may have been in creating this commission, his action had three consequences. First, by scheduling the commission to report after November, President Reagan was able to reduce the level and intensity of debate on Social Security benefits until after the 1982 mid-term elections. Second, the composition of the commission, which the president proposed and Congress adopted, worked to his advantage. This is in keeping with the common practice of other presidents who have shaped the general direction of a commission by selecting its initial members. Because Republicans controlled the Senate, the makeup of the commission ensured that it would be at least reasonably sympathetic to Republican party concerns. Third, since the March 1981 report of the National Commission on Social Security (which Carter and Congress had established in 1977) contained a number of expansionary dimensions, Reagan's establishment of a new commission effectively reduced the attention that otherwise might have gone to those earlier recommendations. The appointment of the new commission so closely on the heels of the previous commission report also served to underscore the frequency with which presidents are now likely to become involved with aging issues through the use of commissions.

Several other aspects of the institutionalized presidency deserve emphasis. The Office of Management and Budget (OMB) has the overall responsibility of helping the president develop his budget proposals. In the Reagan administration, former Michigan Rep. David Stockman worked aggressively to assert the influence of OMB in the formation of presidential budget proposals, including those in the area of aging. The OMB plays a key role in deciding which agency proposals will be forwarded to Congress and in recommending to the president vetoes of congressional bills. With the legislative roles in OMB and the expanded legislative liaison office, as part of the White House staff, relationships with Congress now have a substantially institutionalized dimension. Instead of relying on a few aides to count potential votes and to decide how to help specific legislators, presidents now have several dozen aides to help them gain passage of their legislative programs.

Activities within the institutionalized presidency as well as the actions of presidents as individuals affect the development of policies for the aging. It is essential to assess the extent to which presidents themselves have been significant participants. At the same time, those surrounding the president who are involved with aging policy formation are increasingly important.

The Gubernatorial Role

Governors have had extensive opportunities for leadership in the evolution of policies affecting the aging. Many of our present federal policies, from nursing home regulation to provisions against age discrimination in employment, were developed at the state level first. Furthermore, despite the increase in federal roles and standard setting, major differences among the states continue in aging policies. Governors thus have opportunities for leadership through new innovations and with actions that improve their state's relative position on basic policies such as Medicaid and social services.

Governors periodically have been highly active in aging policy development. Gov. David Pryor of Arkansas became interested in aging issues when he was a U.S. representative. In search of firsthand information regarding existing problems, he served for a day as an orderly in a nursing home. Gov. Milton Shapp of Pennsylvania was interested in social services policy development and was a major promoter of Robert Benedict, his director of aging programs, to serve as the head of the Administration on Aging in the Carter presidency. Minnesota Gov. Wendell Anderson became personally involved in designing and promoting a freeze on property taxes for those 65 and over. Washington Gov. Dixie Lee Ray developed a close relationship with her state's major aging-based interest group, the Senior Lobby. She also worked to prevent cuts in the budget for aging programs in 1979 and 1980 — a time when Washington, like other states, was experiencing mounting budgetary problems.

A number of generalizations can be made regarding the evolution and present characteristics of the gubernatorial role in aging policy development (Lammers 1982). First, governors, like presidents, have become more conscious of the aging in recent years. This renewed interest is reflected in visits to nursing homes and retirement communities during campaigns and in promotions of events such as Senior Citizens

Day at the state capital. Second, governors rarely become substantially involved in the development of specific proposals or in the use of their own political resources to directly push a major policy change. More often, they influence aging policy development indirectly through the actions of their appointees. Third, governors who have been generally expansionist in their approach to state government and to welfare policies may create a momentum that helps increase commitments for the aging. In California in the early 1960s, for example, Gov. Pat Brown, while not a specific promoter of new initiatives for the aging, conducted an administration that was conducive to expanded efforts.

When considering the likelihood of gubernatorial involvement in specific policy areas, two further generalizations can be suggested. Some governors have become involved with the promotion of social services programs for the aging, particularly when state dollars can be maximized through the use of federal matching funds. This promotion can be a significant factor in the evolution of these policy commitments, even though the dollar amounts in many cases are small. Conversely, on a variety of regulatory policies, governors have tended to prefer limited involvement in situations in which they seem likely to confront intense opposition. Governors who take a strong stand on controversial issues such as regulation of the funeral industry, the establishment of generic drug laws, and certain regulatory policies affecting the nursing home industry take significant political risks. The prospect of intense opposition from politically important groups is so great that many governors consciously avoid a policy development role.

In short, governors only periodically have been central actors in policy development for the aging. Like presidents, however, they are beginning to take greater interest in the electoral politics of aging issues. In the future, governors may have increased opportunities to be leaders in aging policy development.

BUREAUCRATS AND THE BUREAUCRACY

The agencies involved in policy development for the aging include several very prominent organizations and an array of smaller units. The Social Security Administration (SSA) and the Health Care Financing Administration (HCFA) within the Department of Health and Human Services (formerly HEW) are the largest federal agencies. A wide variety of persons and organizations representing virtually every cabinet department of the U.S. federal government also are involved.

The Social Security Administration

For very different reasons, the Social Security Administration (SSA) and the Administration on Aging (AoA) have a distinctive importance in policy making affecting the aging. From its small beginning in the 1930s, the SSA has emerged as a large organization even by today's federal standards. By the late 1970s more than 90,000 people worked for the agency. Of these employees, 20,000 operated from the Baltimore offices where the early leaders chose to be located so they would be removed from daily political affairs in Washington. With many of its buildings housing nothing but computers, the SSA stands, in the eyes of many, as an example of organizational efficiency. Administrative costs have been relatively low. Costs for operating the basic Social Security benefits (OASI) were estimated by Robertson (1981, 24) as only 1.9 percent of the program's total budget. The difficulties of administering the Supplemental Security Income program since 1974 and the emerging backlog in computer operations, however, have led to some less favorable assessments of the SSA in recent years.

The top leadership within the administration has been remarkably stable. Between 1936 and 1973, only six individuals held the chief executive position as Commissioner of Social Security. Two of them, Arthur Altmeyer and Robert Ball, were in command for about 27 of those 37 years. Few have questioned the leadership capabilities of those at the top of the SSA or their commitment to developing and expanding a program along the lines they judged to be most appropriate. More questionable has been the willingness of SSA's leaders to consider other approaches and to welcome open political competition over alternative policies (Derthick 1979, 412-428). The role of the SSA, with its commitment to "quiet expansion" during much of its existence thus emerges as an important factor in an assessment of income maintenance policy development.

The Administration on Aging

The Administration on Aging, as a minor organization within the Department of Health and Human Services, stands in striking contrast to the Social Security Administration. Formed in 1965, it has tried to emphasize coordination and participation — objectives of many social services agencies in the days of Lyndon Johnson and the Great Society, but objectives that were not always comfortably shared. In a manner similar to the initial Model Cities programs but with the objective of covering the entire country through state action, the AoA was to serve as a focal point for the planning of federal-state initiatives. It also was to provide a basis for advisory committee actions in each of the states which would facilitate support for aging-related programs.

The evolution of the AoA has produced several basic changes since the 1960s. It began with a tiny budget of $6 million. In the late sixties, however, the nation's attention turned to Vietnam and the problems of the inner cities. As a result, potential interest in expanding the AoA was slow to develop. When the White House Conference on Aging met in 1971, the limited growth of the Administration on Aging was widely criticized. Changes in 1972 and 1973, however, substantially expanded and altered the administration. In March 1972 Congress provided a separate title to expand the nutrition programs, which had been conducted thus far on an experimental basis. This had the consequence of adding a specific administrative role, and a popular program, to the AoA's operations. Then in 1973, in an effort to prod additional service development, Congress established Area Administrations on Aging — locally based units throughout each state that would provide planning, advisory commission activity, and the administration of such programs as the nutrition site facilities and demonstration projects.

With these additions, the AoA budget increased more rapidly. Indeed, some state and local governments had difficulty assimilating the influx of funds. Funding levels nonetheless remained well under a billion dollars as of 1981. While the AoA has been important as a catalytic organization and has administered a growing social services program, it remains a small component within the Department of Health and Human Services, and it is not a major source of funding for the nation's expensive programs in the areas of income maintenance and health care assistance.

The Proliferation of Agencies and Programs

The number of organizations involved with aspects of policy for the aging is remarkably extensive. In a summary table presented by Estes (1979, 80-81), one finds no less than 24 different federal agencies included in a list of some 80 different programs for the aging. A similar sense of fragmentation in programs and agencies is apparent in the annual summaries of program development prepared by the House and Senate Committees on Aging. (See, for example, U.S. House, Select Committee on Aging, 1981).

The problems that are likely to occur as a result of the fragmentation of program responsibility are easily illustrated by considering the number of organizations involved in the related areas of income maintenance policies, job opportunities, and private pensions. Income maintenance programs are administered not only by the Social Security Administration but also by the Department of Agriculture through its responsibility for the Food Stamp program. Pensions are administered separately by the Civil Service Commission, the Railroad Retirement Board, and the Veterans Administration. In recent years, various job programs have been administered by agencies within the Labor and Agriculture Departments. Responsibility for work discrimination issues has been assigned to the Equal Employment Opportunities Commission. Finally, in a particularly awkward instance of shared responsibility, private pension issues have involved the Treasury Department, the Labor Department, and the Pension Benefit Guarantee Board, created in 1974.

There are several consequences of the proliferation of organizations involved with policies for the aging. Administrative responsibility often is divided, and some of the programs in particular agencies are very small. Politically, the wide variety of organizations means that those seeking to maintain support for programs have an extensive set of agencies and corresponding legislative committees and subcommittees with which they must interact. Not surprisingly, lobbyists for aging-based interest groups need to maintain contact with more legislators than lobbyists for a number of other large Washington lobbies (Pratt 1980). Thus the proliferation of programs and agencies affects not only program coordination but also opportunities for political action.

THE LEGISLATORS

Any search for key roles and actors in the development of policies for the aging must give careful attention to the actions of influential legislators, important committees, and the increasingly well-staffed and full-time operations of the U.S. Congress and the state legislatures. Despite the image of Congress as a "stalemate machine," it has frequently played a major role in the development of policy for the aging. Similarly, the part-time state legislatures of the pre-1960s, with their limited capacities for policy development, have given way two decades later to substantially improved policy-making capacities. At both levels of government, it is important to consider the key access points in committee structures, the role of legislative specialists, and legislative voting patterns on aging-related issues.

Congressional Committees

Three different types of congressional committees make decisions affecting aging policy: aging-designated committees, authorizing committees involved with policies affecting the aging, and financially oriented committees. Often the most visible roles, but not necessarily the most influential ones, are associated with the aging-designated committees: the Senate Special Committee on Aging formed in 1961 and the House Select Committee on Aging formed in 1974. The Senate committee became active in nursing home reform in the early 1960s. More recently, the House committee also began to play an important role in focusing attention on issues affecting the aging. The Senate Special Committee on Aging publishes an annual report entitled *Developments in Aging*, which circulates widely among those involved with aging-related issues. It has had a useful impact on policy debates. In both committees the use of hearings has been utilized to help give witnesses recognition in their home communities and to help focus national attention on key issues. Perhaps the most noteworthy example of this process was the action of the House Select Committee on Aging, then chaired by Rep. Claude Pepper (D-Fla.), in promoting the abolition of mandatory retirement in a series of hearings in 1976 and 1977. Despite their importance as a focal point for issue raising, these committees are not allowed to report legislation. As a result, the authorizing committees (so called because they authorize federal programs and limit spending on them), and the financially oriented committees take on major importance.

Many authorizing committees influence aging policy issues. Two of the most important are the House Education and Labor Committee and the Senate Labor and Public Welfare Committee. Often crucial decisions are made at the subcommittee level. For example, the Subcommittee on Aging, Family and Human Services of the Senate Labor and Public

Welfare Committee handles aging legislation as do numerous other subcommittees. According to one estimate, more than 40 different committees and subcommittees have been involved in legislation affecting the aging in the past few years (Binstock 1978, 1838).

Despite the formal separation between the aging committees and the authorizing committees, there is considerable coordination of activity. On occasion, members will serve on one of the aging committees and on an authorizing committee that is dealing with a similar aging-related issue. The elimination of nonmandatory retirement, for example, was aided by some membership overlap between the House Education and Labor Committee and the House Select Committee on Aging. The problems of separate committee structures also are minimized by the extensive interaction — and sometimes even exchanges in positions — of congressional staff members.

Where questions of expenditure are involved, the financially oriented committees take on great importance. Historically, the House Ways and Means Committee and the Senate Finance Committee have been particularly influential on certain aging issues because of their jurisdiction on tax policies. They played a critically important role in decisions on Social Security pensions and Medicare and Medicaid. These two committees are among the most coveted assignments in each house. Membership is generally reserved to comparatively senior legislators. The chairmen of these committees often have developed specializations in Social Security and Medicare and have been extremely influential. Rep. Wilbur Mills (D-Ark.), Ways and Means Chairman from 1958 to 1974, and Sen. Russell Long (D-La.), Senate Finance Chairman from 1967 to 1980, had very important policy development roles. Sen. Robert Dole (R-Kan.) assumed the chairmanship of the Finance Committee when the Republicans took control of the Senate after the 1980 elections. In the early 1980s he used his position to promote Social Security reform.

The other four financially oriented committees are the House and Senate appropriations committees and budget committees. The appropriations committees must approve allocations for all departments. Thus they help determine expansion or reduction in the budgets of such agencies as the Administration on Aging and the Department of Agriculture (with its Food Stamp programs). The budget committees, established under the Budget and Impoundment Control Act of 1974, were created to give Congress greater control over the federal budget.

Their often unenviable task is to determine overall expenditure ceilings and then attempt to keep spending bills within these limits agreed upon by the House and Senate. It was these budget ceiling resolutions that formed an early test for Reagan in his desire to have Congress restrain domestic spending. In recent years the budget committees have had an increasingly central role in determining how much money will be allocated by Congress for aging-related programs.

Legislative Specialization

The emergence of greater specialization on aging issues in Congress has occurred with both the development of expanded staffs and the evolution of more specific interests on the part of members of Congress. The size of congressional staffs doubled in the 1970s; the number of professional staffers with aging-related specialties also increased, not only in the aging-designated committees but also in the Congressional Research Service. In addition, the General Accounting Office, as part of its expanded emphasis on policy implementation questions, has become an important source of analysis for many individuals, including members of Congress, agency officials, and interest group leaders. In recent years GAO investigations have included nursing home rate policies and the operation of social services programs under the Older Americans Act of 1965. The expansion in the involvement of congressional committees and federal agencies in aging issues has been accompanied by a corresponding growth, not uncommon in other policy areas, in the number of university research personnel and private consultants involved.

The development of legislative specialization on issues affecting the aging also has been occurring among members of Congress. Prior to the late 1950s, few legislators specialized in aging-related policies. The enactment of the Social Security Act in 1935 did not produce major instances of specialization, and the next years found pension issues being debated in the financial committees but without strong advocates or specialists. By the late 1950s and 1960s, however, legislative interest began to increase. Rep. Aime Forand (D-R.I.) and Sen. Patrick McNamara (D-Mich.) were active in the areas of health care assistance and nursing home reform, respectively. In the early 1960s, Rep. Mills focused his interests increasingly on questions of Social Security expansion and the development of Medicare.

In recent years the most visible spokesman for the aging in Congress and possibly in the nation has been Claude Pepper. His congressional career has been atypical to say the least; after 16 years of service in the Senate (1936 to 1951), he was elected to the House in 1963. "Senator" Pepper, as he likes to be called, has used his personal convictions, political skills, and the legitimacy gained by his own length of years (in 1982 he was the oldest member of the House — 82) and seniority in Congress to champion the cause of the aging in this country. (Ending months of speculation, Pepper announced on November 19, 1982, that he would give up his chairmanship of the Select Committee on Aging to assume the chairmanship of the Rules Committee, vacated by the retirement of Sen. Richard Bolling (D-Mo.). Pepper said he would continue to serve on the Aging Committee and chair its Subcommittee on Health and Long-Term Care.)

When he was a member of Congress, Sen. Frank Church (D-Idaho) also gave considerable attention to aging issues, particularly as chairman of the Senate Special Committee on Aging from 1971 to 1977. Less senior members often are attracted to the two aging-designated committees and have taken a substantial interest in cultivating a role for themselves in policy development.

Voting Patterns

There are surprisingly few instances in which important divisions have occurred in roll-call votes on aging issues. This is a testament to two basic factors. First, there has been a tendency for issues to be resolved in committee to avoid confronting legislators with the necessity of voting against legislation for the aging in controversial final votes. This is an important manifestation of the general desire among members of Congress to avoid actions that could cause them to be labeled as opponents of the aging. Second, in the days of fairly easy expansion in revenue for the Social Security Trust Fund, gradual expansion in Social Security benefits was not very controversial.

Two dimensions of legislative voting deserve emphasis. First, members of Congress tend to vote for Social Security benefit increases in reelection years, when they are eager to identify with electorally popular proposals (Tufte 1978, 28-37). Second, members' voting patterns on controversial measures generally show strong partisan cleavages, but with the same ideological defections one finds on other domestic policy choices. The Medicare struggle in the early 1960s is a case in point. Republicans and Southern Democrats opposed Medicare, and Democrats with liberal voting records generally supported it. On specific issues, however, this pattern may differ; Southern Democrats' interest is often greater if aid formulas favorably affect their districts and states. It is interesting to note that the Republican party provided the primary thrust for indexing Social Security benefits in 1972. It was motivated in considerable part by the desire to keep the Democrats from claiming credit for the passage of Social Security benefit increases in election years (Derthick 1979, 349-350).

State Legislatures

State legislatures also have markedly altered their policy-making roles and capacities since the 1960s. Before then, most state legislators worked part-time, staff assistance was usually negligible, and sessions often were convened only every other year and then for short periods of time. In this context, aging-related matters generally received peripheral attention. New York was an exception; it developed an important legislative committee role in the 1950s. After 1958 and the major Democratic gains in the state legislature, California also began to develop a substantial legislative capacity for program analysis. The state legislatures dominated by part-time amateurs clearly could respond — as they did with their involvement in setting Old Age Assistance benefit levels. Neither issue raising nor detailed policy analysis, however, tended to be a part of the typical legislative role.

The state legislatures went through a major transformation in the 1960s and early 1970s. Staffs grew rapidly, legislators were more apt to devote full time to the responsibilities of their offices, and the legislatures also were much more equitably apportioned. Some states, such as Florida, Georgia, Nevada, and North Carolina, transformed their legislatures physically through the construction of new capitols or legislative buildings. In many states new office buildings began to emerge as part of larger capital complexes — and with separate rooms for each legislator and a rapid expansion in committee rooms and space for legislative analysts. The expanded capacity had an impact on the potential for policy development, from consumer protection legislation to reimbursement rates for long-term care facilities.

The changing policy-making capacity of the state legislatures also has had an important impact on the emergence of legislators who specialize on aging policy. Prior to the 1970s, many who were interested were drawn to the field on the basis of career backgrounds and, in at least some instances, a direct personal interest. Thus, insurance agents often handled pension matters, doctors health policy issues, and lawyers questions of inheritance and guardianship. Because turnover among state legislators was high, few specialized or sought to advance their careers on aging-related issues.

In the last decade the number of legislators with a substantive interest in aging-related policy issues increased. Interestingly, these legislators tended to be young, perhaps because they found aging policy issues to be a growing area and could use them to gain recognition within the legislative arena. They came most often, although not exclusively, from urban areas and were disproportionately members of a state Democratic party organization. The comparative state study by Dobson and Karns (1979) shows that legislative advocates for the aging were emerging by the late 1970s in a variety of states. Turnover remained a problem, however, and in many states the advocacy structure was quite frail. Yet repeatedly, this level of activity was seen as an expansion over what had existed prior to the 1970s.

Committees at the state level always have been less formally structured than congressional committees, but a few of them, particularly finance and appropriations committees, have been extremely influential in the passage or defeat of aging legislation. State advocates for the aging at points have suffered from the same problems encountered by promoters of aging issues in Congress. It is easier to gain support in a committee specializing on aging policy matters, or in a sympathetic authorizing committee, than it is to gain support in key financial committees. Thus, even if a state has a committee on aging — about half of the states did by the mid-1970s — there may not be a receptive response within the particular committee controlling the budget. In Iowa, for example, the appropriations committees often presented a difficult arena for aging-related proposals, in part because the recognized aging advocates usually had limited influence with those committees (Bruner 1978, 112-120).

The state legislatures, like Congress, raise important questions for persons interested in policy development for the aging. To what extent, and in what ways, has the state legislative role changed in recent years?

Are legislatures more responsive to lobbying from aging-based groups now than in the past? And, from a practical standpoint, what tactics and strategies appear to be successful in the efforts to influence legislators on policy matters affecting the aging? Legislative roles as well as the roles of executives and members of key agencies raise basic issues regarding policy development for the aging.

THE STUDY OF PUBLIC POLICY MAKING

The study of policy development for the aging, as we have seen in the past three chapters, must include several lines of analysis. At a general level, it is important to assess the overall impact of systemic factors and the specific roles of key participants in the policy process. The character-istics of the aging population, social attitudes, economic conditions, and private sector activities are factors that should be considered in a developmental framework. In terms of more proximate forces, the differing contributions being made by key participants need to be considered. It is not enough to simply ask: "Whose political power was used to achieve a given result?" Thus, interest groups may be important as issue raisers but not as bargainers, and bureaucrats may be more important in shaping policy proposals than in building political support.

In several respects, the nature of policy outcomes are significant. Some policy characteristics, such as cost, impact, and visibility, are apt to alter the nature of the responses which emerge from the political process. The separate trust fund status for the Social Security system, for example, often is viewed as a factor that reduced the visibility of expenditures in early years and contributed to the ease of program growth.

Policy responses also must be considered in a variety of evaluative contexts. Does a program distribute benefits fairly? Are the needs of all segments of the older population covered adequately? Does the level of commitment to different types of policies, such as the division between social services and income maintenance, reflect an appropriate division of governmental resources? Are there options in a given policy area that could be expanded with positive results? Are the interests of the aging be-ing given fair support in relationship to the claims being made for governmental assistance by other groups? How may future social changes affect the potential policy responses in a given policy area? Questions also emerge surrounding the prospects for achieving different policies through changes in the nature of the political process. For example, would changes in the strength of interest groups, or the level of decentralization, be likely to achieve improved policy responses?

Chapters 5 through 9 address a number of policy-making and policy evaluation questions. Particular attention has been given to the following actions: (1) expansion of Social Security benefits, (2) the establishment of Supplemental Security Income (SSI), (3) pension regulation decisions in 1974, (4) the establishment of nonmandatory retirement in 1978, (5) the Medicare and Medicaid decisions in 1965, and (6) social services policies and the evolution of the Older Americans Act of 1965. These actions reflect different policy areas, levels of conflict, and policy characteristics. The book concludes with a consideration of emerging issues and possible future directions for aging politics and policies.

V

SOCIAL SECURITY

Policy making for the Social Security system has become increasingly difficult. Thirty-six million persons receive payments from that system's basic programs, and 93 percent of the labor force pay taxes for them. In 1977, the new tax structure for the Social Security system was judged to be adequate for projected payments into the next century. Yet by the early 1980s, the financial shortages of the Old Age and Survivors Insurance (OASI) Trust Fund required congressional approval of inter-fund borrowing in 1981. When that authorization ended December 31, 1982, funding issues had to be confronted yet again. The magnitude of the funding crisis is easily overstated, since references to bankruptcy often ignore the fact that the system has essentially operated since the first benefits were issued in 1940 on a "pay as you go" basis. Furthermore, the deficits being projected in the system constituted only a small portion of the federal government's increasing deficit problem in the early 1980s. Nonetheless, the nation and its leaders could not ignore the need for basic reforms. In this chapter on Social Security we will consider program characteristics, questions of political support, and reform alternatives.

PROGRAM CHARACTERISTICS

Since Congress passed the Social Security Act in 1935, the system has been adapted in response to changing economic and social conditions. New programs have been added, and new objectives have continued to evolve. Often these objectives conflict with specific policy decisions. In these debates, a frequent question emerges: Is Social Security really an insurance system?

The answer to the insurance question depends upon one's definition of insurance. Clearly, the system does not operate in a manner parallel to private pension plans in either the calculation of benefits or in the requirements for financial reserves to pay for future benefits. Yet there is some relationship to earnings in the calculation of benefits, which represents an aspect of the insurance approach as used in the private sector. For survivors and dependents, the system very definitely operates as an insurance against unexpected loss of income.

Major promoters of the system, such as former Social Security Commissioner Robert Ball, argue that the system should be referred to as one of social insurance. In his view (Ball 1978, 1-17), it is both accurate and important for public support to maintain the insurance concept. Interestingly, individual paychecks still refer to Federal Insurance Contributions Act (FICA) withholdings as the label for contributions to the Social Security system. Regardless of one's definition of insurance, it is useful to think of the programs under the Social Security Act as a result of multiple and changing objectives. An understanding of those multiple objectives provides a basis for considering specific program characteristics.

Objectives of the Social Security System

One of the objectives of the Social Security Act of 1935 and the amendments of 1939 was to provide a system of income maintenance for the aging through individual insurance. That objective has been the reason for the largest expenditures: about 80 percent of all payments go to the elderly, and this does not include the costs of health insurance under Medicare. A second objective was to provide a floor of protection for the most needy segment of the older population. This was initially pursued through federal participation in the state-initiated plans for Old Age Assistance. Beginning in 1974, the federal government assumed a larger role with the establishment of the Supplementary Security Income program (SSI). These programs have been explicit in addressing the question of need, with eligibility for SSI dependent upon assets as well as income. A third and more recent objective has been to provide compensatory income to those, regardless of age, who experience sudden loss of income, such as widows, surviving children, and the disabled.

The question of proper objectives becomes more difficult to determine when one considers specific issues. Should Social Security benefits constitute an adequate income without other sources? Some observers believe the objective should be to provide a "floor of protection" rather than a complete retirement income. Yet in the eyes of critics of the system, the expansion that occurred in the 1970s constituted a shift toward the use of Social Security benefits as the basis for sufficient retirement income regardless of other sources such as private pensions (Campbell 1979).

How should the Social Security system relate to existing differences in income levels in the nation and among the aging? This is another hotly debated question. There has been considerable discussion over the extent to which regressive taxes can be justified for current financing. Others question the appropriateness of a benefit structure that is distinctly more generous to the low-income wage earner. Should the contributions of married women be treated with an emphasis on adequacy of retirement income or equity on past contributions? Different conclusions emerge depending upon which objective is emphasized. None of these questions can be answered easily by trying to return to the "real intent of the original legislation." Neither is it possible to conclude from the evidence what the "fair" answers are on these issues. Within the multifaceted Social Security system, legitimate policy goals are often in conflict.

Revenues and Costs

The Social Security system has been financed by separate trust funds, revenues raised equally from employees and employers, and funding on a "pay as you go" basis. These characteristics are rooted in the major decisions made in 1935. Financing from current taxes, rather than through the development of reserves sufficient to pay future benefits without additional contributions, has been a common approach for central governments. In contrast to private industry, governments are able to commit their future taxing capacity as the basis for future payment of benefits. Many national governments, however, do contribute to social security pensions through general revenues rather than by relying solely upon employer and employee contributions (Stein 1981, 183-185). The use of three-way splits between government, employee, and employer is one increasingly popular alternative.

Despite the continuing use of the trust fund approach and the formal exclusion of general revenue, there is some debate as to the extent to which this system avoids a general revenue contribution. First, employers (not employees) are able to deduct their payments as operating expenses and thus reduce their taxes. (The rationale for the tax on employee contributions is that taxes are not paid on benefits.) Presumably, if employers were not deducting the Social Security tax, then they would be paying more substantial corporate taxes into general revenue funds. Second, the level of the Social Security tax often is considered on issues of general economic management. For purposes of macro-economic theory, the distinction between Social Security taxes and income taxes is not important. Economic planning goals thus may require a drop in income and corporate tax levels if Social Security taxes are to be increased. The debate over Social Security tax increases in 1981 and 1982 quickly underscored the interrelated nature of all tax revenues. The separate accounting process does not alter, in other words, the underlying relationship between total government taxing and spending.

The separate funding basis does mean, however, that Social Security financing involves a direct tax (without the use of personal exemptions as with income taxes) and that the financial health of the trust funds operates as a built-in call for modifications in existing tax and benefit structures. The Social Security system has not had to compete directly with other federal programs for support. The Social Security contributions, while highly visible, have emphasized the half of the tax payed by each participating employee and not the employer's contribution.

It is important to know that there are four separate trust funds, not just one, because the financial health of these funds has differed in recent years. Congress has added separate funds as new programs have been developed, so that there are now separate trust funds for Old Age and Survivors Insurance (OASI), Disability Insurance (DI), and Hospital Insurance (HI), funded through Medicare. A fourth fund handles revenues for the supplemental portion of Medicare. In some discussions, the funding for Medicare is kept separate, and discussions then focus on the combined revenue and cost projections for OASI and DI as a combined OASDI fund. The costs of programs for the disabled are only 7 percent of the combined obligations for OASDI.

In operating the trust funds, a calculation is made each year projecting the relationship between revenues already in the fund (exclusive of taxes that will be collected that year) and the likely costs of benefits to be paid out. In times of easier financing, it was not uncommon for OASDI at the beginning of a year to develop reserves that were several times in excess of those to be paid out for the entire year. Building up a reserve in the trust funds also has been recommended by some as a strategy for coping with the retirement of the baby boom generation, especially since they will be preceded (at least demographically) by years of fairly low demands upon the system. As reserves are built up in the trust funds, they are invested in government bonds. The funds earn interest and provide the federal government with an assured customer for financing some of its debt. As excess revenues build up in one or another of these funds, borrowing periodically has been authorized. For example, funds from HI and DI may be borrowed for OASI and vice versa. In 1982, many felt that interfund borrowing simply postponed attention to long-range problems.

Since the mid-1970s, there have been two periods of peak concern in which the reserves on hand at the beginning of the year dropped below half of the benefits scheduled to be paid out in that year, and in which the funds for OASDI were projected to run out within a year or two on the basis of present operating practices. A variety of borrowing options could be developed through new legislation, since deficit financing is certainly not unknown in other operations of the federal government. However, the inability of the trust funds to maintain their self-financing basis in the longer run would require general revenue financing. Low reserves in the trust funds thus are taken as an indication that changes should be made in the benefit and/or tax structures.

Several related factors have contributed to the Social Security revenue problems. Regardless of any change in benefit levels, the maturing of a pension system over time will increase total costs (Wilensky 1975). It is always easier to operate a new system at low cost because there are few eligible retirees in relationship to the number of contributors. As the number of eligible retirees begins to increase, the number of workers who are contributing also may increase. Thus, in the 1950s the Social Security system grew in financially favorable ways. Inevitably, however, the number of new employees that can be recruited into a system begins to decline, and the number of eligible retirees begins to increase. Mounting costs result.

Costs also have been raised by substantially increasing benefits and by reducing the age of eligibility. The age of partial eligibility was reduced from 65 to 62 for women in 1956, and for men in 1961. This step has contributed to a situation in which the average age of retirement has dropped substantially. As a result, literally half of all applications recently have been made by individuals between the ages of 62 and 64. Major benefit increases also were enacted in 1972 and 1977, thus contributing to higher costs and the subsequent revenue shortage.

Short-run problems for the trust funds have been caused by unexpected changes in the performance of the economy. Higher inflation than expected has contributed since 1972 to greater costs as a result of the decision to index benefits to changes in the Consumer Price Index. As a result of high unemployment, less revenue is collected through taxes, while older persons are more apt to apply for early benefits when they have trouble finding jobs. The loss of Social Security taxes for every 1 percent increase in unemployment was calculated by Gwirtzman (1982) to be at least $3 billion. In the long run, high unemployment may reduce future benefit payments somewhat because the level of covered earnings for some workers will decline. Nonetheless, in the short run, a combination of high inflation and unemployment has had a major impact on trust fund operations.

The increase in costs has not been fueled in the past decade by sharp percentage increases in the size of the U.S. older population. The next two decades also will have a distinctly favorable demographic impact in terms of those who reach age 65. Unless there is a sudden surge in the average age of death, the demographic factor gives the nation time to plan for the greatly increased costs that will be precipitated by the retirement of the "baby boom" cohort. In sum, the Social Security problems facing the nation are short-run and long-run. From the late 1980s to 2010, these problems will not be as acute as in subsequent years.

Even without a major demographic shift, the combination of a maturing system and increased benefit levels has produced rapidly increasing costs in recent years. Table 5-1 shows the increases in tax levels between 1937 and 1982 and projections for 1983 to 1990. Although a small percentage of all employees will be paying the maximum dollar amount, the tax percentage and covered earnings level increases have been substantially increasing the tax in recent years. Furthermore, while there was considerable sentiment in Congress for avoiding an additional tax increase in the early 1980s, the warning signs from the OASI Trust Fund indicated that difficult choices had to be made. In looking at those tax rates, it is also important to emphasize that an important body of economic writings, as reviewed by such writers as Schulz (1980, 158), argues that the employer's half of the Social Security tax is borne by the employee in the form of lower wages. While there is disagreement as to the completeness of that shift in the tax burden, it is important not to consider the impact of Social Security taxes only in terms of the employee

Table 5-1 Social Security Taxes

	Taxable Portion of Wages	Tax Rate
1937	$ 3,000	1.00%
1950	3,000	1.50
1960	4,800	3.00
1970	7,800	4.80
1975	14,100	5.85
1980	25,900	6.13
1981	29,700	6.65
1982	32,400	6.70
Projections:		
1983	35,100	6.70
1984	37,500	6.70
1985	40,500	7.05
1986	43,800	7.15
1990	57,000	7.65

SOURCE: Social Security Administration; *The Congressional Quarterly Almanac*, 1977, p. 167; the March 1981 report of the National Commission on Social Security, p. 78; and *National Journal*, Oct. 9, 1982, p. 1706.

NOTE: The tax rate is the combined employee taxes for the retirement, disability, and hospital insurance programs. The employer also pays that percent in taxes. Projections for taxable wage ceilings for 1983 to 1990 may be changed by fluctuations in wage rates.

payroll deductions. By almost any standard, Social Security benefits by the 1980s had become a very expensive public policy.

Benefits

Policy questions are raised regarding the consequences of taxing and benefit levels for different social classes, racial groups, and age groups (Derthick 1979, 252-270). First it is important to recognize that the Social Security tax is regressive. People with lower incomes are paying a larger percentage of their monthly salary. This has been modified somewhat since 1977 in that most people now pay taxes on all of their annual income. There also has been some modification in the regressiveness for those at the lowest income levels through the reduction in income taxes now being achieved on the basis of earned income credits (Stein 1980, 187).

The benefit structure, in contrast, is the least generous to high-income contributors. By design, they receive a smaller proportion of their preretirement income with a lower replacement rate. For a given individual, the progressively less generous nature of the benefit structure is evident by the basic formula. After calculating the average monthly earning (AME) — and adjusting for an expansion in wage rates during a person's working years — an individual's benefit is then calculated on the basis of an annually adjusted formula for new applicants. The formula in 1981 was 90 percent of the first $211 in Averaged Indexed Monthly Earnings (AIME), 32 percent for the next $1,063, and 15 percent for any remainder. In addition, the modest length of the requirements for gaining coverage in early years (which do not reach 10 years until 1991) and the very low earnings required to constitute a period of covered employment have favored marginal members of the labor force. These eligibility requirements and minimum benefit levels have given high rates of return to some low-income persons. The impact among social classes is thus mixed, with different consequences for individuals with different employment situations and life spans. In general, taxes hit low-income groups the hardest, but benefits are higher in relationship to contributions for those with low lifetime earnings.

The distribution of advantages and disadvantages for racial groups also has drawn increased interest in recent years. Blacks have argued that they are discriminated against because they more often pay a regressive tax on the basis of low incomes and yet have reduced total benefits because of a lower average age of death than the average for the total population. Like any group that is characterized by low earnings, blacks may have a rate of return on those payments that is higher than for persons making substantially more money through their lifetime if the age of death is similar to the national average. Continued increases in the life expectancies of minority groups may rectify, at least partially, the present impact on the nation's minorities.

Finally, the Social Security system raises questions about the distribution of benefits and costs between generations. Given the evolution of a mature Social Security system, there is no feasible way for future retirees to receive a rate of return comparable to that received by many early recipients. Before the reader becomes overly envious, however, he or she should remember that the absolute level of those benefits was quite small. Ida Fuller, the first Social Security recipient in 1940, had a generous ratio of benefits to payments, but those payments averaged about $50 a month. The standard of living for the entire nation has improved substantially since those early post-World War II years and should continue to improve through the lifetime of today's younger age groups. The question of benefits for future retirees is complicated by the approaching retirement of the large "baby boom" cohort. Even with a mature system in place, there is no easy way to adjust to problems created by sharp differences in the number of potential retirees.

Are present contributors likely to receive a reasonable rate of return? The answer to this question can be found only after numerous assumptions are made about family size, the incidence of tax, age of entry, and age of death. On the basis of the future benefit levels projected after the 1977 amendments to the Social Security Act, Kaplan (1979, 119-144) reports various rate of return assessments. He concludes that his studies basically support Martin Feldstein's view that the real rate of return (after adjusting for inflation) in a fully mature Social Security system is limited to the growth rate of real wages, or approximately 2 percent. Recent calculations by Robertson, a former chief actuary of the Social Security Administration, are even more sobering (Robertson 1981, 134). He predicts that the generation entering the work force now, between the ages of 20 and 24, probably will get only $1.15 in benefits for every $1 paid in through the combined tax on workers and employers. Future generations, he predicts, will fare even worse, with the benefits on combined contributions often dropping to less than has been contributed.

Ultimately, the intergenerational equity that emerges in the form of rates of return for those retiring in future decades, and particularly for the large "baby boom" cohort, will be determined by the policies that future voters and leaders develop to deal with the problems presented by that larger group of retirees. A variety of results are possible, depending upon different policy choices as well as future birth and death rates and levels of economic performance. Before turning to those policy choices, the political forces that have been shaping recent changes in the Social Security system will be discussed.

THE POLITICS OF EXPANSION

The Social Security Act of 1935 was passed in the context of dire economic conditions for the older population, an attitudinal shift in the midst of the depression, effective presidential leadership, and heightened interest on the part of legislators and lobbyists in pension issues. During the period of gradual expansion between World War II and the late 1960s, the major factors shaping changes in the Social Security system included strong advocacy from within the Social Security Administration, support from key legislators, a general mood in Congress supportive of programs for the aging, and presidential roles involving either modest support or an absence of the desire (and perhaps the political capacity) to slow the movement toward expansion. It is in this period in which Derthick (1979, 62-88) is particularly effective in tracing the important influence of the top leadership within the Social Security Administration in developing new proposals and promoting support for them in Congress.

Program expansion in the 1950s and 1960s was aided by several underlying factors. With the gradual expansion of coverage, and the strong performance of the economy during parts of the postwar period, it was possible to expand the system without sharply increasing taxes. Thus individual tax rates, presented in Table 5-1, remained under 2 percent until 1954, and under 3 percent until 1960, before edging into the 4 percent range in the 1960s. The favorable relationship between benefits and personal contributions contributed to the strong public support between 1935 and 1965 (Schiltz 1970).

The policy decisions we will be examining all occurred in the 1970s and expanded the overall program substantially. In 1972, Congress passed an amendment to the Social Security Act indexing future benefits to changes in the cost of living while also increasing the benefit levels by 20 percent. In 1972, Congress also federalized and expanded federal-state pensions (Old Age Assistance). The new program was called Supplemental Security Income (SSI). Then in 1977, Congress again expanded Social Security benefit obligations by increasing taxes and modifying the manner in which replacement rates were calculated.

The factors common to this five-year period deserve consideration before turning to the more specific political factors involved in the actions taken between 1972 and 1977. Throughout this period, favorable attitudes toward the aging persisted. In 1977, according to Ladd (1977), programs for the aging were those deemed least favorable as targets for curtailment. As a more recent indication of continuing support, a major survey by Hart (1979) found strong support for maintaining the basic dimensions of the Social Security system and more concern with inadequacies in benefits than in the magnitude of the taxes. These indications of support were stronger than those found for general welfare programs.

In terms of demographics, while the percentage growth of the aging population had slowed, the absolute numbers were continuing to grow. What is perhaps more important, however, is that an awareness of the impact of those numbers seemed to gain more general attention in the 1970s than in previous decades. Particularly in the first half of the decade, there was a general expansion in social programs by the federal government. The post-Vietnam budget grew rapidly in a variety of domestic spending categories, fueled in part by the reduction in relative proportions going to the military and in part by the additional revenues which inflation was beginning to bring to the federal till. Political factors, including Richard Nixon's strong reelection effort in 1972, and then the resurgence of Congress in the wake of Nixon's slide to resignation in his second term, also contributed to a general period of domestic policy expansion.

The Indexing of Social Security

One of the striking ironies of Social Security benefit expansion is that the desire for indexing, which when accomplished became a significant factor in benefit growth in the past decade, came most forcefully from those wanting to curtail benefits. The idea was anything but new. Rep. James Byrnes, a Wisconsin Republican, advocated indexing in 1958, and some form of indexing was widely used in many industrial nations by the late 1960s.

The Republican party supported indexing in its 1968 platform, and a number of Republican legislators advocated indexing in 1969. A major motivation for some was to try to hold down the bidding contests which tended to emerge in election years (Derthick 1979, 349-357). For Republicans in Congress, indexing promised the desired result of some — reduced benefit increases; others favored it because they hoped it would reduce the likelihood that the Democratic party could claim credit for further increases in benefits. Some conservatives, primarily those outside Congress, opposed indexing because of its potential costliness. Within the Democratic party there was some interest in indexing, but such key figures as Rep. Wilbur Mills (D-Ark.) were opposed initially because they wanted to see larger increases prior to the establishment of an indexing system.

The resulting controversy produced delay and then disagreement over the appropriate formula to employ. The House passed an indexing formula in 1970, but the Senate balked and the final compromise measure died in conference. Finally, in 1972, an indexing formula was passed as part of a package increasing SSI and Social Security benefits by 20 percent. As an indication of the confusion surrounding that legislation, Congress realized only belatedly that the formula gave a double indexing advantage to some recipients. The 1977 amendments to the Social Security Act rectified that problem.

Several forces contributed to the establishment of indexing in 1972. The decision occurred at a time when inflation was viewed as a problem for the aging, but indexing was not viewed as an unduly expensive solution. In 1972, a 3 to 4 percent inflation rate seemed high; virtually no one anticipated the double-digit levels that would occur by the end of the decade. More directly, indexing was the result of legislative maneuvering and the mixed desires to either contain or expand the system, coupled with the desire among Republicans to avoid Democratic opportunities for election advantage in the politics of Social Security. President Nixon supported the change but was not a key actor in these developments. As a president primarily involved with foreign affairs, and who became increasingly isolated in the White House after the discovery of the Watergate break-in in June 1972, he was in no position to provide strong leadership. Lobby groups helped focus attention on the indexing issue, and the Social Security Administration provided important analyses of alternative approaches and future costs. In short, indexing came into being in 1972 primarily as a result of legislative maneuvering and a general sense within Congress and the executive branch that programs for the aging were good things to support, especially in an election year.

The Establishment of SSI

The legislative history of the Supplemental Security Income (SSI) program is most unusual. Few would have suspected in the spring of 1969, as Nixon unveiled a major program for welfare reform, that the end result would be passage almost four years later of a modified assistance program for the needy aged. With a further touch of irony, the actual start of those benefits and Nixon's resignation both took place in 1974.

The establishment of SSI expanded federal assistance to the needy aged, blind, and disabled through Old Age Assistance. Whereas the earlier program shared costs (with greater assistance going to programs in the less wealthy states), the new program provided a floor of assistance to be financed fully by the federal government. (Newly uniform eligibility tests included both income limits and ceilings on assets.) The states could still supplement the federal assistance with their own benefits, and a few added substantial amounts. The federal minimum assistance levels, while uniform, were very low — initially only $140 a month for individuals and $210 a month for couples. Although administered by the Social Security Administration, the program was funded from general revenue.

The roots of SSI emerged in 1969 when President Nixon, to the surprise of many observers, embraced a broad program of welfare reform (Moynihan 1973). Despite a surprising victory in the House, the initial proposal never succeeded in the Senate. By 1971 and 1972, Nixon's orientation had shifted from welfare reform to other issues (Burke 1974; Bowler 1974). Hearings did continue, however, despite the increasingly bleak legislative outlook for the program. By 1972, while it was clear that the total welfare reform package had no chance of success, an interest in salvaging some of its aspects remained. While a divisive debate continued over the larger program, both Rep. Mills and Sen. Russell Long (D-La.) emerged as supporters of SSI as an acceptable partial reform. Nixon indicated his willingness to support SSI, and the presence of these three supporters contributed to a remarkable lack of conflict over this portion of the welfare reform proposal. An assistant to Sen. Abraham Ribicoff (D-Conn.) summed up some of the ironies of SSI's success:

> People were so concerned about Title IV (the family provisions) that no one paid any attention to Title III (provisions pertaining to aged, blind, and disabled adults). If SSI had been on its own it never would have made it. Also, it passed because it looked like peanuts next to the family programs. (Bowler 1974, 47)

SSI passed surprisingly quickly and easily in 1972 for several reasons. First, the costs were perceived as being modest in relation to other welfare reform issues. The greater federal share meant an actual increase in total cost of only two to three billion dollars for all categories of SSI recipients over what had been contributed previously. Second, because the plan would most help those who were receiving low benefits in the poorer states, there was an obvious constituency advantage for Southern Democrats (among them Mills and Long) to support this plan. Third, liberals had an interest in an expansion of SSI as a way to reduce the problem of minimum benefit increases. SSI was seen as a more direct route because of its income and assets test. Fourth, in terms of legislative strategies, the support by Mills, Long, and Nixon meant that potential conservative opposition was less likely to emerge. Fifth, mass member groups, such as the National Council of Senior Citizens, were interested in SSI. Finally, increased financial aid for the aging was generally seen by legislators as an appropriate campaign issue in an election year.

The 1972 Benefit Increases

The third key decision in 1972 involved the 20 percent expansion in benefits for current Social Security recipients. This was the most costly direct change and, in a period of debate over the inflationary impact of increased government spending, the one around which it should have been easiest to rally opposition. Yet Congress passed that increase as part of the final 1972 reform package.

The forthcoming election was a major factor in its passage. As Tufte (1978, 28-63) points out, Congress tends to expand benefits in election years. That tendency can be traced back to the 1950s and was becoming more pronounced in the size of the increases in the decade prior to the 1972 amendments. (A 20 percent increase, however, did constitute an unprecedented direct expansion of benefits.) Evidence of political motives marked the presidential election as well as legislative campaigns. Candidates began bidding for credit on this issue; gradually the increase moved from 5, to 10, to 15, and finally to 20 percent. This latter figure was introduced by Rep. Mills shortly before the New Hampshire primary. Mills was flirting with a bid for the presidential nomination. Nixon initially opposed that figure as highly inflationary, although he took a decidedly different position during the campaign, with a mailing to all recipients in late October which implied credit for those increases.

An analysis of interest group roles by Pratt (1976, 154-168) shows that aging-based interest groups were actively involved, particularly the National Council of Senior Citizens (NCSC). According to Pratt, this group was instrumental in the final passage of the 20 percent increase for several reasons. First, because of the ties between their long-time leader

Nelson Cruikshank and members of the Advisory Council on Social Security there was an important early opportunity to promote the 20 percent increase in background discussions. Second, NCSC leaders made efforts to recruit the support of Sen. Long, who was initially opposed to the more extensive increases. In his role as chairman of the Senate Finance Committee, Long was in a very important position to influence Senate decisions on the size of the benefit increase. Third, there were major efforts to generate grass-roots support among the three million members of NCSC. This grass-roots lobbying is seen as an important factor in reminding members of Congress of the importance of having a good voting record on Social Security benefits in an election year.

The conclusion reached by Pratt particularly stresses the importance of lobby efforts such as those undertaken by NCSC:

> Taken in its entirety, the study of the Mills-Church Amendments illustrates the substantive and often disregarded manner in which interest groups influence congressional decisions. Obviously, NCSC could not have wielded the kind of influence it did in the absence of favorable conditions in the political environment — the upcoming presidential election in which Wilbur Mills was an aspiring candidate, the prestige of the amendment's sponsors, the apparent "surplus" in the Social Security Fund, and so forth. But had NCSC, or some like-minded group with similar resources, not intervened, the legislative result would almost certainly have been different.

The 1977 Amendments

The 1977 amendments began a period in which the "graying of the budget" was producing a different — and more difficult — policy process (Hudson 1978). First, the impetus for action was not an upcoming election, but rather the forecast of deficits in the major trust fund, OASI. The cost issue was substantial, in contrast to 1972 when projected future revenues were seen as sufficient to fund the proposed expansion. The program was billed by its opponents as the largest peacetime tax increase ever proposed. There was also an unusually large number of proposals being considered, including President Jimmy Carter's April 1977 message to Congress and diverse actions by the two most critically involved committees — House Ways and Means and Senate Finance. As a result, a particularly wide range of interest groups became involved. In part because the process was more divisive than in the past, the role of the Social Security Administration was less central. As in the past, its analyses

103

of future revenue projections and the modifications in the replacement rate were important. Nonetheless, the final actions taken by Congress differed in several areas from those favored by Robert Ball, the Social Security Commissioner.

The reform process began when President Carter submitted a reform package to Congress in April containing major changes. To meet emerging financing needs, he proposed not only to increase taxes, but to make two other funding changes. First, in periods of high unemployment, some general revenue funds would be used to help make up the deficit stemming from reduced payroll tax contributions. Second, the pattern of equal taxes for employees and employers was to be broken with a slight increase in the tax on employers. The failure of Congress to accept either proposal indicates the continuing problems of presidential leadership in this area.

Alternative proposals were then bandied about in Congress, and after considerable disagreement and partisan divisions, a solution was finally enacted. The range of alternatives which emerged in the House, and the level of disagreement, reflected in part the greater difficulty Rep. Al Ullman (D-Ore.) had in chairing the Ways and Means Committee in a period of reduced willingness to rely upon direction from committee chairmen. Interestingly, a Ways and Means Committee proposal to include federal government employees passed in committee, before going down to a solid defeat on the floor of the House. The Senate also produced intense political maneuvering before reporting out a final bill. This included a rare tie vote which Vice President Walter Mondale broke in favor of Carter's proposal that a higher tax be levied on employers than on employees. That position, however, did not survive in conference committee.

A wide variety of lobbying activities was generated on this legislation, not only from the aging-related groups but from many other groups with specific interests. Government employees lobbied very hard in opposition to being included in the Social Security system, as did most state and local groups. Employer groups were firm in their view that the size of their contribution should not be increased. The business community was easily mobilized on this issue because there was a shared stake of significant proportion which affected all businesses. Insurance companies argued that this plan would decrease investment in private insurance plans. State and local governments and charitable organizations also lobbied that they should be given a lower contribution requirement because of the financial difficulties they would face in meeting the increasing employer taxes. Rather than a policy-making process largely confined to the network of groups and individuals specializing in aging policy matters, the pattern of interest group involvement became considerably broader, involving many of the most important organizations in American politics.

Politically, the ultimate decisions produced a set of increasingly partisan actions in both the House and Senate. When the final vote in the House was taken on the measure sending the bill to the Senate, the vote in favor was Republicans, 3-121; Northern Democrats, 134-19; and Southern Democrats, 41-35. Upon passage of the final bill, Speaker Thomas P. "Tip" O'Neill, Jr. (D-Mass.) claimed: "The philosophy has not changed on the Republican side since 1935. If I've ever seen an issue that's a Democratic issue, it's this." On the Senate side partisan divisions were less intense. On the final bill sent to conference committee, the Republicans voted 17-14 in favor, the Northern Democrats 25-2 in favor, and Southern Democrats in support, 12-2.

To some extent, the policy actions taken in 1977 represented a response to the impact of increasing claims on a trust fund financed only by a fixed tax rate. Once the issue of reform was seen as inevitable, however, a wide variety of groups, interests, and political leaders became involved. Several of those interest groups were influential in pressing their own claims, such as the government employees who rejected inclusion in the Social Security system. In a more general sense, the partisan impact was also substantial, with the Democrats providing the impetus for a final reform which increased taxes more substantially than some of the early proposals. These factors, plus the public's generally supportive attitude, came together to produce a major tax expansion. But these actions and the decisions on indexing and earlier benefit increases did not end the controversy as had been hoped. By the early 1980s, the nation was left with another revenue predicament in the trust funds and increasing concern as to what might be done to achieve more effective reform of the Social Security system.

The Early 1980s

Tensions over Social Security policy were even more dramatic in 1981 and 1982, but there was an initial reluctance to make difficult decisions. On May 12, 1981, President Reagan proposed a series of reforms that would have had a substantial impact on several aspects of the Social Security system. The greatest controversy surrounded his proposed reduction in benefits for retirees between the ages of 62 and 65. Additional provisions included a delay in the cost of living increase from July 1 to October 1 (since 1977 the beginning of the government's fiscal year), and an elimination of the minimum benefit provision for those whose covered earnings would result in very low monthly payments. In addition, reductions in the scholarship assistance for dependents were to be made.

The response in Congress to Reagan's proposals was one of instant resistance, with the Democrats taking the initiative. A mere eight days after Reagan had introduced his proposals, the Senate voted unanimously to reject, in principle, the changes being proposed. Following that action, the Reagan administration backed away from its initial reforms. In August Reagan proposed that the Social Security system be given yet another commission study. As for the reactions in Congress, there was a proposal in the House, authored by Rep. J. J. Pickle (D-Texas) to increase gradually the age of benefit eligibility to 66, and to reduce marginally some other benefits. (Given the likely sponsor in the Senate, John Heinz (R-Pa.), promoters tried to lighten a sometimes rather somber topic with references to the Heinz-Pickle bill.) The proposal for increasing the age of eligibility for benefits was defeated in committee, leaving the major issue by the end of the year one of resolving the status of the minimum benefit program. Congress initially went along with the president's proposal in the context of his major victory on the budget reconciliation act in August 1981, but then quickly began to have second thoughts. With Reagan himself changing his position by October, Congress acted at the end of the year to restore the minimum benefit for those who became eligible prior to January 1, 1982.

Proposals to cut Social Security aroused an impressive increase in interest group activity. Besides the actions of the established groups, there were broad coalition efforts by Save our Security (SOS). Leadership was provided by some of the same officials who had been involved with the development of the program in recent years, including Robert Ball and the official leader, Wilbur Cohen. In addition to an extensive letter writing campaign, their activities included a mass rally on July 21, 1981 (Congressional Quarterly 1981, 2329-2346). These groups then began pointing toward the controversies which would develop, following the release of the commision study after the 1982 congressional elections. Social Security politics clearly was changing as the search for possible reforms became more urgent.

THE REFORM AGENDA

The costly stakes involved in Social Security reform give future decisions a vital importance for all Americans. Given the difficulties of pursuing one's favorite reforms in a complex system, the present scene almost seems to bear out H. L. Mencken's sage comment that for every complex problem there is a solution which is simple, straightforward, and wrong! Yet despite the complexities inherent in the Social Security system, there are decisions of major importance which can be taken in the 1980s. Because budget pressures are an important force for reform, this decade is extremely important. Since the 1990s are apt to create reduced pressure on the financing of Social Security, the present period of political interest may be a critical juncture in terms of devising policies which will be in place as the baby boom generation begins to retire in the next century.

The following discussion thus examines a series of issues involving benefit levels, the position of the poorest recipients, the lack of adequate coordination with other public sector plans, and the case for and against the use of general revenues. The important related issues of possible changes in the average age of retirement and the degree of reliance upon private systems are discussed in Chapter 6. To introduce the following discussion of the reform issues, it is useful to consider this basic question: Why is there so much disagreement among those who study the Social Security system?

Sources of Disagreement

Discussions among specialists on different aspects of the system often show disagreement concerning not only overall values but also seemingly "factual" questions. It is not surprising that experts, like the general public, will have different value positions on such issues as the degree of emphasis on equity versus adequacy in benefits or the appropriateness of requiring individuals in future years to work to an older age before becoming eligible for benefits. Questions such as these simply raise basic value questions about which disagreement is to be expected and, at least periodically, to be encouraged.

Problems for analysts also emerge on seemingly more straightforward questions. There are often limitations in the basic data that permit differing interpretations. Surveys of the major reasons for retirement, for example, often find health factors emphasized strongly. Yet to an unknown degree, this response is apt to be given because it is deemed to be more socially acceptable than other answers, such as being bored with one's job. As a result, forecasts of future retirement rates based upon the impact of changes in the health status of the older population must be undertaken cautiously. Yet in assessing income at the lower levels, a different problem arises. It seems clear that some income is going unreported, in part because of a fear of reduced benefits from various means-tested programs such as Food Stamps and Medicaid. Yet the magnitude of that under-reporting is difficult to calculate.

Difficulties also occurred surrounding differences between studies that trace individuals over an extended period (longitudinal studies) and studies that focus on recent behavior (cross-sectional studies). Studies focusing on current behavior (for example, studies of who retired last year) are easier to conduct. Yet it it often difficult to sort out the effects of a given policy by looking only at the aging population at a single point in time. Studies of individuals over time are methodologically more accurate, but are often difficult — and expensive — to conduct. Finally, efforts at predicting the overall performance of the Social Security system are also difficult. On issues such as the future cash flow of the trust funds, even minor shifts in inflation and unemployment can have sharp short-run impacts. The complex nature of the research task will require expanded efforts to reduce problems surrounding existing analyses. It is nonetheless possible to see a number of reform possibilities quite clearly in the existing studies.

Benefit Levels

Are present benefit levels too high or too low? In terms of personal finances, a retired person does not have economic needs that match preretirement levels. In part, Social Security benefits (in contrast to private pensions)[1] are not taxable, thus producing greater spending power

---

[1] This difference is based upon the general principle in tax policy that taxes should be paid either on money going into a pension plan, or on money coming out, but not on both. Social Security payments are thus taxed initially but not the benefits; the reverse is true for private pensions requiring contributions.

for comparable sums of preretirement income. Some work-related expenses, such as clothing and transportation costs, also decline. Although the cost of supplementing Medicare may be substantial in some cases, there is at least a major assist with most forms of health costs (other than long-term care). Finally, a variety of other free or subsidized benefits, from Food Stamps to consumer discounts, are of some help.

The percentage of preretirement income needed to maintain a similar standard of living varies for different income levels. The analysis undertaken by the National Commission on Social Security (1981, 155-157) focused on needed net take-home pay as a percentage of gross earnings for different income levels. To maintain a comparable life situation after retirement, they concluded that a person earning $4,000 prior to retirement would need to have a net income of 83 percent of that amount after retirement. For a person earning $25,000 the figure dropped to 65 percent. The figure for married couples shows a similar relationship, with combined incomes at the $4,000 level requiring 86 percent after retirement, and the $25,000 level incomes requiring a 71 percent replacement after retirement.

Despite the increases in benefits in recent years, those who are dependent solely upon Social Security benefits in their old age will not have incomes replacing their previous earnings at these levels. The replacement rate, which calculates the relationship between past earnings and Social Security benefits, has been projected in the 1977 Social Security Amendments. For those who retire in the future at age 65, the replacement rate is projected at 52 percent for single workers if they have been earning the minimum wage, 41 percent if they have been an average wage earner, and 31 percent if they have been covered to the maximum level. For couples, the respective figures are 78, 62, and 47 percent. To meet this goal, the benefit formula is adjusted each year for the new group of individuals reaching age 62.

As of July 1981, the average retiree age 65 and over received $374.00 in monthly benefits, and the average couple received $640.00. For a widow or widower, the average was $348.00. The maximum benefit was $752.90, the minimum benefit $170.00. It also should be remembered in considering benefit policies that while the 1977 law stipulated intended replacement rates for future retirees, the aging population still includes a significant number of previously retired individuals who are receiving limited amounts of assistance and who may actually live below the poverty level. Thus the question of future benefits and the issue of aiding those in greatest need deserve attention.

Indexing and Future Benefits

The question of changes in benefit levels for present and future retirees has been tied in the last several years to the question of indexing. For current retirees, this is an understandable result of a situation in which the annual cost of living adjustments constitute major increases in benefits and costs. As of July 1, 1981, for example, the increase of over 10 percent for benefits being paid from the OASDI trust fund added almost $15 billion to projected obligations for the coming year. With sums of this magnitude, even the timing within the year can make an important difference in budget totals. The Reagan administration's proposal that the cost of living increase be postponed in the future until October 1 is a case in point.

The appropriateness of the existing indexing procedure for present retirees has received considerably more debate than when it was passed in 1972. Some have argued that the economic needs of the aging are not accurately reflected in the changes that occur in the standard cost of living index. The Consumer Price Index (CPI) includes a substantial housing cost factor, for example, and the aging do not often buy homes. (Renters, of course, also face direct increases insofar as rents reflect inflationary tendencies.) Conversely, the aging spend a larger percentage of their income on heating costs and on medical care than does the average consumer. Interestingly, efforts on the part of the National Commission on Social Security to produce a separate cost of living index for the aging did not produce results substantially different from those produced throughout the 1970s by the overall CPI. Yearly indexing has been a means of expanding benefits across the board, which proponents of policy advances for the aging have generally endorsed. A change in the approach to indexing, perhaps through a modified index, could be used to somewhat reduce benefits for everyone. An important but not readily answerable question is the extent to which savings from a decrease in indexed-benefit costs would be used either to focus attention on the most important expenditure areas within the overall program or to use those unspent funds to reduce total program costs.

Indexing procedures used to compute the benefit base figure of the new group of retirees each year have become highly controversial, and for a simple reason: technical differences can have a massive impact on future benefit levels. Since wages and prices increase over an individual's lifetime, it has been deemed appropriate to make some adjustment for this in computing average monthly earnings. (In the private sector, the same issue is generally addressed by taking an average wage for the last few years rather than a total career average in computing pension benefits. Because of differences in the amount of change between prices and wages, however, some have argued that it is more appropriate to index on the basis of price changes. While the technical procedures are complex, the result is very simple: the wage indexing formula yields substantially larger future benefits than would price indexing. Hsiao (1979) has argued that price indexing is the more equitable approach and the one which will allow the system to maintain its financial soundness in the next century. The National Commission on Social Security (1981), on the other hand, has taken the position that a shift from wage rate adjustment to price adjustment would inappropriately reduce benefits for future retirees. It claims it also would reduce retirees' replacement rates and make the rate of return on their investments much lower than for the present generation of retirees.

In the next few years, expansion or curtailment of benefits seems destined to be debated on the basis of rather technical formulas and not on the seemingly more straightforward basis of stipulating benefit levels in specific dollar amounts. The basic issue nonetheless remains. The system is growing more costly, yet those who depend solely on it have at best modest incomes and some live in poverty.

Minimum Benefits and SSI

Despite the increases in public programs, a sizable portion of the older population remains below the poverty level. Figures differ depending upon how generously the provisions of services are included in net income calculations. In one of the most favorable assessments, Clark and Barker (1981) place the percentage of families living in poverty (after the impact of transfer income, such as Medicaid, and taxes) at 6.1 percent in 1981. With the official figure for those in poverty again exceeding 15 percent by the early 1980s, it is very evident that a significant segment of the aging population, including some who are receiving Social Security benefits, suffer serious economic hardship. While the percentages may seem small, this group numbers at least two to three million persons. Possible reform in the two basic programs — minimum benefits and SSI — deserve careful attention.

The minimum benefit approach has an obvious capacity for reducing poverty among those who qualify for Social Security benefits, but it also has a serious flaw. To increase the incomes of those who qualify for Social Security benefits and have no other income, substantial sums are spent on individuals who have qualified for the minimum under Social Security but actually use this income to supplement other pensions and income sources. In 1977, Congress moved to create a special minimum benefit based upon the needs of those who had worked for a longer period of time at low wages. The regular minimum benefit was then placed at a base figure of $122 per month (with only inflationary adjustments to be included in the future). The use of special minimum benefits did not develop sufficiently to alleviate the basic problem, however, so that by 1981 the pattern of minimum benefit.allocations going to those with substantial alternative revenue sources remained.

The evidence from a recent General Accounting Office report summarized by the U.S. House Select Committee on Aging (1981) illustrates the continuing problem. As of 1981, among the 3.1 million recipients of the minimum benefit, 15 percent received federal pensions averaging $900 a month, 10 percent depended on working spouses earning an average of $13,700, and 2 percent relied on retired spouses with federal pensions averaging $12,500 a year. From a different perspective, some also have argued that the use of minimum benefit formulas is a violation of the individual equity aspects of the Social Security system. This has produced proposals for financing of the minimum benefit through general revenue (Ball 1978, 430).

The controversy in 1981 over minimum benefits illustrates the difficulties with this program. The Reagan administration argued that the thrust of their proposed cuts in minimum benefits would be to reduce payments to those who had other sources of income, and for whom the low level of eligibility benefits was a function of their short time of covered service and not a life history of low individual and family earnings. It was nonetheless unclear from the evidence presented to Congress just how substantial a shift to SSI actually would occur. There appear to have been approximately 2 million persons among the 3.1

million individuals receiving the minimum benefit who would not be eligible for SSI either because their incomes were too high (from other sources such as government pensions), or they were between the ages of 62 and 65. It was more difficult to determine how many individuals among those who were potentially eligible actually would apply (Congressional Quarterly 1981, 119-121.) The congressional action of continuing minimum benefits for those who apply prior to January 1, 1982, temporarily resolved the issue, however. To function efficiently as a policy for providing a minimum income for those in need, the minimum benefit provision needs to be combined with measures which sharply reduce its application where individuals or households have other forms of retirement income.

Despite SSI's rather unorthodox birth within the legislative process, the basic intent of providing a minimum income level for all aged persons (as well as the blind and the disabled) contained a very sound strategy. The basic policy provided a mechanism through which individuals could be aided directly on the basis of need rather than through the more indirect method of expanding minimum benefits under OASDI. The SSI program avoids payments to those who are not in economic need, including those who may have minimally qualified for Social Security benefits.

The evolution of SSI has, at the same time, not fulfilled the role some had envisioned for reducing poverty among the aging. Although the federal floor has been indexed for inflation, the federal payment level remains below the governmentally defined poverty level for individuals. For those receiving full benefits but not state supplements, the monthly levels as of July 1980, were $357 for a married couple and $238 for a single individual. In 1979 the monthly poverty index level for a nonfarm, two-person family with a head of household age 65 or more was approximately $350; the one-person level was about $290.

Variation among the states, which some criticized under the preceding program of Old Age Assistance, is still substantial. While some of those variations reflect differences in the cost of living, they also reflect differences in the states' willingness to confront the problems of the poor elderly. Thus while a few states, such as California and New York, tended to have substantial supplements for a large number of recipients, the majority of the states either had few recipients receiving supplements or gave token amounts to a larger number. This program dynamic is reflected in the expenditure of $1.4 billion among the 50 states (Grimaldi 1980). Qualifications for free services, such as medical assistance, could be an important additional component of SSI. Nonetheless, it is not difficult to see why SSI has not reduced more dramatically the number of older persons living at or near the poverty level. As an additional complication, the serious financial problems facing the states in the early 1980s suggested the likelihood that without federal assistance, there would be little growth, and possibly reductions, in SSI benefits. Less substantial benefit increases (in which the state supplements to SSI do not have to be indexed for inflation) and/or an increased tendency to deny eligibility in marginal cases may occur in the future.

When compared with the minimum benefit approach, SSI also has two limitations. The administrative processes required to administer a means-tested program quickly become quite complex and are more costly than for benefits administered without a means-test. While there is some evidence that the resistance to accepting "welfare" is declining among the aging (Binstock 1979, 1711-1717), recipients of assistance have a more positive feeling if they believe (even if incorrectly) that the benefit was based upon their level of earlier contribution.

Despite the problems associated with SSI, it remains a very direct tool for confronting the problem of poverty among the elderly. In fact, the National Commission on Social Security (1981, 248) recommended a 25 percent increase in benefits. As a testament to the increasing coverage of the older population through Social Security benefits and other sources of income, there has *not* been a sudden increase in beneficiaries among the aging even in the wake of substantial efforts by the Social Security Administration in 1974 to expand awareness of the program. With a total 1979 cost of $5.4 billion for the federal government and $1.9 billion for the states, SSI stands as a program in which dollar commitments can be directed very straightforwardly toward the goal of meeting the economic needs of the least economically fortunate of the older population (as well as the blind and the disabled).

The Earnings Test

Policies that reduce Social Security benefits for those who work after age 65 have been intensely criticized by spoksmen for the aging. The reduction of benefits (on a $1 for $2 earned basis) for those who are otherwise eligible for larger benefits simply because they have current earnings above $6,000 and are less than 70 years old is viewed by opponents as not only unfair but stupid. The question of fairness surrounds the equity issue. If you paid in all those years but happen to want to work past age 65, a reduction in benefits based on those current earnings is seen in the critic's eye as unfair treatment. From an individual insurance perspective, the question often raised is: "If I paid in the money, why should I be penalized for continuing to work?" It is also judged to be doubly unfair that taxes have to be paid on those earnings whereas no taxes have to be paid on Social Security benefits. Finally, the shortsightedness of the policy is argued in terms of its potential for reducing labor force participation on the part of those over the age of 65. In the face of these arguments and the political pressures behind them, Congress gradually has made the earnings test more lenient. It even has seriously considered eliminating it altogether.

Despite the seeming persuasiveness of the case for elimination or at least curtailment, there are important grounds for supporting alternative strategies. Both the National Commission on Social Security (1981, 140-153) and Ball (1978, 264-280) support an earnings test. In their view, eliminating the earnings test would not significantly encourage additional work. One of its advantages, they claim, is to provide an additional benefit for that small segment (about 10 percent) of the population that works past age 65 and disproportionately tends to be enjoying both good health and a satisfactory income. With an emphasis on the importance of adequacy in Social Security benefits as a part of the total income for the aging, it is argued that the present limit of $6,000 allows individuals at the lower earnings levels to engage in a reasonable amount of work without being penalized and is thus not a barrier to labor force participation.

Fundamentally, those who oppose elimination of the earnings test point to its relatively high cost. According to the National Commission on Social Security (1981, 146), abandonment of the earnings test for those age 65 and over would cost at least $2 billion as of 1982, and the cost of eliminating the earnings test for those between 62 and 65 would be an additional $4 to $5 billion. With the money required to eliminate the earnings test, the federal government as of 1982 could virtually double its spending on the means-tested Supplemental Security Income program (SSI).

To meet some of the objections to the earnings test, supporters have proposed a variety of alternatives including a system of expanded tax credits for those who continue to work after age 65. In Ball's view (1978, 278-280), the present 3 percent tax credit should be increased to at least 7 percent. In the views of its proponents, the tax credit approach constitutes a much less expensive and more direct way to encourage labor force participation on the part of those beyond age 65. Overall, the earnings test issue raises very pointedly the tension in the Social Security system between the objective of equity for past contributions and a concern for using available funds to provide economic support for those with limited incomes.

Public Employee Systems

Although most of the reform issues now evolve around benefit questions rather than eligibility changes, the existence of independent pension systems for federal employees and some employees of state and local governments presents a continuing problem of coordination between systems. There are about 3.7 million state and local employees and 3 million federal employees. Just as with private pension plans, some individuals, particularly at lower levels of employment, may find themselves without clear claims on any of the pension systems in which they have participated. At the same time, the ability of some employees to "double dip" by taking advantage of eligibility in several pensions (all of which have been designed to provide a basic adequate income) raises questions of fairness and, in some state and local systems, difficult choices between pension costs and needed services.

Pension plans for federal, state, and local employees have developed outside the Social Security system for several reasons. Federal employees received coverage in 1920 and were thus not included in the initial planning for the Social Security system in 1935. Some of the state and local plans also predated 1935, and many more were developed prior to 1950, when Congress gave state and local employees the option to be included. This optional strategy was utilized because of the constitutional question as to whether the federal government could require state and local employees to join. In the wake of decisions by state and local employee groups, about 70 percent are now included. In some instances, individuals are covered under both the Social Security system and state or local plans.

The continued resistance among various public employees to partici-pation in the Social Security system has been motivated by a calculation of relative benefits. The most intense opposition has come from some local employee groups, particularly in the area of protective services. In the eyes of policemen and firemen, a move to place them in the Social Security system would jeopardize their benefits under existing plans. (There is no requirement that individuals cannot be a part of both, but the suspicion has been that the public will not be so willing to support these often very generous existing plans if individuals also are included under Social Security.) For federal employees who contribute, in effect, on a 38 percent basis to their plan, the official position as voiced by the National Association of Retired Federal Employees has been adamantly against a merger. Although Ball (1978) argues that the recent benefits added to the Social Security system make it more competitive for federal employees, there has been little indication of a change in sentiment on the part of federal employees.

The costs of state and local pension plans are likely to be more con-troversial throughout the 1980s. It has been too easy in the past for political leaders to bargain with local employee groups to grant future pension benefits in exchange for a less substantial current wage increase and the resulting necessity for tax increases. An accurate assessment of the problem is compounded by poor record keeping in some of the 2,394 plans presently in existence. As part of the poor management in some plans, the actuarial tables which have been used have been seriously out of date and thus understate future costs. Many plans have a substantial re-serve, however, in contrast to the "pay as you go" basis used for the Social Security system. Existing assessments such as the one by Stein (1981) have given the overall system fairly good marks for its ability to meet obligations that will arise in the future. The problem is that there are quite a number of states with stagnant economies and declining central cities in which there is no real assurance of a future ability to pay (Tilove 1976).

If more of the state and local plans face difficulties in the next years, then there may be additional pressure from voters and public employees to expand inclusion within the Social Security system. The state and local plans, excluded from the reform provisions enacted for private sector plans in 1974, are major targets for reform. One part of that reform effort surrounds the proposed Public Employee Pension Plan

Reporting and Accountability Act, which would attempt to build a more effective system of reporting and develop adequate financial reserves.

"Double Dipping"

An unsuccessful candidate for governor in California a few years ago experienced considerable political embarrassment when it was pointed out during his campaign that, if elected governor, he would qualify for four different pensions. This situation, although somewhat extreme, dramatizes the serious policy question raised when individuals qualify for several pensions and receive from each benefits that are designed to be minimally adequate by themselves. The number of "double dippers" is quite large. In 1976, about 45 percent of the civil service and foreign service retirees also were eligible for Social Security benefits (Price and Novotny, 1977). If the plans in each instance were geared closely to total contributions, then one could simply argue that individuals should be allowed to contribute to the development of retirement income wherever they were working. The problem, of course, is that the formulas have tended to reward disproportionately those who have fulfilled the minimum eligibility requirements.

Some individuals are eligible for pensions at remarkably young ages, which complicates the double dipping question. It is not uncommon for members of a police or fire pension system to be able to retire with benefits equaling half or more of their final salary after 20 or 25 years of service. This means that such individuals can draw a pension while turning to a full second career — and also develop pension rights in that second career track.

The situation for retired members of the armed forces raises similar issues. When Social Security was extended to the armed forces, the existing career system was not touched. The military system provides a minimum pension of 50 percent of basic pay after 20 years of service and a maximum of 75 percent of basic pay after 30 years or more of service. This policy allows retired military personnel to draw substantial pensions, plus Social Security benefits when they reach 65 (or 62 for reduced benefits). In addition, if they put in five years with the federal government, they then also qualify for benefits under the system for federal employees. (Retired regular officers working at federal jobs do, however, have to take a cut in their military pensions. As of 1978 they could receive annually a pension retirement sum of $4,320.36 plus half the remainder they were eligible to receive while working for the federal government.) Members of the armed forces who do not fill their 20 year requirement suffer a major penalty in loss of potential retirement income.

A variety of steps can be taken to reduce the opportunities for individuals to profit inappropriately from participation in multiple pension systems. In 1982, as concern over Social Security financing mounted, the inclusion of all public employees in the system began drawing additional interest. Even if that is not done in total, two practical steps can be taken in developing specific plans. First, increasing the years needed for eligibility would reduce opportunities for qualifying for several plans in a single lifetime. Second, plans could be written stipulating that the benefits would not be paid until the individual either became unable to work or reached a stipulated age. Because of worsening financial pressures and the growing concern with questions of fairness, public employee pension systems constitute an important reform area for the 1980s.

Revenue Sources

There is a continuing debate over the appropriateness of financing aspects of the Social Security system through general revenue rather than the present payroll tax. In addressing that debate, it should be remembered that the payroll tax supports not only the major pension benefits funded through the OASI and DI trust funds, but also through the Hospital Insurance (HI) trust fund, a portion of the expenditure for Medicare. The distribution of the 6.7 percent tax rate for 1982 was divided as follows: Hospital Insurance under Medicare, 1.30 percent; OASI, 4.575 percent; and DI, .825 percent. The Supplemental Security Income program (SSI) is not financed as part of the payroll tax. However, the SSI benefits are the first aspect of the assistance to be reduced when other sources of income, including Social Security benefits, are received. This has helped to keep costs down for SSI and has minimized general revenue contributions.

The increased financial pressures in trust fund operations in recent years have produced considerable interest in funding at least some portion of the Social Security system with general revenue. Proponents cite the regressive nature of the payroll tax which, unlike the income tax, makes no allowance for family size or unique financial demands such as high medical bills. In addition, the payroll tax is often seen as having been designed when the components of the system were substantially fewer, and when there was a greater emphasis on the individual insurance dimension. Today, with benefits geared toward low contributors and programs such as Medicare partly aided, it is seen as inappropriate to have these costs supported by a payroll tax. Moreover, the present payroll tax structure, when compared with the income tax and the ease with which it can be adjusted, often is viewed as unfortunately inflexible.

The most frequent specific suggestion is that the Hospital Insurance component under Medicare be financed entirely through general revenue. This has been the basic legislative position of the American Association of Retired Persons (AARP) for several years. Similarly, the National Commission on Social Security (1981, 9) recommended that the general revenue funds be used for Hospital Insurance if and when the combined employer and employee tax reached 18 percent. President Carter's proposal in 1977 that some general revenue funds be used when high unemployment reduced short-run revenues constitutes one interesting alternative strategy.

Those against a shift to general revenue have tended to be adamant in their opposition. In 1981, the Reagan administration made a firm commitment to avoid using general revenue. For some, the use of general revenue funds is seen as an opportunity to expand the program which cannot be exercised as long as the Social Security system is based upon a payroll tax. One could argue in response that in its first half century of operation, the separate tax actually contributed to the ease with which the system has grown. From a different perspective, some have argued that funding Social Security from general revenue, and thus breaking the tie with the concept of an individual's earned right to a pension, would create, over time, pressures for a means-tested program. This is seen as a likely consequence of legislative frustration with the mounting costs on the one hand, and yet payments of benefits to some older persons who have substantial other sources of income. A means-test, from the standpoint of long-time leaders within the Social Security Administration, would lead in the long run to an inadequate program for major segments of the older population.

Changes in the last several years have importantly modified, at least in the short run, the nature of the general revenue debate. Given the current competition for tax dollars, a shift to general revenue financing does not promise an easy resolution of the underlying issue of Social Security costs. The decision in 1981 to undertake a major three-year income tax reduction and to index future taxes (beginning in 1985) to avoid the impact of inflation on tax brackets seemed likely to intensify sharply the competition among existing programs for general revenue support. According to a national poll in late 1982 by the *Los Angeles Times* (Nov. 21, Sec. 1, p. 1), a clear majority of the nation's voting age population was in favor of this shift in financing. Overall, there do not seem to be compelling reasons for avoiding some shift to general revenue, but this step is surely no panacea.

A Final Perspective

By late 1982, some predicted that the short-fall in the OASI fund (prior to interfund borrowing) might exceed $50 billion annually by the mid-1980s. Even with borrowing among funds, the revenue short-fall over a seven-year period was projected by some to be in excess of $150 billion *(Los Angeles Times, Dec. 12, 1982, p. 1)*. The necessity for new decisions was becoming increasingly clear.

The proposals offered by the National Commission on Social Security (1981, 100) showed significant opportunity for reform without a sizable change in total costs for the combined trust funds. These reforms included as additional expenditures such items as partial credit to women for child raising years in computing eligibility for benefits and continuing benefits for marriages ending in divorce. The commission proposed to save revenue by increasing normal retirement benefits gradually to age 68 and maintaining earnings tests to age 72. These changes, which may seem fairly minor, can have a substantial impact on the overall program. With the harsher economic conditions that had emerged by 1982, some of the choices became more difficult.

In confronting reform issues, it is essential that the options not be viewed in an overly narrow or predetermined manner. Projections of problems several decades ahead serve as a warning that alternative policy strategies need to be developed, but they should not be taken as firm signals of future disruption of the Social Security system. The present system is the result of design as well as economics and demography, and future systems also can reflect a variety of design components. Evolution in program design will occur despite the constraints on making changes. In that evolution, two important issues will be changes in labor force participation and the scope of private pension systems.

VI

EMPLOYMENT, RETIREMENT, AND PENSIONS

Changes in the average age of retirement and in the use of private pensions profoundly affect the Social Security system. Private pensions are important not only for the 45 percent of the labor force who participate but also because of the economic significance of the investment funds, now well in excess of $400 billion. Questions of both control and future size involve major economic stakes. Clark and Barker (1981, 4) describe the fundamental impact of retirement ages on Social Security. If one assumes that the entire labor force retired at age 60, the cost of retirement benefits in 1978 would be two and one-half times greater than if everyone retired at age 70. Even a one-year increase in the average age of application for Social Security benefits would have a major favorable impact on present and future funding problems.

The policy processes surrounding the issues of retirement age and private pensions show striking variation. It was surprisingly easy to expand opportunities for voluntary employment past age 65. Proposed increases in the age of eligibility for Social Security benefits, however, have produced major controversies in Congress. Reform efforts directed toward expanded regulation of private pensions in the early 1970s also dramatized the high level of conflict that can occur on policies for the aging. To begin our consideration of politics and policy in these areas, it is important to examine changes in retirement patterns.

RETIREMENT PATTERNS AND POLICIES

The average age of retirement in the United States has decreased sharply in recent years. Prior to the 1930s, formal retirement policies were uncommon in the public and private sectors. In this fluid situation,

123

in which opportunities for income other than through continued work were very limited, retirement simply was not a common practice. The age of eligibility for benefits under the Social Security Act of 1935 was 65, and this age gradually began to be adopted in the retirement plans that became more formal after World War II. For a variety of reasons, the years since World War II have seen a sharp decline in the average age of retirement, especially for men. (See Table 6-1) The forces producing this change, and the voluntary policies and requirements that can be used to alter that pattern, deserve careful attention.

The Declining Age of Retirement

The basic data on retirement patterns show a particularly strong shift toward early retirement on the part of men. In 1920, about three-fifths of men age 65 and over were employed, and by 1940 the figure had dropped to two-fifths. By the late 1970s, only one out of five men age 65 was employed. It is important to note, however, that the figures for women, while still much smaller, have increased slightly since 1940. A major decline also has occurred in labor force participation on the part of men in the 60 to 64 age bracket. Between 1955 and 1978, participation at that age level dropped from 82.5 percent to 62 percent. Unlike men's labor force participation rates, however, rates for women in the 60 to 64 age bracket rose between 1955 and 1970 before declining slightly from 36.1 percent in 1970 to 33.1 percent in 1978. A similar pattern is apparent in more specific categories. In the federal civil service, for example, the average age of voluntary federal retirement declined from 64.3 in 1963, to 62.9 in 1969, to 61.4 in 1973. In many industries the practice of retiring after 30 years of service makes retirement parties for those in their early sixties and even late fifties a common occurrence.

In the early 1980s there were slight indications that this pattern was not continuing to move downward into lower age brackets as was the case in past years and that it might begin to reverse slightly. Given the magnitude of the shift that has taken place in the past several decades, however, a much larger shift would have to occur to alter the size of Social Security costs that have been created by early retirement.

The first question to pursue in considering the decline in average age of retirement is obvious: Why are people leaving the labor force at an earlier age in such large numbers? Explanations include poor health, lack of job opportunities, and the availability of retirement income. An

Table 6-1   Labor Force Participation by Sex and Age, 1890-1980

	Male *Age 65 and Over*	*Female* *Age 65 and Over*
1890	73.9%	8.3%
1900	68.3	9.1
1910	58.1	8.6
1920	60.1	8.0
1930	58.3	8.0
1940	41.5	5.9
1950	41.6	7.6
1960	30.5	10.0
1970	25.8	9.1
1980	19.1	8.1

SOURCE: W. Kip Viscusi, *Welfare of the Elderly* (New York: John Wiley & Sons, 1979), p. 154. See also U.S. Department of Commerce, Bureau of the Census, *Historical Statistics of the United States, Colonial Times to 1970, Part I*, p. 132; U.S. Department of Commerce, Bureau of the Census, *Statistical Abstract of the United States, 1981*, p. 381.

increasing amount of research has been undertaken on this question, including studies by Boskin (1977), Munnell (1977), and Clark and Barker (1981).

The initial studies of retirement decisions, which were primarily conducted by the Social Security Administration, tended to emphasize poor health as the primary reason for retirement. A study of retirees in 1941 and 1942 indicated that only 5 percent of a sample of applicants for Social Security benefits retired voluntarily and while in good health. A 1951 survey paralleled those early findings; only 3.8 percent indicated that they had retired voluntarily and in good health. In the 1960s, the responses indicating a preference for leisure began to increase, but health factors still received strong emphasis. A study of retirement decisions in the early 1970s, also using Social Security Administration data, reported that 52 percent of men age 60 to 65, and 54 percent of men age 66 to 67, who left the labor force between 1969 and 1973 cited reasons other than health or job displacement as their main reason for retiring (Munnell 1977, 64).

Various economic analyses based on income patterns rather than interview responses have given a sharply different emphasis. According to Boskin (1977, 1), the previous emphasis on health was highly inaccurate. In his view, availability of income, whether through Social Security benefits or other sources, constitutes the overriding factor behind retirement decisions. Clark and Barker (1981, 25-50) also emphasize the availability of income, including both Social Security benefits and private pensions.

The reasons people retire obviously do not fit into simple and distinct categories. It seems clear that the health-based explanations have included an effort to give what is perceived as the socially acceptable answer in a society in which the work ethic has long been highly regarded. There are also some grounds for arguing that the health factor will continue to decline in the future. In terms of survey responses, only 24.2 percent of men eligible for reduced Social Security benefits (age 62 to 64) in 1976 gave health as the main reason for retirement, and among women of the same age the figure was only 8.9 percent (Coberly 1980, 3). Furthermore, given the movement in our society away from physically demanding jobs, the number of people who are simply "worn out" is likely to decline.

According to Barfield and Morgan (1974, 70), health, income, and job satisfaction factors tend to be interrelated:

> Economic factors provide the basic enabling framework for the retirement decision. If one can afford to retire, then his decision will be affected by his health and by his attitudes toward work and retirement. But if one feels economically unable to retire, only rather severe problems with (say) health or work may induce retirement.

Given a situation in which people are retiring for a variety of reasons, strategies for modifying the tendency for earlier retirement appropriately involve a multiple focus. Before turning to those voluntary and eligibility-based policy alternatives, however, we will consider the rapidly changing position of the older worker in the labor force of the 1980s and beyond.

The Need for Older Workers

Demographic conditions, so often cast as the chief villain in aging-related policy discussions, are creating a major opportunity — perhaps even an economic imperative — for expanded employment among the aging. The reasons for this shift are obvious and dramatic. Because the birthrate began dropping very sharply in the 1960s, the number of newcomers to the labor force will be substantially smaller in the 1980s. In retrospect, the 1970s was a period in which the labor market accommodated not only a large number of newcomers but a substantial proportion of women. The decline in the number of teenagers entering the labor force is thus destined to increase the importance of retaining older workers.

In the short run, fairly immediate economic forces will dictate the number of workers who are employed and the wages they receive. In the recessionary years of 1981 and 1982, the older workers too often joined younger age groups in the unemployment lines. In the long run, however, the pool of available workers is an important factor in the operation of the economy (Gillaspy 1980, 135, 138). To help spur economic growth, it will be necessary to expand the pool of available workers after about 1983. Yet to expand that pool, few options emerge.

The basic alternatives are foreign workers, increased employment for women, or greater use of older workers. Many European countries that did not experience a high birthrate after World War II began to import workers from foreign countries in the 1960s and 1970s. Yet in the United States, the prospect that needed workers will migrate from neighboring countries is not promising. Canada, which has a population age distribution similar to the United States', will provide few individuals for migration. Mexico, while a growing source of unskilled and semi-skilled labor, probably will not be an extensive source for employment in skilled occupations (Gillaspy 1980, 137). More and more women are working, but this annual increase in the rate of female labor force participation may not continue in the future in light of the recent increase in the percentage of women having children (Easterlin 1978). Thus, pressures to retain older workers through various incentives and modified job designs are very likely. Signs calling for older workers on a part-time basis in McDonald's franchises in Los Angeles in the early 1980s may well reflect the beginnings of an important shift in employment policies nationwide. Employment policies that promote increased use of older workers constitute a major opportunity in the coming years. Both private sector and public policy strategies will be considered.

Job Satisfaction and Opportunity

One obvious way to expand labor force participation among the aging is to increase job satisfaction and opportunity. In this regard, the concept of work distribution throughout the life cycle is important. It is essential to break down the notion that work must be continual throughout one's life and then cease at a designated age (McConnell 1980, 69-71). Opportunities for part-time work for older workers are increasing, as Jacobson (1980, 1-17) emphasizes.

Work activities can be redesigned to increase employee satisfaction in various ways. Initiatives in Sweden to manufacture cars through a group effort rather than on an assembly line basis constitute one of many possible approaches in trying to make work activities more satisfying. Flexible scheduling, or "flextime," is another appropriate strategy in some work situations. Although widely used in Europe, flextime in the United States is a fairly recent development. The 1978 legislation on federal employee work schedules led to experiments with flextime for many federal government employees. With various specific formats, flextime allows workers to arrange a portion of their hours on the job to fit their own needs. While a core of required hours for all employees is generally necessary, some of these plans have allowed individuals to adjust to the very sharp differences in the distribution of their most productive work time throughout the day. Four-day weeks with 10-hour days are another variation with some potential for increasing interest in continuing in the labor force.

The redistribution of work throughout one's lifetime is important from several perspectives. It could help alleviate "burn out," a common problem in some jobs. Adapting the university concept of sabbaticals to other career areas might address this problem and also provide opportunities for employees to update their skills, which is essential in this era of rapid technological change. (Not all sabbaticals, in other words, need to be spent writing books!) In redistributing work throughout the life cycle, greater attention also needs to be paid to recruiting those who may have dropped out for a time, perhaps to raise a family.

Part-time work stands as an extremely important step in prompting more extensive use of older workers. Some firms already allow individuals after age 55 or 60 to begin reducing their weekly hours. While this strategy may cause a few persons to work less extensively than they otherwise might, it may keep some people from retiring entirely — thus becoming eligible earlier for pensions and, after age 62, Social Security. Other firms seek part-time employees, regardless of their age, as a conscious hiring strategy. As a result some firms, such as Macys in New York, now employ more than half of their workers on a part-time basis. Today many firms are reporting substantial expansion in their use of part-timers.

The encouragement of policies that promote greater job satisfaction and part-time opportunities will require concerted action in a wide variety of contexts. Governments at all levels can help by reexamining their own personnel policies. Government employment policies are particularly important not only as examples but because they influence approximately 17 percent of the total labor force. One of the early federal experiments with second career planning was started for air controllers in 1973 and was abandoned in the wake of very modest accomplishments in 1978 — ironically, only three years before the air controllers' strike (Jacobson 1980, 20-24).

Tax incentives also can be increased and some present disincentives eliminated. If the earnings tax on Social Security benefits does emerge as a deterrent to part-time employment, then those levels should be reconsidered. All pension plans, public and private, also need to be reexamined with an eye toward increasing the opportunities for part-time employment. In developing private sector plans, it will be necessary in some professions to try to address union leaders' fears that part-time workers are more difficult to organize. A variety of community groups now exist to help major industrial employers place older workers and promote new job design ideas. Converting these initial steps into a more substantial movement will require public and private sector assistance. Fortunately, the likelihood that older workers will be seen as an increasingly valuable resource in the next few years should constitute a major force for more extensive efforts.

Eliminating Mandatory Retirement

One obvious hurdle in the quest for more extensive labor force participation on the part of older workers has now been surmounted. Only rarely are individuals now retiring because of mandatory retirement policies. Since 1982, when university professors under the age of 70 became exempt from mandatory retirement, the categories of employees who may be retired prior to age 70 simply on the basis of their age include only high-level corporate executives and a few individuals in hazardous occupations. The 1978 legislation making mandatory retirement illegal prior to age 70 rather than age 65 (which had been accepted in most contracts) was an amendment to the Age Discrimination in Employment Act (ADEA), a law passed in 1967 to prevent discrimination

129

against employees in the 40 to 65 age bracket. As we shall see shortly, these steps passed with surprising speed in the late 1970s.

The elimination of mandatory retirement for most individuals younger than age 70 will not necessarily produce a major shift in retirement patterns. Indeed, one of the factors contributing to the speedy passage in Congress was the realization that most individuals were retiring prior to age 65 anyway. As Schulz (1980, 18-19) commented: "When you get down to hard numbers, we're talking about thousands of people and not millions."

Initially, the 1978 law both encouraged and discouraged continued employment among older workers. In the wake of greater publicity about the question of when one should retire, some personnel officers were beginning to report more interest on the part of workers in exploring the possibility of continued employment. Conversely, there were early indications that the documentation requirement for employers wishing to terminate an individual was having an unexpected consequence. Termination could no longer be ensured at age 65 without a documented case. Thus there was an incentive for employers to build cases for dismissal regarding workers in their early sixties who might previously have been simply retained until their automatic retirement at age 65. From an economic productivity perspective, this step might be justified, but it also raised questions about the coordination of early termination with pension plans and other benefits. More generally, while the virtual elimination of mandatory retirement was perceived as a great victory by a portion of the aging population, it seems doubtful that the short-run impact on labor participation rates will be substantial.

The Age of Eligibility

Few questions have been more politically explosive in recent years than proposals for modifying retirement patterns through increases in the age of eligibility for Social Security. A suspicion that eliminating mandatory retirement for those under the age of 70 was a first step toward increasing the age of eligibility contributed to some opposition from labor unions. President Jimmy Carter's secretary of commerce, Juanita Kreps (who has studied labor force participation and the aging), drew sharp criticism when she suggested during the debate on mandatory retirement that a change in the age of eligibility for Social Security benefits also would ultimately have to be considered.

In the spring of 1981, Ronald Reagan quickly learned of the political explosiveness surrounding proposed changes in the age of eligibility for Social Security benefits. The president and his advisers apparently felt that reducing benefits for retirees between ages 62 and 64 would be acceptable if accompanied by a complete elimination of the earnings limit on those who began receiving benefits at age 65. The intense political response in Washington, including the formation of new groups such as Save Our Security (SOS) and the quick rejection in Congress despite its support of the new president's initiatives in some other areas, underscored the strength of opposition to an abrupt and substantial shift in the age of eligibility.

The political controversy in 1981 was intensified by three factors. First, Reagan's proposal did not include a phasing-in process; it would have started immediately. Thus individuals trying to plan their retirement would have been confronted suddenly with different rules and would have had to face the nagging uncertainty of whether or not they would miss their best opportunity if they did not retire under the old rules. Second, his proposal came in a context in which a variety of other programs were being curtailed and thus became a popular rallying point for those who were concerned with the general contraction of social programs. Third, many observers did not agree that the current financing problems required a major policy shift.

The more politically acceptable and equitable manner of introducing a change in the age of eligibility would be with a phasing-in process. Several variations of this scheme have been proposed. Clark and Barker (1981, 62-64) suggest that the age of eligibility for benefits be raised one quarter a year in the 1990s, thus reaching 68 by the year 2007. A similar position was taken by the National Commission on Social Security. The proposals that involve a phasing-in have the advantage of allowing individuals to plan for their future. They also have the important political advantage of not disturbing benefits for those who have the greatest concern — namely, the currently retired and those who are close to retirement. A 40-year-old individual might view a change in eligibility as a means of preventing convulsions in the system as the baby boom cohort retires a few years later and thus feel that such a plan was in his or her own best interest. Persons who would be affected 15 or 20 years in the future are far less apt to mobilize politically than those who are at or near retirement.

Is a policy of encouraging later retirement by denying substantial benefits prior to age 68 or age 70 wise? Opinions vary. Some argue that individuals are often physically worn out prior to their early sixties and that an increase in the age of eligibility would constitute a serious hardship. This view is forcefully expressed by Elizabeth Duskin of the National Council of Senior Citizens in her dissenting opinion in the National Commission on Social Security's report (1981, 330-334). Others argue that the availability of greater leisure time through earlier retirement is one of the benefits gradually derived as part of a higher standard of living in American society. It is a benefit, they say, that should not be given up easily. Problems with Social Security costs in the future should not be taken as reasons for shifts now in public policy, some claim. A final view is that more reliance should be placed on voluntary incentives to continue working, such as improved work conditions and opportunities for part-time work.

Proponents of an increased age of eligibility nonetheless have a strong case. The future cost saving would be substantial and might make it possible to avoid serious problems as the baby boom generation begins to enter the Social Security benefit rolls. Proponents also claim that the health disadvantages of early retirement become less important in light of longer life expectancy. They also stress the need for older workers because of the slackening number of new workers entering the labor force.

The extent to which work is viewed as a positive experience is perhaps the major issue in this debate over the age of eligibility for retirement benefits. For those engaged in interesting and rewarding jobs, the prospect of an additional year or two may be seen as a favorable step or at least a reasonable policy. Yet for those who view employment as tedious and/or frustrating, an expansion in the age of eligibility is viewed as a step backward. Perhaps not surprisingly, the most union oriented of the aging-based interest groups, the National Council of Senior Citizens, has shown the greatest resistance to an increased age of eligibility.

It is important, in viewing this debate, to link the question of disability provisions with the age of eligibility for Social Security. Clearly, use of the disability provisions would increase if the age of eligibility was increased, thus reducing the total savings involved. If the age of eligibility is increased, it also will be important to consider the adequacy of present disability policies and eligibility criteria. If those policies are watched carefully, then a number of proposals for gradual increases in the age of eligibility deserve serious consideration. Voluntary incentives might fulfill the ultimately very necessary task of moving the age of retirement upward rather than in a continuingly downward direction. Nonetheless, in the long run it may be necessary to increase the age of eligibility as a cost-saving step. Whether through voluntary means that stress opportunities or through the process of denying benefits until a more advanced age, it is clear that policies devised now will not only help in the short run but may be mandated by the demographic forces unfolding in the next century.

PRIVATE PENSION PLANS

Individual retirement decisions and the financial future of the Social Security system are greatly affected by private pension plans. Although growth tapered off after the rapid expansion of the 1950s, in the next two decades private plans continued to grow annually by about 3 percent in the proportion of the labor force covered by them. By the mid-1970s, more than 7 million individuals were receiving private pensions, and the average annual payment was just over $2,200. In studies of specific industries, the replacement rate was about 25 percent, thus standing substantially below the figure being projected for Social Security benefits (Schulz 1980, 133). Overall coverage was also substantial, including more than 30 million workers and about 45 percent of the labor force. Major issues today include the extent to which private pensions encourage early retirement, the appropriate future scope of private pensions in relationship to Social Security benefits, and the adequacy of the 1974 reforms in protecting employees from losses of expected pension income.

Like Social Security eligibility requirements, private pension system rules can have an important impact on the employment practices of older workers. Many private pensions have been written with provisions that encourage early retirement, such as the promise of full pension benefits after 30 years of service. Pension plans also tend not to reflect the growing interest in part-time work. Stein (1980) and the President's Commission on Pension Policy (1980) thus consider the development of pension systems with incentives for later retirement an important reform.

The appropriate scope and magnitude of private pensions are other controversial issues. Proponents of maintaining or expanding the use of private pensions have stressed these pensions' greater flexibility in relating to the problems of particular industries. They also see them as creating opportunities for personal choices among employers that are not present if only a single, Social Security system option is available. Some individuals may be attracted to particular employers because of the pension benefits offered.

Skeptics of extensive reliance upon private plans have offered a variety of counterarguments on some of these issues. First, private plans are seen as inequitable in their tendency to discriminate against marginal members of the labor force who never remain in one company long enough to develop a firm or "vested" pension right. Second, it is doubtful whether private plans can be expanded substantially beyond their present scope of coverage in the labor force. Thus, if policy makers assume that individuals can combine Social Security benefits with a private pension, then those who are employed by small or marginal firms, and those firms seeking to minimize personnel costs, would be placed at a disadvantage. There are early indications that the 1974 reforms have led to the termination of some plans covering individuals employed by small and marginal firms. Workers might be better off without the false hopes raised by financially unsound plans, but they are still in need of some method of developing retirement income. Third, because private pensions are not indexed for inflation, and the periodic voluntary adjustments for retirees in some firms do not produce an overall response even approximating the present levels of inflation, the long-range results are seen as increasingly inadequate for those seeking to depend primarily on private pensions for retirement income. (These issues are extensively reviewed in McGill 1979.)

The expansion of the Social Security system in the 1970s increased dissatisfaction among those seeking to avoid a decline in the use of private pensions and personal savings. The argument has been that a heavy reliance upon the Social Security system discourages savings and thus contributes to a shortage of investment capital in the economy. In part, it has been argued that the pay-as-you-go basis of the Social Security system, as distinct from the substantial reserves that are generated by private pension plans, is disadvantageous in not facilitating the development of investment capital (Campbell 1979).

Some also claim that the availability of Social Security benefits serves to reduce savings. Early writers argued that the availability of Social Security benefits tended to increase savings because individuals saw the goal of a reasonable retirement income becoming feasible. More recent researchers, such as Feldstein (1976) and Munnell (1974), disagree, however. They are of the opinion that Social Security benefits decrease savings, but they differ on the magnitude of the change in behavior that can be attributed to the availability of benefits. Taking a perspective emphasizing intergenerational transfers, Barro (1977, 161-170) has argued that there is not a substantial net loss of tendencies to save.

The investment issue produces different responses among analysts. First, in terms of the resource created by private pension funds, the question is raised as to how investment decisions are going to be made surrounding those funds. Drucker (1976) has seen the magnitude of these funds leading to a potential for a form of "pension fund socialism." In a harsher account of present investment practices, Rifkin and Barber (1978) have argued that present pension funds should be used for investments that will be of greater benefit to the workers who have contributed to the creation of those pension funds. In terms of the potential problem created by Social Security in undercutting investment capital, Schulz (1980) has claimed that it also would be possible for the Social Security system to begin to create more substantial reserves. Such a policy would help to prepare for the high demands on the system after the year 2010. In addition, if investment in specific types of projects is judged to be lacking, there are precedents for using federal incentives and, on occasion, federal investment funds to promote those activities.

The future evolution of public and private plans will probably take a middle course between attempting to create totally adequate public sector plans and sharply increasing private plans at the expense of public programs. In evaluating one's preferences, these four points should be kept in mind. First, while private plans do not directly enter one's tax bill and thus do not have direct, visible costs for nonparticipants, consumers nonetheless pay for those plans through higher prices. A sharp shift toward programs such as those in major Japanese firms would reduce public visibility and conflict but not eliminate the underlying economic costs that the working population bears for those who are retired. Second, the advantages of public and private sector plans — and also their limitations — would seem to suggest the importance of continuing to divide roles. Third, while the saving question should be monitored carefully, it is important to remember that savings and investment can be promoted in an economy in a variety of ways. Fourth, efforts to increase the use of private sector pensions inevitably will raise the related question of how to further improve those plans and reduce the inequities for marginal members of the labor force along the lines begun in 1974.

To what extent did the 1974 reforms succeed in adequately protecting the rights of individual employees? This is the final issue we will consider in assessing private pensions. The Passage of the Employee Retirement Income Security Act (ERISA) in 1974 constituted an intricate legislative compromise on a policy question that had been actively debated for the better part of a decade. In 1958, legislation calling for a reporting procedure had been enacted, but it had very limited effect in the wake of misuse of some pension funds during that period of rapid expansion. The legislation passed 16 years later, while unusually complex and subject to a variety of administrative interpretations, resulted in numerous protections.

First, ERISA established tighter vesting requirements. (A vested right in a pension plan means that, regardless of further contributions or employment, an individual has a right to a pension on the basis of terms originally agreed upon.) The law gave three options for vesting, but the most commonly chosen option has been for vesting after 10 years. Second, ERISA protected individuals against loss of pension benefits up to $750 per month if the company that offered the pension is unable to meet its obligations. Technically, the benefits are provided by the Pension Benefit Guarantee Corporation, which is funded by a small contribution from the firms that operate private plans. Third, the legislation tightened funding requirements of pension plans to avoid future failures. Fourth, it created limited opportunities for changing plans from one employer to another; in other words, it made some plans "portable." This provision was limited, however, and the lack of a more substantial opportunity for changing pensions from one employer to another was criticized by those who basically favored a national system of private pension plans. Fifth, in an effort to weed out weak and questionable plans, it instituted stricter reporting requirements.

Action also has been taken through ERISA and the more recent Economy Recovery Act of 1981 to increase opportunities for retirement saving by the self-employed (through Keogh Plans) and others who want to begin Independent Retirement Accounts (IRAs). In each instance, individuals may deduct those savings from current taxable income, thus delaying tax payment until the money put aside is used during retirement (and at a time when they usually will be in a lower tax bracket). The limit as of 1981 for Keogh Plans was $15,000 for a self-employed person. For IRAs, the limit was $2,000 per individual and $2,250 for a married couple. This legislation was promoted both as a way for individuals to shoulder greater responsibility for their own retirement and as a policy that was likely to help the economy by producing investment capital through increased savings. From the initial responses it appeared that those plans were likely to grow in significance and in their possible impact on private savings and public support for Social Security.

POLITICS, PENSIONS, AND RETIREMENT

Strikingly different political processes have surrounded the recent reform of policies involving pension and retirement age policies. The pension reform issue was widely publicized in 1964, when former employees of Studebaker Corporation lost most of their pensions as a result of the collapse of that automobile manufacturer. Yet a full decade passed before Congress passed a pension reform bill in 1974. Progress was equally slow initially on the issue of nonmandatory retirement. Prior to the 1970s, little interest was expressed in eliminating mandatory retirement. By 1977, however, a major reform bill had passed both houses of Congress, and the new law was signed by the president in early 1978. The differing politics surrounding these two issues are indicative of the opportunities and constraints facing efforts to modify pension and retirement policies and the importance of several major sources of policy development (Lammers 1980).

The Politics of Pension Reform

The political process surrounding pension reform produced controversy, delay, and often bitter legislative battles (McGill 1975, 37). The process began with executive branch studies in the 1960s. Several bills were then proposed. After President Lyndon B. Johnson's major reform proposal was defeated in Congress, a more limited bill was proposed by President Richard Nixon in 1971.

The legislative committee responses were lengthy and often highly contested. Business spokesmen from the U.S. Chamber of Commerce and from smaller business and trade groups often indicated a willingness to go along with some aspects of minimum vesting standards but generally balked at proposals for ensuring against company default. Proposals for

137

portability and for an extensive shift to multiple employee plans also produced sharp opposition. Business spokesmen preferred administration by the Treasury Department and fought possible Labor Department oversight of the new law.

The AFL-CIO and the United Auto Workers frequently pushed for measures that would strengthen the proposed legislation. Labor spokesmen also expressed concern over the question of pension fund control. Unions that enjoyed substantial control over their funds wanted to maintain that control, while others voiced concern about the amount of discretion going to management. The business-labor struggle also was manifested in jurisdictional squabbles among congressional committees and between the Treasury and Labor Departments. Nixon's proposals for individual plans for the self-employed and for those without other major plans were attacked as tax shelters for the rich.

To speed House action, the Senate passed an initial measure in September 1973, but that strategy was to no avail. The House Ways and Means Committee could not agree on an alternate version. Finally, legislation reached the House floor in February 1974. After three days of debate over Labor and Treasury jurisdiction, the extent of the plan termination insurance, and the plans for the self-employed, the House passed an amended bill. But the controversy lingered. It took five months for the House-Senate conference committee to agree on the final language. The bill totaled 202 pages — a testament to the complexity of the issues and the elaborate nature of the compromises involved. More than a decade after the initial proposals had begun circulating in the executive branch, a significant step forward had been taken in the area of pension reform.

The Quiet Passage of Nonmandatory Retirement

The political process leading to the elimination in 1978 of age 65 as a lawful mandatory retirement age was markedly less controversial than the one surrounding pension reform. For several decades a few spokesmen for the elderly had been voicing opposition to retirement policies based solely on age. Preparations for the 1961 White House Conference on Aging had produced some discussions of retirement policies, and there were sporadic comparisons between the rigid American policies and the greater flexibility allowed in some European countries. Nonetheless, the dominant emphasis in discussions of work and retirement in the 1960s and early 1970s was on private pension reform. At first, interest in employment policies was focused primarily on discrimination against older workers. In response to this concern, about half the states passed age discrimination legislation prior to Congress's passage of the Age Discrimination in Employment Act (ADEA) in 1967.

The desire to eliminate age requirements for retirement emerged very quickly in the mid-1970s. State legislative committees and executive departments dealing with the aging began to question, as of about 1974, the appropriateness of mandatory retirement on the basis of age for at least some groups of employees. Interest in the use of court procedures to challenge mandatory retirement laws grew in several employment areas, with teachers making a significant contribution. By 1976, this issue had become politically attractive; both the Republican and Democratic party platforms supported nonmandatory retirement. In Congress, Rep. Claude Pepper (D-Fla.) became the leading spokesman on this issue. A bill reported by the House Education and Labor Committee easily passed the House, 359-4. On the Senate side, somewhat greater controversy emerged. A few changes in the legislation were approved, and floor amendments softening the bill received fairly substantial support. All amendments were defeated, however. The Senate bill also passed by a comfortable margin, 88-7. In early 1978, the House-Senate conferees reached agreement on a final resolution. Congress had acted swiftly. As industry leader Harrison Givens, Jr., noted: "It came into being so rapidly — astonishingly so, to many people." (Givens 1978, 51)

Sources of Policy Development

How did socio-economic conditions and political forces differently affect the development of ERISA and nonmandatory retirement policies? This question will be addressed in terms of the model of policy development presented in Figure 2-1 on page 27.

Systemic Factors. Among the systemic factors, economic conditions and public attitudes had a significant impact. Because both bills passed within a four-year period, differences in the size of the aging population were not substantial. Economic conditions, however, were more important in the elimination of mandatory retirement before age 70. Passage of ERISA in 1974 seemed to flow from the underlying political dynamics and not from current economic conditions. For nonmandatory retirement, however, 1976 and 1977 were clearly good years for passage in that decade because the economy was on the rebound from the 1974 recession and unemployment was somewhat less widespread. Thus Walker and Lazer (1978, 14) concluded that passage was much easier because unemployment problems were declining when nonmandatory retirement was being considered.

Public attitudes concerning pension reform and the elimination of mandatory retirement were similar. Both issues appear to have had broad electoral approval. The evidence on nonmandatory retirement was more extensive, however, and it received greater emphasis in the legislative debate. Electoral support from all age groups in the population for nonmandatory retirement was overwhelming. Data gathered for the National Council on Aging by Louis Harris (1975) showed a resounding 86 percent of the electorate in agreement with this proposition: "Nobody should be forced to retire because of age if he wants to continue working and is still able to do a good job." A clear majority (66 percent) indicated strong rather than only limited agreement. Perhaps even more significantly, there was no indication in any of the polls of a reduced commitment to nonmandatory retirement proposals among younger segments of the population. Any possible conflict of interest surrounding job prospects was apparently overcome by an antipathy toward the arbitrariness of age-based retirement criteria.

By 1971 members of Congress were beginning to perceive pension reform as a very popular issue. A sharp increase in the number of bills being introduced in the early 1970s by legislators not associated with the initial efforts indicated a perceived advantage in being on record in favor of pension reform. The list of pension plan abuses circulated by Ralph Nader and other consumer advocates received substantial discussion within an electorate that appeared to be growing uneasy with existing pension practices (Nader and Blackwell 1973). In short, the general public clearly supported both measures.

The differences in policy impact on key interests were nonetheless very pronounced, and those differences contributed to the greater difficulties confronting pension reformers. There is no question that the stakes are high in private pension reform. Private pensions cover more than 30 million individuals and generate more than $400 billion in investment funds. Furthermore, ERISA's requirements for vesting within 10 years did present the prospect of increases in pension costs. Greenough and King (1976, 171-172) reported the results of a McGraw-Hill survey of

491 large firms showing that the new vesting rule was adding about 2 percent to pension costs. They also emphasized that the impact differed substantially from one industry to another. Other proposals being debated, such as widespread portability of plans and the use of multi-employer plans, also would have raised costs. From the government's standpoint, indirect costs of approximately half a billion dollars were involved as a result of further tax credits going to firms developing more extensive plans. The tax loss issue was insignificant, however, in the overall debate.

It became clear quite quickly in the debate over nonmandatory retirement, on the other hand, that the costs to private industry would be small. In some cases the potential for higher salaries from later retirement could be more than offset by reduced training costs for new employees, plus lowered retirement benefit costs (Walker and Lazer 1978, 77). Furthermore, Sen. Jacob Javits (R-N.Y.) and other congressional proponents of the new legislation were careful to make clear that employers were not being asked to abandon age-based criteria in designing pension plans and incur major new costs which such a change would have demanded. Finally, it was widely concluded that the number of persons who would not choose to stay on past a mandatory retirement age under age 70 was quite small, perhaps as few as 200,000 persons. As a result of these calculations, several firms that were considering testifying against nonmandatory retirement in state capitals and on Capitol Hill decided to abandon their opposition. From the government's standpoint, eliminating mandatory retirement before age 70 not only did not require major new costs but also promised some relief in the costs of Social Security benefits. Clearly, by 1976 and 1977 the cost issue was significant for many political leaders. From a cost perspective, the sources of greater conflict and delay on ERISA than on nonmandatory retirement are very evident.

Political Participants. The ERISA debate was characterized by important roles for many key actors in American politics, particularly several major interest groups. Presidents made some contributions with their development of initial proposals. In Congress, various legislators took an interest, particularly in the Senate, but no single champion of pension reform emerged. The major participants in the lobby struggle were business and labor, represented by the U.S. Chamber of Congress, the AFL-CIO, and many small individual firms and organizations. Particularly in 1973 and 1974, consumer groups helped popularize the issue.

The leadership and lobbying pattern was much different for non-mandatory retirement. By 1976, both political parties were on record in favor of reducing mandatory retirement provisions. President Carter also endorsed that basic concept in 1977, but he did not play a major role as legislative support grew. In Congress, Rep. Pepper was a strong champion through his chairmanship of the House Select Committee on Aging, an important focal point for supporters of nonmandatory retirement.

The lobby process for eliminating mandatory retirement at age 65 produced a different configuration of interest groups than is usually found on aging-related issues. Some business groups opposed, as did a few individual firms, but the issue did not produce the intense lobbying that occurred on ERISA. On the other hand, spokesmen for organized labor were (at most) only mildly supportive. They were concerned about the possible impact on the age of eligibility for Social Security benefits and existing contract provisions for retirement. (The final language sought to minimize any impact on agreements presently in existence.) In addition, spokesmen for the nation's colleges and universities expressed grave reservations over impacts on their salary costs, as well as opportunities which could be restricted for young Ph.Ds. (As a result, the final bill excluded college and university faculty until 1982.)

Reflecting its more middle-class orientation, the American Association of Retired Persons (AARP) made the issue a major legislative priority and rallied support for the measure among the aging. The National Council of Senior Citizens (NCSC), however, did not play a significant role because its members, like many union members, were uncertain about the consequences. A number of employee organizations, including school teachers and public employees, also mobilized in support of the curtailment of mandatory retirement. In short, low stakes and strong public support made it possible for leaders and lobbyists to increase the age of mandatory retirement to age 70 in a period in which low levels of unemployment reduced potential intergenerational conflict on job opportunities.

CONCLUSION

The study of policy development and policy alternatives reveals several important conclusions. Regarding policy development, the two case studies clearly reveal the importance of differences in policy impact. The substantial effect on private firms foreseen with the passage of ERISA produced much greater conflict and involvement by key political figures than occurred for nonmandatory retirement. The perception of greater impact on the private sector also contributed to the delay in developing pension reform and the lengthy set of compromises that were required to win passage. Conversely, in the nonmandatory retirement case, speedier passage was possible because of a more limited perception of private sector impact, strong indications of electoral support, and skillful leadership in rallying the support of lobby groups and legislative leaders. In the policy analysis framework developed by Lowi (1964)', these differences could be viewed as illustrative of the differences between a redistributive policy (such as ERISA, with its cross-cutting impact on major economic groups in American society) and a regulatory policy (such as nonmandatory retirement, in which policy adjustments were made with less conflict and a smaller range of participants).

Regarding policy alternatives, there is clearly a major opportunity for improved use of older workers in the coming years. The decline in the number of younger workers entering the labor force means that older workers will be an increasingly important resource. Moreover, the increasing costs of private and public systems of financial support for the aging are likely to produce strong incentives to maintain older workers in the labor force.

The political processes surrounding the development of job-related reforms in the private sector show some grounds for anticipating more substantial reforms in the future. Given the importance of economic conditions and the cost impact on employers in determining the success — or defeat — of legislation, it is especially encouraging that these factors seem likely to lead to greater reform in the 1980s. As older workers become more important, efforts to retain workers by increasing employment opportunities and job satisfaction are likely to increase. However, as our examination of pension reform suggests, major changes in the pension system, such as the adoption of a compulsory system of private pensions, are likely to generate substantial conflict. The number of compromises involved in ERISA, on issues such as portability of plans and assurances of adequate funding, may make it necessary to confront pension reform issues fairly often. These issues will take on particular importance if there is an effort to expand the use of private pensions as an alternative to reliance upon Social Security benefits. In short, employment and pension issues are likely to have, and should have, a prominent position on the issue agenda of the 1980s.

143

VII

HEALTH AND LONG-TERM CARE

When older Americans are asked what concerns them most, they often reply: the availability and cost of health care. This response is very understandable. The general improvement in Americans' health that has occurred in recent years has not altered the fact that the aging are major users of health services. As of 1977, some 29 percent of all expenditures on health in the United States went for the needs of those 65 or older. Despite the adoption of Medicare and Medicaid in 1965, the aging were paying about one-third of the total cost — a personal expense averaging more than $600 annually by 1977. Actions by the Reagan administration and Congress in the early 1980s, combined with rapidly inflating health costs, substantially increased those personal expenditures (Gibson and Waldo 1982). About 5 percent of the older population reside in nursing homes at any single point in time, yet as many as 25 percent are likely to spend a portion of their senior years in a nursing home. Thus, while Medicaid and other assistance programs pay for more than half of those total nursing home costs, many elderly persons fear that they will have to face long-term care costs that easily could exceed $1,000 a month.

The importance of the health care system to the aging is also evident in the extent of actual use. A survey conducted by the U.S. National Center for Health Statistics (1978) found that 70 percent of persons age 65 and over had seen a physician within the previous six months. The aging are the highest user group by a substantial margin. Whereas the average person 65 or older had 6.5 physician visits in a year, the average for other age groups was 4.6 visits. The aging also were more apt to enter hospitals, and they tended to stay longer. Eighteen percent of the individuals age 65 and over had at least one hospital visit in 1977, compared to 9.5 percent for all other age groups, and they stayed an average of 11 days, in sharp contrast to 4 days for the under-65 age group.

The question of health policy for the aging is also very significant in the context of national health care costs and the resulting debate over cost control strategies and national health insurance. The aging comprise an important segment of a health care system that is rapidly growing more expensive. Before 1966, prices for medical services increased by 3.2 percent per year, while the Consumer Price Index advanced at approximately 2 percent per year. Between 1966 and 1971, medical prices outdistanced consumer prices by an annual rate of 7.9 percent compared with 5.8 percent. Despite higher inflation throughout the 1970s, health costs continued to increase more rapidly than overall prices.

Hospital costs were expanding at a level well above the general inflation rate by the late 1970s and early 1980s. In 1980, average rates were more than four times as high as in 1967. The proportion of the nation's gross national product devoted to health care also expanded rapidly. Cost increases changed that annual allocation from 7.2 percent in 1970 to 9.8 percent in 1981. The total dollar allocation in 1981 was $286 billion. Moreover, in 1980 and 1981 total health costs increased by more than 15 percent (Gibson and Waldo 1982). These increases in the face of a slowdown in inflation were particularly sobering. Thus, increasing health costs for the aging are closely tied to a pattern of generally increasing health costs for the nation.

Has the increased commitment to health care for the aging resulted in an improvement in their health status? The evidence is mixed. Some factors suggest it has. In recent years the number of individuals over the age of 75 as a proportion of the aging population (over 65) has increased. Thus one might expect an overall worsening of health status when all individuals age 65 and over are compared for different decades. Indeed, the number of impaired days per year for the aging rose between 1973 and 1978 (National Commission on Social Security 1981, 332). On the other hand, the number of acute conditions among persons age 65 and over has declined significantly since 1965. Similarly, the percentage of the aging with some degree of limitation due to chronic conditions has declined (Davidson and Marmor 1980, 1-7).

Segments of the aging population are healthier than their counterparts in earlier decades. As a result, the elderly constitute an important human resource in terms of assistance with volunteer programs and employment at advanced ages. Nonetheless, even those who are in fairly good health require more health care than individuals in younger age groups. At the same time, the needs of those who are in poor health present a critical challenge to the nation's health care system. To begin confronting key policy issues, it is important to consider first the basic program components.

HEALTH CARE POLICIES

Recent health policies are best understood in the context of a gradual evolution of governmental commitments at all levels. In the 1930s and 1940s, sporadic efforts occurred on the part of state and local governments to extend health care to the most needy segments of the older population. County hospitals, for example, provided in some instances a measure of health care for the needy. Following passage of the Social Security Act of 1935 and the resulting establishment of Old Age Assistance, interest in nursing homes also increased. Typically, new homes would be developed by private organizations, but there was some interest in state regulation in the more progressive states by the late 1940s. Although the federal government avoided a direct commitment to health care when it passed the Social Security Act, such programs as the operation of Veterans Administration (VA) hospitals provided some health assistance to a segment of the older population. Indirectly, some older persons also experienced improved health care through the Hill-Burton Hospital Construction Act, which was passed in 1946 and extended in 1954. With an emphasis on improving hospital care in rural settings and in states with low personal income levels, the act provided assistance for hospital construction and, to a lesser extent, long-term care facilities in hospitals and separately constructed nursing home facilities. The dominant pattern in the 1930s and 1940s, however, was one of private payment for physician and hospital services. Instances of unattended or underattended medical needs were all too frequent.

Medicaid

The cautious steps taken in the 1950s provided a basis for the Medicaid program that was established in 1965. With an initial enactment in 1950 and a more extensive provision in 1956, the federal government agreed to provide some financial assistance to those states that wished to make medical assistance payments to individuals who were receiving Old Age Assistance. The Old Age Assistance program, which

147

was transformed into the Supplementary Security Income (SSI) program in 1972, had involved a federal sharing of program costs since 1935 for individuals without other means of support such as regular Social Security benefits or private pensions. In the 1950s, that program structure was viewed as a logical administrative vehicle for providing health assistance to the same category of individuals. Technically, these payments were termed "vendor payments" because the money often was paid directly for services provided, such as payments to hospitals, doctors, or (in a few instances) nursing homes.

The federal matching formula was designed to be more generous to poor states with the hope that some form of medical assistance would be developed in a large number of states. The more substantial efforts, however, generally were made in the more prosperous and progressive states (Stevens and Stevens 1974). Because the program's clientele was generally a small proportion of the older population in a state and the benefit structures were usually very restricted, the total impact of the program on health care for the aging was quite small.

The Medicaid program enacted by Congress in 1965 represented a major expansion in federal assistance to the states for the provision of health care to needy persons. In 1960, the Medical Assistance Act (MAA) provided increases in federal contributions to state programs that assisted individuals who met restrictive eligibility requirements. The act was popularly known as the Kerr-Mills program after its sponsors, Sen. Robert Kerr (D-Okla.) and Rep. Wilbur Mills (D-Ark.) (Oklahoma and Arkansas were among the states to profit most substantially from the matching formula's more generous provision for states with low per capita incomes.) The MAA program was expanded in 1961. By 1965, when Medicaid came into being, 44 states operated an MAA program of some kind.

The establishment of Medicaid in 1965, as an outgrowth of earlier programs that utilized matching grants and strict eligibility criteria, had two major consequences for the nation's attempt to provide health assistance to the low-income elderly. First, because Medicaid also covered individuals who were eligible for financial assistance through the related program of Aid to Families with Dependent Children (AFDC) and programs for the disabled and the blind, the administrative problems associated with operating a program of "welfare medicine" were intertwined closely with the problems confronting the aged who sought medical assistance on the basis of need. Second, discretion in establishing eligibility criteria for those who were not eligible for Old Age Assistance (now SSI), or other categorical aid assistance programs, was left to the states. As a result, individuals with similar incomes and comparable medical bills could be aided in some states but not in others. It all depended upon whether the particular state allowed individuals to subtract their medical bills from annual income to determine those in the "medically needy" category. As of 1977, 28 states had made some provision for the medically needy. Because of the discretion allowed the states, the medically needy category became an important target for budget cutters in the early 1980s.

Under Medicaid, the states are responsible for providing numerous services, including inpatient services; outpatient hospital services; physician services, whether rendered in an office, hospital, nursing facility, or patient's home; X-ray and laboratory services; skilled nursing home services; and optional services which include a wide range of services from dental care to prescription drugs and home health care. The number of services provided and the level of assistance (such as the maximum number of days of home care) vary considerably among the states. For whatever services a state chooses to provide, as well as the required services, the federal government will provide matching funds with a formula giving the most wealthy states 50 percent of total costs and the poorest states up to 83 percent of total costs.

Important pricing and regulatory policies also evolved as a result of state discretion. In contrast to Medicare, in which only a reasonable rate standard is used, the prices for physicians and for long-term care (but not for hospital care) are determined by a definite fee structure. Since the fees allowed for physicians are generally somewhat below prevailing levels, some physicians will refuse to take Medicaid patients. Nursing home rate structures have been hotly contested in most state capitals. In addition, although the federal government has exercised a stronger role since 1972, states have considerable discretion in both policies and enforcement efforts pertaining to nursing home regulation.

Although the aging represent a minority of total users of the Medicaid system, they generate a major component of the total costs. This seeming anomaly occurs because of the impact of nursing home costs on total budgets. As of 1979, the aging comprised 16 percent of all individuals who received some assistance through Medicaid, but their payments for medical care comprised 37 percent of total program costs. In those expenditures for the aging, nursing home costs have comprised about 75 percent of total costs. In sum, about 15 percent of the older population is dependent upon Medicaid for health care, but because the individuals who are dependent are often in nursing homes, the operation of Medicaid constitutes a particularly important aspect of the nation's health policy for the aging.

Medicare

In 1965, a more general program of health care for the aging also was adopted — Medicare. The initial debate over Medicare focused on hospital insurance. A more accurate (but politically less attractive) label for the program might have been "Hospicare." In the legislative deliberations conducted on the initial proposal in early 1965, however, rival plans were combined to produce the more extensive Medicare program that was ultimately adopted.

Medicare is a health insurance program for the aging sponsored by the federal government through the Social Security Administration and divided into two basic components: Part A, hospital insurance (HI), and Part B, supplemental medical insurance. Part A pays for hospital care and for a restricted amount of skilled nursing care and home health services. All elderly persons who are eligible for Social Security benefits are automatically eligible for Medicare's hospital insurance. (Recipients of railroad retirement benefits and those who have been disabled for more than 24 months are also eligible.) As of 1980, Medicare paid for up to 90 days of hospitalization per "spell of illness." The patient must pay the first $144 for hospitalization. Medicare assumes the rest of the cost for the first 60 days. Between the 61st and the 90th day, the patient must contribute $36 a day as co-insurance. A patient also can develop a reserve of 60 days from previous years, but if that is exhausted assistance terminates. Nursing home coverage is restricted to 100 days, and assistance can be given only for skilled nursing facilities that have been entered following a hospital stay of at least three days. Medicaid rather than Medicare has been the primary source of public assistance for nursing home residents. As a result, individuals who are not eligible for Medicaid because their incomes exceed the eligibility requirements are not given long-term assistance (assistance for more than 100 days).

The supplemental medical insurance portion of Medicare, Part B, covers physician services, hospital outpatient services, home health care (in addition to the assistance provided by Part A), diagnostic laboratory and X-ray services, and a variety of miscellaneous services. All individuals who are eligible for Part A also are eligible for Part B. The monthly rate, which had been increasing gradually, reached $12.20 as of July 1, 1982, and the pressure in Congress for further increases was considerable. Many states, however, assist the low-income aging with the payment of that monthly fee. In addition, the person receiving medical assistance must pay the first $60 of his or her annual medical expenses for a calendar year and generally at least 20 percent of the remaining expenses. Private insurance plans, often referred to as "medigap" insurance, are available for those who desire more inclusive and extensive coverage.

Several important health expenses are either excluded or given limited support through Medicare. Besides the major limitation on long-term care costs, the eligibility requirements for home care have limited Medicare assistance. The important category of drug costs for medical treatment not given by a doctor also is excluded, thus requiring many elderly persons to pay substantial monthly sums for routine drug costs. Eye glasses and examinations, hearing aids and examinations, dentures and routine dental treatment, and cosmetic surgery also are excluded. (For a more detailed review, see Ball 1978, Davidson 1980, and Lowy 1980.)

The Costs

Despite the limitations and exemptions in present policies, the costs of Medicare and Medicaid have increased rapidly in the past decade. The total annual cost of Medicare by the end of 1981 reached some $44.8 billion. The funding for Part A, the hospital insurance portion, came almost entirely from the Social Security tax, and constituted 1.30 percent of the 1981 tax rate of 6.65 percent. Funding for Part B, the supplemental medical insurance portion, came from a combination of the annual premiums and general revenue contributions. As of 1981, 71 percent of total financing was from general revenue for Part B, and the general revenue contribution for both programs was 23 percent, which amounted to approximately $9 billion.

Costs for Medicaid also have become increasingly substantial for the federal government and for state governments. As of 1981, the total program cost for all categories of recipients had grown to $31.3 billion, with the federal government contributing 55 percent or about $17.5 billion, and the states contributing $13.8 billion. In 1981 the Reagan administration sought a cap on federal expenditures. Although Congress resisted that proposal, it did vote to reduce payments to the states by 3 percent in 1982, 4 percent in 1983, and 4.5 percent in 1984. Because of the importance of Medicaid as a funding source for long-term care, along with its support of a substantial number of poor elderly, these changes had major significance for the aging in the United States.

MEDICAID AND MEDICARE POLITICS

The passage of Medicaid and Medicare in 1965 represented the culmination of a lengthy political struggle. Three points need to be stressed before turning to those policy controversies. First, the Medicare debate focused almost exclusively on assistance with insurance payments; the organization of health services or the method of determining fee structures received little attention. As a result, increases in the cost of doctor and hospital services have been one of the major consequences. Second, the Medicare program emerged late in the debate. The primary focus prior to 1965 was on assistance with hospital costs. Third, Medicaid was given much less attention and was in many respects a rather hastily conceived program. This is one reason for the problems with it today.

Health care needs and general societal attitudes were two underlying factors contributing to the 1965 legislation. While political factors help explain the expanded federal commitment, the major health care needs of the increasingly large aging population constituted an obvious focal point for substantial lobbying efforts on the part of older Americans. The number of persons age 65 and over expanded by more than one-third between 1950 and 1960, adding a net increase of more than three million persons. At the same time, older Americans were less apt to be covered by private health insurance plans. This absence of coverage occurred as the aging, once they retired, lost the benefits of group plans and were forced to seek individual policies at substantially higher, and often unaffordable, prices. Thus as of 1959, only 33 percent of the aged in families with less than $2,000 in annual income carried health insurance, and the figure for all retired aged households was only 42 percent (Feingold 1966, 181). These statistics, which were often communicated by letters and political expressions of frustration, underscored a very basic problem for many older Americans.

Public support for some form of health insurance assistance for the aging was strong. Opinion surveys from 1943 to 1965 generally indicated a relatively stable two-thirds majority of Americans favoring some government assistance in the financing of personal health services (Marmor 1970, 3). Comparable levels of support were not always found for more specific proposals. Yet by 1965, Gallup would report no less than 63 percent of the public approved of the medical insurance program about to be adopted by the 89th Congress. Thus, while general electoral support had not been sufficient to prompt adoption of national health insurance proposals in the 1950s, this support, along with the more specific political actions that were taking place in the early 1960s, constituted one of the factors contributing to the passage of Medicare.

Several federal officials had an instrumental role in designing the proposals that became the focal point for the health insurance debate. Following the defeat of President Harry S. Truman's national health insurance proposals in 1950, top officials in the Federal Security Agency proposed that future plans for national health insurance focus on hospital care for the elderly. This was judged to be a more acceptable step politically than a more general plan, since the aging could be easily defended as beneficiaries who were needy and deserving. Whereas most other countries began a system of national health insurance by insuring segments of the industrial labor force, the United States in 1965 became the only advanced industrial nation to begin a system of health insurance by extending coverage to the aging. After that initial policy design contribution, the bureaucratic role became less important. The molding of a more substantial program design in 1965 actually took officials in the Johnson administration by surprise.

Presidential Action

Presidential roles were very different for Dwight D. Eisenhower, John F. Kennedy, and Lyndon B. Johnson. President Eisenhower responded to the initiatives developing in Congress rather than enthusiastically leading with his own proposals. After initially indicating complete resistance to the health insurance measures in Congress, the Eisenhower administration under the leadership of Arthur S. Flemming (as secretary of the Department of Health, Education and Welfare) did produce a plan with the Medicare label. This proposal focused upon state action, covered hospital care, and included only those who were judged to be in need of assistance on the basis of a means test. (Ironically, the Medicare label persisted on the plan which emerged in the early 1960s even though the program design was fundamentally different.) Overall, scholars generally agree that Eisenhower did not play an important role in the Medicare issue (Marmor 1970; Sundquist 1968).

President Kennedy, in sharp contrast, was very interested in health care for the aging. As a senator, he favored increasing existing assistance above the levels the Eisenhower administration had proposed, and he endorsed the modest legislative response in 1960 which emerged as Kerr-Mills. Repeatedly during the 1960 presidential campaign, Kennedy criticized Richard Nixon and the Republicans for their opposition to stronger legislation and promised a major proposal for hospital insurance for all older persons regardless of economic means. This was known in the public debate as the King-Anderson bill after its sponsors, Rep. Cecil King (D-Calif.) and Sen. Clinton Anderson (D-N.M.). In addition, Kennedy continued to cultivate interest group support through his encouragement of the National Council of Senior Citizens and other organizations. Thus, whereas Eisenhower had almost no interest group meetings in the White House or major addresses relating to health care for the aging, such events occurred frequently throughout the Kennedy administration. These actions included, most notably, an address to a rally of senior citizens at Madison Square Garden in New York City in May 1962. Despite Kennedy's initial interest, he was not successful in altering opposition to the King-Anderson bill among key members of the Ways and Means Committee, including its skeptical chairman, Rep. Mills.

President Johnson also was a strong public advocate of expanded health care for the aging. He gave the issue substantial attention in the 1964 presidential campaign and then promoted the symbolically important designation of H.R. 1 and S. 1 to the hospital insurance legislation as the first session of the 89th Congress got under way in 1965. Johnson's advocacy contributed to public support for Medicare and to the sense in Congress that a major program would be approved in 1965. In evaluating Johnson's role, however, it is important to emphasize two qualifications. First, the more comprehensive program which ultimately emerged, with its coverage of doctor costs as well as hospital insurance, was the result of Ways and Means Committee actions and not those of

Johnson or his top health policy planners in the Department of Health, Education and Welfare (HEW). Second, Johnson was helped dramatically by the strong showing of the Democrats in the 1964 congressional elections. The Democrats gained a net increase of 37 new seats in the House and in looking at the total number of individual changes, the National Council of Senior Citizens projected an increase of more than 40 additional votes.

Legislative Action

Actions within the legislative arena were important at several points in the evolution of Medicare. In the context of the Eisenhower administration's limited interest in the 1950s, the actions of individual legislators, in particular Rep. Aime Forand (D-R.I.), were important in providing a focal point for those interested in health insurance for the aging. At the same time, the importance of committee structures and committee chairmen, particularly in the early 1960s, contributed to the difficulties facing supporters of expanded health insurance proposals.

The most dramatic impact, however, came with the decision taken by Ways and Means Chairman Mills to promote an expansion of the King-Anderson bill and its provisions for hospital insurance. Perhaps sensing that a bill of some kind could be passed over his objections, he decided to maintain a major role in shaping the final bill by promoting expanded coverage (Marmor 1970, 65). Mills surprised virtually everyone involved with the health insurance controversy by combining major ingredients of plans that were being presented as alternatives to King-Anderson and then by steering the more extensive bill through committee. Since some opponents to King-Anderson had been advocating partial voluntary coverage of doctor costs, as well as an expansion of the vendor payments through the existing American Medical Association (AMA) program, many AMA spokesmen and Republican legislators found it particularly difficult to oppose measures which they had supported even though they had proposed those policies as alternatives to the initial King-Anderson bill and its inclusive provision for hospital insurance. It was thus an unusual instance of policy synthesis which Mills promoted and which emerged fairly quickly in 1965 as Medicare and Medicaid. In effect, the hospital insurance proposals of the King-Anderson bill became Part A of Medicare, the doctor proposals instigated by Rep. John Byrnes (R-Wis.) became, in expanded form, Part B of Medicare, and Medicaid filled the role of the means-tested approach that had been a part of the AMA's alternative as it sought to contain the scope of the final federal program.

Interest Groups

The position of interest groups for and against an expanded health care commitment has been debated extensively. Harris (1969) and other writers have emphasized the role of the American Medical Association as a factor contributing to the inability of Congress to pass a major health insurance proposal earlier than 1965. Conversely, Pratt (1976) has stressed the role of the National Council of Senior Citizens.

The AMA. The American Medical Association invested heavily in its opposition to national health insurance for the aging. After it mobilized to help defeat Truman's proposals in 1949, the AMA continued to voice strong opposition. Campaign contributions and money for public relations work came forward very extensively. In his assessment, Marmor (1970, 53) draws an interesting conclusion:

> The AMA has few resources for coercing individual congressmen to change their votes, especially senior, autonomous figures on committees like Ways and Means. That a coalition within the committee shared some of the AMA's ideological predispositions should not lead one to assume that the AMA controlled the votes. This is not to say the efforts of pressure groups opposed to Medicare were unimportant, but rather that they were important in other ways. The AMA and its ideological allies brought the issue to public view in terms likely to place Medicare advocates on the defensive. Their impact was evident in the character of the debate over medical care for the aged and especially in the narrowing of Medicare proposals to exclude coverage of physicians' care.

One of the most crucial consequences of the AMA's involvement may have been its focusing of the debate away from questions involving the pricing of health services. Marmor very correctly emphasizes the importance of the AMA in placing Medicare advocates in a position in which the fear of explosive controversy prevented this issue from being raised. Focusing only upon controversies that do occur can obscure the underlying relationships that are actually shaping policies. (On the importance of nonissues, see Bachrach 1980.) Ultimately the AMA reached a position by 1965 in which the impact of other political forces made it impossible for it to defeat a proposal which was regarded with considerable dismay within the organization, especially by key organizational leaders. As both Sundquist and Marmor emphasize, the election of 1964, with the large Democratic majorities it produced and the expectation that action would take place, became the immediate key ingredient which had previously been lacking as Medicare proposals languished in legislative committee.

Aging-based Lobbies. Similar arguments can be made for aging-based lobby activities. The actions of various ad hoc groups in the late 1950s and the mobilization of the National Council of Senior Citizens (NCSC) in 1960 and 1961 clearly contributed to the amount of interest that was being expressed among legislators on the question of health care for the aging. The leaders at NCSC, furthermore, were sensitive to the subtleties of legislative politics. They brought 1,400 older persons to the opening session of the 89th Congress in 1965 to ensure that Speaker John W. McCormack (D-Mass.) would keep his commitment to appoint a pro-Medicare majority on the Ways and Means Committee. Yet their actions in the Kennedy period were not sufficient to alter the overall position taken in the key legislative committees. Thus, while the actions prior to 1965 can be judged to have contributed to the growing interest in the health care issue, it took the major changes occurring in the wake of the 1964 election for a sufficiently favorable political environment to emerge.

Conclusion

Multiple forces shaped the final legislative product in 1965. The need itself was substantial, program design focused on a comparatively favorable clientele group, organizations of senior citizens emerged more forcefully than at any time since the 1930s, and both Presidents Kennedy and Johnson were strong public supporters of an expanded program. Because of the extensive public role of Kennedy and Johnson, it is easy to underemphasize the importance of legislative action. Key bargaining activity and program redesign took place within the legislative arena, and ultimately the large Democratic majorities in Congress after the 1964 Republican debacle ensured final passage of a fairly substantial bill. Yet rather than providing long-term answers to the problems of health care and the aging, those 1965 decisions, in retrospect, marked simply one important step in the evolution of health care policies affecting the aging. As one consequence, the post-1965 increase in the use of long-term facilities has become a controversial aspect of health care policies.

LONG-TERM CARE

The nation's long-term care facilities have constituted an increasingly central and expensive policy commitment for the aging. By 1978, there were 18,722 long-term care facilities, and the total number of beds had grown from 510,000 in 1963 to an impressive 1,349,000 in 1978. (About 10 percent of those beds were used by patients younger than 65.) Total costs also have grown rapidly. More than $22 billion in public and private funds was spent in 1981. Federal and state Medicaid payments were predicted to increase from about $8 billion in 1980 to between $24.8 and $31.0 billion by 1990 (General Accounting Office 1982, 9). Understandably, nursing homes have become the focal point for considerable analysis and reform activity.[1]

The Sources of Growth

Dramatic changes have taken place in the number, structure, and basic operation of long-term care facilities. Dunlop (1979, 67) describes those changes:

> In 1964, the typical nursing home was an older, wooden-frame building, two or three story converted house, containing perhaps forty beds, owned and operated by a husband and wife, with an LPN supervising staff activities during the day shift. Today, the Life Safety Code with its extensive provisions and the information and reporting requirements for participation in federal funding programs — principally Medicaid — has produced typically a single story fire-resistant facility of sixty beds frequently owned by a corporation or partnership of investors and often managed by a salaried nursing home administrator.

While evaluations of the quality of patient care continue to vary widely, it is important to recognize that several physical and managerial aspects of today's nursing homes have undergone substantial change.

Surveys conducted by the National Center for Health Statistics reveal the changing organizational patterns of the nursing home industry. The number of proprietary homes (operated on a for-profit basis) has increased substantially, with a resulting decrease in the number of governmental and nonprofit facilities. The growth in proprietary homes

---

[1] In recent years, nursing homes have increasingly been referred to as "long-term care facilities." These include skilled nursing facilities (SNFs) and intermediate care facilities (ICFs). References to nursing homes and long-term care facilities are used interchangeably in this chapter.

began as early as the 1940s. In 1960, 60 percent of all beds were in proprietary homes. By 1977, proprietary facilities contained 69 percent of all beds and represented 76.6 percent of all nursing home facilities. With increasing facility size, by 1977 only about 13 percent of all facilities had fewer than 50 beds and about 18 percent had more than 200 beds.

Despite the impressive growth in facilities and use in the past 15 years, the nation actually has had a lengthy period of gradual growth in the rate of assignment or institutionalization in long-term care facilities. (Institutionalization rates refer to the frequency of admission to nursing homes per 1,000 elderly persons.) Manard (1976) and Dunlop (1979) emphasized the gradual increase in the percentage of older persons in nursing homes since the 1940s, with the rise in the number of persons in those facilities occurring due to both an increase in the size of the older population and an increase in the rate of institutionalization. The nation has been experiencing steady growth — not a sudden surge — in the rate of institutionalization.

The factors that have produced the increased rate of institutionalization deserve careful attention. Despite the seeming association between Medicaid and increased use, several other factors are important. Dunlop (1979, 29-47) stresses demographic factors such as the growing proportion of very old persons within the older population and the number of elderly women living alone. As both Moss and Halamandaris (1977) and Dunlop emphasize, the policies adopted by the states in the late 1960s to reduce the use of mental institutions also contributed to an increase in the use of long-term care facilities.

The greater level of public assistance available after 1965 also has had an impact on the tendency to locate older persons in nursing homes. Medicaid does not emerge as a strong factor after 1965, however. In part, there already was fairly substantial public assistance in some states through the vendor payment programs of the 1950s and early 1960s. It also should be remembered in evaluating the public spending impact that Medicare has always played a limited financial role, thus leaving the public sector influence primarily to Medicaid and the individuals who have been able to qualify for that means-tested program.

The evidence regarding levels of family support also shows a different pattern than one might suspect. Despite the increasing numbers of older persons who are institutionalized, the primary method of providing long-term care for the frail elderly is *not* in institutions but through family and friends. According to a 1977 General Accounting Office study of the Cleveland area, 63 percent of the extremely impaired elderly and 92 percent of the greatly impaired elderly lived in the community, not in institutions.

Fundamentally, the study revealed that most of the care provided to these people was being provided by family and friends. The significance of informal care also is apparent in findings which show that at comparable age levels, married people use nursing home care only one-third to one-fourteenth as extensively as do nonmarried persons (Pollack 1980, 476). Spouses, in short, are providing far more long-term care than are the nation's nursing homes.

Despite the extensive use of family support systems, many elderly persons undoubtedly have been unnecessarily assigned to long-term care facilities. Some 10 to 20 percent of the individuals in skilled nursing facilities and 20 to 45 percent of those in intermediate care facilities are receiving levels of care that are too high, according to a 1977 Congressional Budget Office survey. Yet it is not entirely clear whether unnecessary institutionalization is a primary cause of the increased rate of nursing home use. Given the waiting lists to get into nursing homes in many areas, some of those who have been placed in them unnecessarily might have had their places filled by others, with a resulting lack of reduction in the overall rate of institutionalization among the aging.

An awareness of the factors contributing to nursing home use is helpful for several reasons. The magnitude of the care now being provided with limited formal assistance is important to bear in mind since attempts to strengthen family and community support for the elderly constitute an important policy effort. Similarly, the continuing problem of unnecessary nursing home use raises questions on humanitarian and cost grounds concerning improved methods of screening patients. Alternative strategies, such as social services and day care centers, obviously deserve attention. Yet the growing numbers of very old persons and persons living alone underscore the necessity of maintaining a large number of long-term care facilities in the future even if strategies for alternatives to traditional nursing homes prove highly effective.

The Reform Movement

Nursing home reform has been a controversial and highly emotional political issue. The rapid expansion in the size of the industry in the late

1960s and the laxity of public controls in many states contributed to the extensive reform efforts. Some of the new owners were highly opportunistic and at points downright dishonest, as the Moreland Commission investigations in New York revealed (Smith 1981). Too often the care of patients was tragically inadequate, with problems ranging from neglect and inadequate services to demeaning treatment and actual physical abuse. The titles of widely read books describing these conditions, such as *Tender Loving Greed* by Mendelson (1974) and *Too Sick, Too Old, Too Bad* by Moss and Halamandaris (1977), indicate the emotion-charged nature of the controversy over nursing home policies.

Aging-based interest groups, local groups spawned by concerned family members, consumer groups, religious and labor groups, and spokesmen from the public interest law movement have been involved in campaigns for more extensive controls. The wide range of coalition activity that has emerged is vividly reviewed by Horn and Griesel (1977). Perhaps the most important resource of these groups has been their ability to capitalize on the negative public image of the nursing home industry. This negative view was intensified by the widely circulated accounts of abuses in New York in the mid-1970s. The number of *New York Times* articles on nursing homes increased from less than 100 in 1974 to well over 500 in 1975. In the context of investigations in New York, one operator committed suicide, six went to jail, and many of the state's political leaders found their reputations severely damaged (Smith 1981, 13).

Despite the popularity of attacks on the nursing home industry, the reform movement has faced major limitations. Getting sustained action from the aging-based interest groups was often difficult, and there were problems in keeping the reform coalitions together (Vladick 1980). Furthermore, the reformers lacked an ability to compete with industry lobbies for campaign contributions on behalf of key legislators. Too often reformers lacked the specialized legal assistance necessary to compete with industry attorneys in hearings involving technical aspects of rule making. Public interest law attorneys and the now curtailed Legal Services Corporation were a major help in this regard, however. At points the reformers also gained the assistance of reform-minded legislators motivated by a variety of factors including genuine concern and a realization that supporting nursing home reform was a good political position in developing an electoral following.

The political influence that the nursing home industry has been able to display, while clearly substantial, also has shown some limitations. Disagreement within the industry itself has been a major weakness. The organizations that primarily represent the private sector have split both nationally and in some states. The largest group, the American Health Care Association (AHCA), formerly known as the American Nursing Home Association, has seen the development of a splinter group, the National Council for Health Care Services (NCHCS), which represents the 18 major nursing home chains. That division also persists in a number of the states. In Ohio, for example, there has been an even larger growth of separate organizations, with each favoring different approaches to reimbursement policies. Ironically, one of the possible consequences of the staunch attack on the nursing home industry may be that it will become more cohesive in the face of its defensive political position (Smith 1981, 152). Overall, however, divisions within the nursing home industry have been a political weakness.

Lobbying skills and close ties with state and national legislators have been an important resource. The AHCA, NCHCS, and (to a lesser extent) the association of the nonprofit (AAHA) maintain full-time lobbying and research staffs in Washington, D.C. In some states, these staff operations are rather prominently (and often quite comfortably) located a short distance from the state capitals.

Many close ties with legislators have been built in state and national politics. At the state level this often has been easy because of the frequency with which a nursing home in a small town will constitute an important source of employment. In an industry that employs 750,000 persons nationally, a local payroll can be very important to a small community. The very ethos of a business operation, which some reformers find so questionable, also can give a nursing home operator a good relationship with legislators who are used to interacting with businessmen in a variety of settings. While some of these relationships may be less direct at the national level, it has been possible for the industry to develop friends in Congress as well, particularly in states with high rates of use and heavy reliance upon privately operated homes (Vladeck 1980, 62). At its worst, as came to light in New York, this relationship has involved ownership by legislators who are responsible for developing policies for a state's nursing homes. Fortunately, greater publicity, closer public scrutiny, and fewer opportunities for quick profits in the nursing home industry have made the charge of kickbacks and direct conflict of interest less common since the mid-1970s. It is nevertheless rather surprising to find that despite its political resources, the nursing home lobby has not been particularly successful in wrestling financial commitments from Congress or the state legislatures.

The legislative arenas in state and national politics have been important for the development of nursing home policies. This has involved an extensive issue raising role as exemplified most notably by hearings for more than a decade by the Senate Special Subcommittee on Long-Term Care (a subcommittee of the Senate Special Committee on Aging), commonly known in the 1970s as the Moss Committee after its chairman, Sen. Frank Moss (D-Utah). Those hearings, in Washington and throughout the country, helped to nurture the nursing home reform movement. Legislators at the state level also have been identified with nursing home reform. At points, specific policy approaches on fairly technical issues such as reimbursement rates have been developed with a substantial legislative impact. At the same time, the congressional role has been hampered by the divisions in committee jurisdictions, particularly between the aging committees (the Senate Special Committee on Aging and the House Select Committee on Aging) and the financially oriented committees. From time to time Congress has taken an interest in reform, but its overall effort at actually implementing change has shown major weaknesses (Vladeck 1980, 204-206).

The president most visibly identified with nursing home reform was Richard Nixon. In a major address delivered in August 1971, he outlined an eight-point program that focused on enforcement and included such steps as expansion of the HEW enforcement staff, federal reimbursement for the full costs of the states' inspection efforts, and the creation of an Office of Nursing Home Affairs within HEW to coordinate policy development. Prior to the convening of the White House Conference on Aging later in 1971, Nixon appears to have been concerned that his administration was vulnerable on the nursing home issue (Vladeck 1980, 66-67). As an indication of possible reasons for Nixon's concern, and also a testament to the importance of state efforts, it should be noted that the push for reform in several states was gaining national attention by 1970 and 1971. Nursing home reform constituted one of several steps taken by the Nixon administration at the end of the president's first term in a concerted effort to capture the support of the aging in the 1972 election. In assessing that role on nursing home reform, Vladeck questions whether there was ever a strong enforcement effort on the part of Nixon and his appointees in HEW, but he emphasizes the importance of Nixon's role in promoting greater public interest in the issue.

The role of agencies in the development of nursing home policy may be more formidable than is apparent from the existing literature. Policy design activities and the quiet registering of political influence can easily take place in the bureaucratic arena. Specific regulatory steps with major consequences can emerge at the agency level, as this example from the Nixon administration testifies. Prior to his 1971 initiatives on nursing home reform, Nixon, working through HEW, developed less stringent rules for the availability of nurses within long-term care facilities than the Moss Committee had envisioned in asking HEW to develop specific rules. This was a case in which lobby pressures from the industry and the personal interests of legislators whose support the Nixon administration was trying to court came together in an important bureaucratic rule making endeavor (Vladeck 1980, 61-62). More recently, important new proposals on such issues as patients' rights have received added impetus from agency action (Demkovich 1979). Because of the complexities surrounding nursing home policies in the areas of regulation and reimbursement rates, key agencies' technical skills often had an important impact on nursing home policies.

The roles involved in the development of nursing home policies clearly have been shared by a number of actors in the political process. Legislative committees, state and national interest groups, and (somewhat secondarily) President Nixon contributed to the heightened interest in nursing home reform in the early 1970s. Industry lobby efforts and federal and state agencies have had important roles, however, in the shaping of specific policy components. In the actual implementation of policies, the courts as well as the bureaucracy also have had a significant impact. Given this pattern of policy development, it is essential to consider the actual results. Has the reform movement been effective?

Policy Responses

The degree of success that the reform movement was able to achieve through federal and state action varied in different geographic areas and from one aspect of the reform agenda to another. A review of major policy changes provides some indication of the effectiveness of the reform efforts and also a guide to current policy issues. Numerous attempts have been made to develop reimbursement policies that provide the funding needed for a reasonable quality of care while preventing excessive financial gain. Efforts also have been taken to improve the quality of care through more extensive regulation. The federal role in regulatory and financial policies has increased gradually since the early 1970s. Nonetheless, the states continue to have considerable discretion in developing Medicaid policies (Lammers and Klingman 1981b).

Regulatory Policies. Regulation of nursing homes has become vastly more extensive since the early 1960s. Regulatory policies in the 1940s and 1950s were very weak and often poorly enforced. Even in the more progressive states, a person could become a nursing home administrator with such minimal qualifications as a high school diploma and good character references. Unless prodded by the dramatic impact of a major nursing home fire, state legislators often were slow to enact fire codes or improve enforcement efforts.

In the wake of the nursing home reform movement in the 1970s and the expanding federal role in funding and regulating homes, overall regulation has increased substantially. Homes that prefer not to take Medicare or Medicaid patients are required to meet state requirements only and can avoid federal certification. Because 90 percent of all facilities are federally certified, federal regulations become an important basic standard that is extended and amplified in some states.

The Social Security Amendments of 1972, which modified the legal definition of nursing homes to clarify the type of care being rendered, contributed to an increase in regulatory efforts. By 1974, the states were reimbursed for the entire cost of certification (or licensing) programs. As a result, state inspection activities increased. By the late 1970s, regulations had been developed in an increasingly substantial number of areas. In all federally licensed facilities, the Life Safety Code (for fire protection) has been required, and many states also have expanded their own fire code requirements. Staffs are more carefully regulated, both in terms of qualifications for administrative credentials and in staff-patient ratios. The level of required nursing personnel is clearly spelled out in the federal regulations. In recent years, a major effort has been under way to establish the rights of patients and their families to see a facility's annual inspection reports, obtain more complete billing information, and participate in evaluation processes.

While increased regulation has transformed some aspects of the nation's nursing homes (Dunlop 1979), many problems remain. The quality of care often falls short, as Manard et al. (1977, 135) point out:

> Our interviewers found that most old age institutions are nice places to visit, and our data show that they are indeed places to die; but they are not good places to live. In fairness to the elderly people who must spend the last years of life in them, the regulations and programs that affect old age institutions must be changed to give a higher priority to improving them as places for living.

After reviewing extensive legislative investigations, Moss and Halamandaris (1977, 127) paint a picture of very limited change as of the mid-1970s in the nation's nursing homes. In their view, no less than 50 percent of them were substandard. Before confronting the reform issues raised by these sobering evaluations, it is important to consider briefly the financial aspects of nursing home operations.

Financial Policies. Developing satisfactory reimbursement policies has proven difficult. First, it has been difficult to develop reimbursement standards that relate directly to the quality of the care being rendered. Several interesting proposals have emerged recently for reimbursement based upon the amount of improvement that occurs in a patient after the initial diagnosis following admittance to the nursing home. While potentially more effective than present approaches, these standards are not likely to be implemented in the foreseeable future because of their perceived administrative problems. Reimbursement policies have been shifting gradually from a flat rate basis (such as $23 per day) to a proscriptive basis in which likely costs are agreed upon in advance, with incentive systems for cost containment if actual costs are lower. In an extensive analysis of rate policies and total costs, Buchanan (1981) concluded that proscriptive reimbursement systems, coupled with incentives for containment, constituted the most effective type of system for containing total costs. As of 1982, this system was used in about half of the states.

Reimbursement policies inevitably have raised the question of appropriate levels of profit for nursing home owners. Unfortunately, the issue of reasonable profits is not always readily answered. In the late 1970s, nursing homes were not particularly profitable ventures in most states.

166

The profit margins (profit as a percent of the annual revenue) were lower than for many industries. Moreover, some corporations that initially had sought major operations were considering leaving the nursing home field (Buchanan 1981, 15-17). Nursing home owners in New York City were finding it particularly difficult to make a profit or sell their properties.

All too many investors in the nursing home industry have made a profit through illegal practices (Moss and Halamandaris 1977). Among the practices they cite are charges for services not provided, kickbacks from drug firms, blatant fraud in the handling of patients' records for the purposes of billing state Medicaid offices, and questionable real estate transactions. Nursing homes have been seen as secure investments by many lending institutions because of their guaranteed public payment and high demand; as a result, loans often have been obtained relatively easily. Interest charges can be deducted from the operating costs while equity is being built up in the facility. Since rates often have involved a rate of return in relationship to the most recent purchase price of the investment, it has been profitable to resell homes at increasingly large figures to increase the rate of reimbursement. This all too often has been undertaken in a highly manipulative manner.

Despite the practices that have resulted in very high profits for some owners, the nursing home chains have not been viewed as particularly good stock market investments for several years. The reimbursement levels for Medicaid patients have been quite low by many standards. As of the late 1970s, state daily reimbursement rates were often in the $20 to $25 range — a strikingly low figure in relationship to hospital costs. For that matter, it is also rather low in relationship to hotel costs. Nonetheless, reimbursement at a rate of $25 a day is expensive from a public policy standpoint: at that figure it costs more than $9,000 annually to keep an individual in a nursing home, and many stay for several years. It is thus not surprising that reimbursement issues as well as regulatory policies have generated keen political interest.

Future Policies. The creation of more satisfying long-term care facilities is not an easy task. Yet some regulatory processes can be strengthened, as well as enforcement efforts, and the question of seeking improved care through additional financial support deserves careful attention. During the Carter administration, there was some interest in the Department of Health and Human Services (HHS) in tightening regulations pertaining to long-term care facilities. Several of the provisions in the legislation being considered involved such patients' rights issues as billing information, visiting privileges, and nursing home resident councils. Another area of concern was mistaken distribution of medication. (As one indication of the continuing problem in this area, industry leaders strongly objected to the proposed goal in that legislation of no more than 5 percent of all medications being given incorrectly.)

While industry representatives are always the first to complain of the paperwork and costs involved in complying with new regulations, other observers have questioned the effectiveness of an expanded regulatory approach. As Caldwell and Kapp (1981, 40) point out:

> The inconvertible fact . . . is that the most comprehensively written and vigorously enforced regulations in the world can only work to a small degree to protect individuals from abuses. Compassion and respect for individuals can not be regulated. Until they are somehow achieved, we must find small comfort in providing dependents with a set of legal rights to accompany those misfortunes that are beyond government's power to abolish.

While some are more optimistic, it does seem clear that major gains through more extensive regulation are difficult to achieve.

What practical steps can be taken to modify regulatory provisions? An informal network often can provide support for nursing homes and also give a quiet nudge to personnel to make a more concerted effort. Some of the industry's attempts to build community support groups are, in effect, public relations campaigns and need to be viewed cautiously. Yet such basic community processes as small town gossip about the food at the local nursing home can be an effective control device.

The second important but difficult step is to close the worst homes in operation. In some states, those who are concerned with nursing home abuses will indicate privately that closing a few of the homes with the worst performance records would cause a major overall improvement in the quality of care. Yet despite all of the legislation passed in recent years, permanent closings have been very rare. In part, the legal authority given to those pursuing the enforcement efforts has been limited, and in some instances the political ties of owners have contributed to a lack of more vigorous enforcement. Since nursing homes are major employers in some communities, the closure step is also resisted because of the loss of jobs. The decision whether to close a home is further complicated when there is a shortage of facilities in the area.

Several prospects for closing the worst facilities are worth pursuing. In some instances, it may be more important to pursue aggressive enforcement rather than the passage of additional technical requirements. One approach would be to give patients a role in the evaluation process (LaPorte and Rubin 1979, 108). Vladeck (1980) discusses the possibility of involving health care professionals more closely in the evaluation process. Health care professionals in a particular city or geographic area often are best informed concerning the adequacy or inadequacy of certain facilities. The advantage of Vladeck's proposal over the existing annual inspection process is that it would focus on the overall quality of care and place less emphasis on meeting technical requirements. Better coordination between licensing and enforcement activities is greatly needed as well as stronger legal authority for the enforcement agency.

Since Medicaid pays about half of all the funds for nursing homes, policy making in the state capitals on financial issues has been extremely controversial. The political pressure generated by the revenue squeeze of the early 1980s is likely, in the short run, to prohibit major increases in financing of long-term care facilities. The industry has not enhanced its position with some of its actions in past controversies or with its desire to conceal the real estate aspects of certain transactions. If higher levels of compensation are to occur, considerable care must be exercised to increase the likelihood that improved patient care will result.

An important case can be made in favor of increased reimbursement rates. Increases in the minimum wage have helped make labor costs a major expense for facilities in which more than half of the total expenses are for salaries. Higher labor costs also must be expected if long-term care facilities are to recruit personnel with more training. Recent analyses by the General Accounting Office (1982, 2) point to an increase in the level of dependency and disability on the part of individuals who have been entering nursing homes in the last several years. In one respect, this is a favorable development, insofar as it indicates that there is now less unnecessary institutionalization taking place. Nonetheless, if the trend toward greater levels of disability increases (as was predicted by the GAO), more extensive and more expensive levels of care will be needed. Some increases in levels of compensation, along with improved reimbursement structures, should be pursued. The importance of reducing both the suspicion and the actual instances of fraud and abuse dictates the appropriateness of greater scrutiny of nursing home operations by both elected officials and the public.

Ultimately, the evolution of the nation's nursing home policies has to be considered in light of the numbers of individuals who are to be placed in those institutions and the extent of the alternative systems of service that are available. At the present time, nursing home capacity is being used at a relatively high rate, and a rate which produces waiting lists in some areas. Enforcement of existing regulations is often difficult, since few politicians or agency officials like to force individuals to move when they may not have any other place to go.

The prospect of building substantial new capacity, however, raises the unpleasant prospect that we will continue to assign individuals to nursing homes who could function without full-time institutional care if that were available. As an alternative, Vladeck (1980, 221-241) has proposed that we use some of the nation's presently under-utilized capacity in acute care hospitals (but at lower payment rates) while at the same time creating additional social services and housing options for those who do not require placement in a nursing home. It is hoped that this would reduce utilization of nursing homes in the next few years and make it easier to close some of the least desirable facilities.

There are political constraints (from hospitals at least as much as from the nursing home industry) that surround proposals for more than incremental changes in nursing home policies. Vladeck's proposals have the major advantage of focusing concern on a wide range of issues. We do indeed have inappropriate uses of nursing homes by many who do not need that care when initially assigned, and we clearly face a situation in which there is some excess capacity in the nation's acute care hospitals. Furthermore, as Vladeck points out, the continuation of present policies will produce a demand for more nursing home beds by the late 1980s. The pursuit of nursing home reform and the key issue of alternative facilities and services is never an easy task. Yet for the more than one million older persons who spend their days in nursing homes, reform is crucial.

ISSUES AND ALTERNATIVES

Any assessment of health care issues must address not only hospital and physician costs but also the promising alternatives that can provide the nation's older population with more appropriate and often less expensive health care.

New Approaches

Expanded uses of preventative health care, modifications in the emphasis on medical approaches, and increased research opportunities are encouraging new developments. The health of the aging in the coming years will be shaped by the extent to which preventative health measures are implemented. The joggers one sees on the parkways of Washington, D.C., as well as the decisions of the nation's health planners, will have a major impact on the health status of the future aging population. Fortunately, Americans of all ages are becoming more concerned about personal health. This may not dramatically reduce the need for health care on an individual basis, but it seems likely that the age at which individuals are in need of extensive care may increase.

Good health is strongly related to environmental factors. The environmental relationship for the aging is particularly important in terms of the vulnerability of the aging to various forms of cancer. Since cancer is often caused by environmental factors, the health of present and future older persons will be significantly influenced by the extent to which more healthy environments are provided for the aging as well as for all Americans.

An increasing number of observers have been stressing that health policy for the aging should place less emphasis on a "medical model" and the often extensive use of acute care facilities. LaPorte and Rubin (1979) note the importance of increasing concern with the social aspects of living conditions in long-term care facilities. In their view, many individuals need a caring environment more than medications and medical attention.

Similarly, important policy differences need to be considered surrounding the extent to which care for the aging emphasizes safety and medical care, versus personal autonomy and dignity, even if this involves a measure of risk to the individual (Kane and Kane 1981a). As we shall see in Chapter 9, the movement toward hospice care in the last several years is an important attempt to modify the nature and focus of medical care in the United States.

In some areas of medical research, important advances are being made. It is essential that recent efforts to improve our understanding of

171

senility be continued and expanded. At least half of the residents of long-term care facilities are suffering from some form of senility. Thus a significant breakthrough in the development of new forms of treatment could have extremely important consequences. Research sponsored in part by the National Institute on Aging has led to some success in developing treatment for Alzheimer's disease and other types of senility. In sum, selectively focused medical research, greater emphasis on preventative medicine, and less medically oriented treatment modes can have important consequences for the health of the future aging population and the magnitude — and cost — of the physician and hospital care which is required.

Cost Controls and the Health Insurance Debate

The organization and financing of hospital and physician services are an important aspect of health policy for the aging. As Feder, Holahan, and Marmor (1980) have persuasively argued in a major review of policy alternatives, it is essential that very specific issues be confronted in our planning for the implementation of future reforms in the nation's health care system. In retrospect, the absence of greater concern with organizational and pricing aspects of health care in the establishment of Medicare and Medicaid was a major failing, a failing, it is hoped, that will not be repeated.

Several alternative policies for organizing health services have had major advocates in recent years. Feder, Holahan, and Marmor (1980, 3-6) have classified these approaches in three basic categories. One series of proposals have focused on catastrophic coverage, with select covering of additional groups. President Carter's proposals fell into this category which essentially involves narrow coverage and a minimum federal role. At the other extreme are proposals emphasizing wide coverage and a large federal role. The Kennedy-Corman proposals in the 1970s (with their provision for universal scope, comprehensive coverage, and public financing) are major examples of this approach. As a middle category, plans have been advocated with wide coverage but a limited federal financial role. These plans seek to utilize employer-based plans and tax credits but not direct federal financing. As one variant of this type, the Reagan administration in 1981 began considering a voucher plan in which individuals would be given vouchers to purchase health care. A major objective of the various voucher approaches has been to try to increase competition in the delivery of health services. As of the early 1980s, political support for a Kennedy-Corman type of coverage clearly had eroded. Proposals that involved a less extensive and less directly expensive federal role were more popular in Congress.

Davidson and Marmor have evaluated a variety of systems of national health insurance for the aging, including the existing Medicare and Medicaid approach, on such criteria as range of services being covered, extensiveness of eligibility, financial costs, and ease of administration. They conclude (1980, 121) that from the standpoint of the aging, under *any* of the proposed systems of national health insurance, "eligibility would be broader and less burdensome to establish, more services would be covered (except in states with the most generous Medicaid programs) and they would be less heavily weighted toward acute care, cost-sharing would be reduced, and administration would be simplified." From this perspective, it is clear that the aging have a major stake in the financing and organization of health services.

Regardless of the outcome of the national health insurance debate, changes are imperative. No matter who is paying the bill, health care costs must be contained. If public rate setting mechanisms are to be employed, as in the Canadian system, then issues of organization and representation need to be addressed. Through the 1970s, emphasis on cost containment involved such strategies as trying to avoid the construction of unnecessary facilities and efforts at establishing review processes before some forms of treatment would be authorized. The effort at controlling new construction, through certificate of need requirements, was an important policy effort for both acute care hospitals and long-term care facilities. (With certificate of need programs, hospitals had to show a need for expansion before new facilities could be built.)

The Reagan administration gave initial indications of substantial hostility to several of the existing cost control strategies. Indeed it was not always evident that such mechanisms as certificate of need programs and Professional Standards Review Organizations (PSROs) had been particularly effective in containing costs (Levin 1980). There was at the same time an interest in seeking greater competition, particularly among acute care hospitals, as a means of cost control. The result of actions in the early 1980s on the cost control issue seemed likely to have substantial implications for the aging. If costs are not more effectively contained, then out-of-pocket costs could expand sharply. Rising costs, coupled with a continuing absence of catastrophy insurance, would be especially devastating.

The position of long-term care facilities and in-home services stands as an additional issue in the organizing and financing of the nation's health care system. As we will see in the next chapter, the in-home-care programs raise difficult financial questions. A national health insurance plan that would cover long-term care services for all individuals (not only those who pass a means test as in Medicaid) also would be very costly. Analyses by LaPorte and Rubin (1979) and Pollack (1980) show that various alternatives can be developed. This is an extremely important area for careful policy analysis. On the one hand, a sudden effort to absorb all long-term care costs into a national health scheme would have major — and not necessarily positive — consequences not only for costs but for the type of care available for the frail elderly. Yet avoiding inclusion, as has occurred in some of the national health insurance proposals, ignores an area in which present policies place major, and seemingly unfair, burdens on some individuals who are unable to qualify for Medicaid assistance.

Health care issues thus promise to be important and controversial in the 1980s. Since 1965, considerable progress has been made in assisting the aging with health costs. Yet the limited initial attention to cost control provisions, and the limited eligibility for some services under Medicare, continues to make the impact of personal, out-of-pocket health costs an important issue for older persons. The aging have a tremendous stake in Medicare and Medicaid reform and in the larger questions involving the financing and structuring of the nation's health care system.

VIII

HOUSING AND SOCIAL SERVICES

Housing and social services programs constitute an important aspect of the nation's policy efforts for the aging. Reform in the quality and extensiveness of nursing home use depends to a considerable degree upon the alternatives available to older persons as they begin to fail and can no longer function without some assistance or a change in living arrangements. Costs also raise crucial issues. In 1982, the federal and state financial commitments for housing and social services were very small in comparison with the expenditures for Social Security, Medicare, and Medicaid. Nevertheless, programs in these areas were major budget-cutting targets of the Reagan administration.

According to a study by Laurie (1981) for the General Accounting Office, as many as 10 million older persons *not* in institutions could use a meals program; the annual cost for these social services could exceed $5 billion. Although hypothetical, Laurie's analysis points to the importance of developing targeting strategies in social services programs and of considering the extent to which the private sector rather than the public sector should finance needed services. In the area of housing policy, the cost of developing large numbers of publicly financed units comparable to those in Britain and the Netherlands is politically unrealistic. Nonetheless, a wide variety of more financially feasible housing alternatives are available. Because housing policies are often contingent upon the availability of social services, this chapter examines social services first. In this section we will explore funding for social services, the politics of social services, and a number of individual policy issues.

SOCIAL SERVICES

Social services for the aging involve an extensive array of programs to help individuals in widely differing circumstances. This fragmented

175

program structure frequently has led to confusion about program labels (Lowy 1980). In general, social services can be categorized in three groups: 1) periodic services, which include information and referral assistance, legal services, home repair, transportation services, and crisis intervention; 2) services on a more frequent basis, which include homemaker services, telephone reassurance, and social opportunities provided by senior centers; and 3) services that focus more fundamentally on health-related problems.

The health-related category has included a variety of specific forms in recent years, often including some emphasis on nonhealth-related objectives. In the 1970s, nutrition programs providing hot meals once a day grew quite rapidly. (Individuals who live in separate rooms in congregate living quarters may receive three meals a day.) A few adult day care centers for individuals needing some care during the daytime also began to appear during the decade. Although objectives in some of the day care programs have been partly social, services such as physical rehabilitation and therapeutic health care are an important part (Weiler 1978). Growth also has occurred in the area of home health care (Oktay and Palley 1982). By 1980, home health care programs for individuals of all ages were costing $2.5 billion. These programs involve visitations by licensed health practitioners with nurses providing much of that assistance. There also has been a rapid increase in the use of home health aides who provide personal health care assistance, usually under a nurse's supervision. Thus social services programs range from infrequent counseling to daily meals and regular visits by a nurse.

Social Services Funding

The large number of specific programs is partially a consequence of the diverse funding sources. In addition to the funding provided by state and local governments, programs have been funded through four federal sources: Medicare, Medicaid, amendments to the Social Security Act of 1935 (Title XX), and the Older Americans Act of 1965.

Important restrictions are placed on the health-related assistance provided by Medicare and Medicaid. Under Medicare, individuals may receive up to 100 home health care visits per illness if those visits are ordered by a physician. In 1977, this involved services to slightly less than 700,000 individuals, with nursing services being provided most frequently and a third of that group being assisted by home health aides.

The use of Medicaid to fund social services (for those who met the program's eligibility requirements) was extensive in some states but virtually nonexistent in others.

After a slow start in the late 1960s, social services programs covered by the Social Security Act of 1935 began to grow very rapidly. In 1974 a ceiling of $2.5 billion was placed on total spending, and each of the states was given a maximum allocation based upon its population and its ability to match federal contributions with a 25 percent contribution of its own (Derthick 1975). The 1974 legislation, which added Title XX to the Social Security Act, required significant public participation in program choices and strengthened support for persons eligible for assistance programs (such as the Supplemental Security Income (SSI) program) on the basis of need. Because the aging must compete for Title XX funds with many other groups, the amount of funding available has varied considerably from state to state. The U.S. House Select Committee on Aging (1981) estimated that in 1980 one million older persons received some assistance through Title XX programs, with the largest dollar amount ($570 million) going for homemaker chore services. The more directly health-related programs, such as adult day care, however, received very limited support. Gilbert and Specht (1982) provide an excellent discussion of Title XX financing. In the early 1980s great uncertainty surrounded all programs under this title. The Reagan administration obtained reduced funding for Title XX programs in 1981 while eliminating several state requirements. The new program was labeled a social services block grant.

The fourth source of funding for social services, the Older Americans Act of 1965, emerged in an effort to stimulate and coordinate programs for the aging. Both health-related and general social services programs have been developed on an experimental basis, but the largest emphasis has been in the area of nutrition programs. Initially begun on a demonstration basis with a fairly strong emphasis on dietary problems of the frail elderly, the programs expanded in the 1970s while gradually giving more emphasis to the social aspects of the daily meals (Posner 1979). Given its modified statutory position in the Older Americans Act, the nutrition programs (which began under Title VII) are commonly known as the Title III program. Although initially very small, the budget for programs under the Older Americans Act has grown. In 1981 the total budget for all programs (except the separately funded community service employment program) was $673 million.

177

Social Services Politics

America's Slow Start. Social services have been substantially slower to develop and more fragmented in their implementation in the United States than in most other advanced industrial nations. In Sweden, for example, 1 percent of the nation's eight million inhabitants work as either full-time or part-time home helpers, while in the United States the number of persons so employed is a tiny fraction of the labor force (Kahn and Kamerman 1977, 94). In Canada, development of social services for the aging also has been more extensive than in the United States (Kane and Kane 1981b).

The slower early response appears to have evolved from the same general set of constraints affecting income maintenance and health care policies. At a time when substantial and innovative programs were being developed in some countries, in the United States political leaders emphasized the importance of individual and private action. Little lobbying was done for major expansion. As some policy responses began to take place in the early 1960s, the medical and hospital lobbies were instrumental in promoting health care by health professionals. In addition, the chosen policy design tended to work against increased commitments. In contrast to the trust fund status of the Social Security system, social services programs have had to compete more directly for financial support in the congressional budgetary process.

The fragmentation in America's responses can be traced to several sources. When comparing the United States to Western European nations, it is important to remember that planning a social services system for all of Sweden involves about the same number of people in a major metropolitan area in the United States — Los Angeles, for example. The diversity and size of this nation undoubtedly has contributed to the lack of cohesion in program development. Moreover, there is an emphasis in American legislative politics on visible projects for the individual constituencies of the members of Congress, and this inevitably leads in some measure to a fragmentary approach. Fenno (1978) and Hale and Palley (1981) have stressed the importance of members' constituency ties. Legislative credit-claiming may well have contributed to separate but visible types of social services programs. The development of a number of different programs has the political advantage of giving an appearance of responsiveness even though the actual financial commitments behind them may be quite small.

Passage of the Older Americans Act. As Hudson (1974), Pratt (1976), and Estes (1979) emphasize, an important new step in social services policy development was taken in 1965 when the Older Americans Act was passed. Two points need to be kept in mind in considering that policy development. First, the act profited by the general momentum surrounding President Lyndon Johnson's domestic agenda in 1965. Second, the initial appropriation was extremely small, only $7.5 million. Funding increases also came slowly at the outset, standing at $23 million in 1969. By the early 1980s, while still not large by the standards of major Washington programs, the budget was approaching three-quarters of a billion dollars.

Beginning in 1958 with the initiatives of Rep. John Fogarty (D-R.I.), Congress began to discuss ways in which the states could take a more extensive role in assisting the aging. The states themselves had begun to experiment with advisory groups that could be used as forerunners for the proposed State Units on Aging (SUAs). President John F. Kennedy endorsed a program of incentives for state action in 1963, and during the Johnson administration interest in expanding federal programs to help state and local governments grew. In 1964 the Office of Economic Opportunity was established, and two years later the Models Cities program was enacted. The mood in Congress and the White House made some response in the area of aging particularly appropriate. Passage of the Older Americans Act of 1965 is not surprising in light of the domestic policy developments in the mid-1960s.

Pratt (1976, 117) stresses the importance of lobby action, particularly on the part of the American Association of Retired Persons (AARP), in gaining passage of the act. Perhaps at least as important was the general disinterest of potentially important opponents. Primarily involved in the fight over Medicare, the American Medical Association did not lobby actively on this legislation. Underlying these opportunities for success was the large Democratic majority in Congress following the 1964 elections and the general political climate, which was conducive to growth in domestic programs.

Amendment of the Older Americans Act. The Older Americans Act has produced several fairly intense political controversies in the eight

179

extensions that have occurred since 1965. The most extensive changes were made in 1973, when Congress — dissatisfied with the lack of initial progress — increased funding and restructured the program. The 1973 amendments set up Area Administrations on Aging (AAAs) in major geographic areas in each state. Close to half of these area agencies were located in regional planning commissions, and some were based in nonprofit agencies with no direct tie to government. By 1978, the number of AAAs had reached 558, and the total planning effort included more than 600 planning and service areas.

As developed in 1973, the area agencies had multiple responsibilities. First, they were to develop comprehensive plans for the provision of services in their area. Second, they were to promote a pooling of funds from other sources, such as general revenue sharing, to meet needs for services. Third, they were to contract or manage the provision of such specific programs under the Older Americans Act as nutrition sites and social services centers. In 1978 the Older Americans Act was amended again. These amendments placed greater emphasis on targeting resources and less emphasis on pooling resources among different agencies. As we have seen, the Older Americans Act has gone through numerous changes since its establishment in 1965. Resulting programs and advocacy efforts need to be reviewed from several perspectives.

Results of the Older Americans Act. Dobson and Karns (1979) draw a picture of limited impact on the part of the networks of state and local agencies established under the act. In part, agencies were troubled in the early years by a rapid turnover of personnel. Perhaps more fundamentally, the advisory council process has tended to generate conflicts over such questions as whether to support quietly a few of the agencies' programs or to push vigorously for new policies. (Advisory councils in other areas have had similar problems.) The councils' concern for representational issues and often a rapid turnover of membership has reduced lobbying effectiveness. In their interviews of state legislators in 29 states in 1977, Dobson and Karns found limited legislative contact with the state units and local area agency councils. According to Dobson and Karns, legislators only rarely felt that the advocacy undertaken by the advisory councils was of major significance. Estes (1979) presented a similarly skeptical view in her work on implementation of the Older Americans Act.

Some researchers focusing more substantially on political actions at the local level have reached different conclusions. Williamson, Evans and Powell (1982) stress the overall importance of the local networks which have been created. Similarly, Decker and Whelan (1982) emphasize the importance of the local advocacy network in their review of recent experiences. Often writers who emphasize the effectiveness of advocacy efforts focus on actions which, while helpful, produce quite modest expansions in social services programs. Conversely, those who see more limited effectiveness in advocacy activities, such as Binstock (1978, 1840), tend to view advocacy activities in relationship to the magnitude of policy efforts that would be required to meet the broader definitions of existing needs.

The attempt to create advocacy roles through the use of state and local advisory councils can be helpful in developing social services programs with a fairly narrow focus. Councils have less impact on programs with a broader range of policy concerns affecting the aging. The advisory council roles often are particularly useful when there is little organized activity on behalf of the aging. One of the useful roles of the formal structures actually may be in providing an initial set of activities from which more independently based advocacy activities can emerge. Once other activities begin to develop, the flexibility offered independently based interest groups may allow them to develop political styles and roles which surpass the formal aging network in their pursuit of political influence.

Has the act, in turn, led to effective pooling of funds and coordination of social services programs? There are few strong indications that it has. In part because of the difficulties with this objective, pooling was given less emphasis in the 1978 amendments to the Older Americans Act. In 1978, Joseph Califano, Secretary of the Health, Education and Welfare Department, testified that more than $440 million had been pooled from other agencies. These funds and services primarily came from such sources as Title XX, Medicaid, ACTION, the Legal Services Corporation, general revenue sharing, and CETA's job training programs. Estes (1979, 183-187) stresses that even if fairly generous estimates of the size of these pooled services are accepted, the average allocation per person age 65 and over would be small — between $19 and $20 annually.

The aging network, both in Washington, D.C., and in the states, has been able to promote some pooling of funds which has been useful for

181

specific recipients. When viewed in terms of either the optimistic assessments made for the Older Americans Act initially, or the magnitude of program development which many would like to see occur, the gains have nonetheless been quite modest. The classic problem, of course, is one of relative organizational strength. Because the budgets within the aging network have been very small in relationship to other programs, there has been an obvious need for tapping other sources of funds to expand the range of programs for the aging. Yet because of their own modest financial resources, organizations in the aging network have little to offer in return, and they also may have fairly limited political power to bring to bear on those pooling decision processes. In the third area of major activity, the direct management of programs, the role of state and local units on aging has expanded.

Social Services Issues

The increasing costs and political controversies involved in the development of social services raise three critical policy questions. First, can family support systems be used in lieu of expanding commitments to social services? Second, are present social services policies likely to foster dependency on the part of the aging? Third, to what extent can social services — perhaps with improved coordination — be envisioned as alternatives to traditional nursing homes?

Family Support Systems: The Forgotten Alternative? In discussions of social services and nursing home utilization a frequent topic of debate is expansion in the use of family structures to care for the aging. Without question, some increase in the use of family structures could be developed. It is also clear that some of our existing policies inappropriately discriminate against the use of family support systems. Yet it is less clear that a major expansion could take place, and even more doubtful that an expansion could take place in a context in which social services were being reduced.

Several limitations have to be confronted regarding the proposition that families can be used more extensively as a substitute for social services or long-term care facilities. First, much of the care now being given to the frail elderly is provided by family members. While the number of adult children caring for their parents within three-generation families has declined, a great deal of care is being provided by spouses and other family members, such as maiden aunts. Second, the rapid increase in the proportion of women in the labor force has increased the pressures on the women "in the middle" who are seeking to care for a family, maintain employment, and in some instances provide care for a parent or in-law (Brody 1981). Third, because women have married more often in recent decades, there are fewer single women available to provide family-based care. Fourth, because of the recent decline in family size, there are fewer adult children in the typical family who can care for an elderly relative. Regardless of predominant values concerning the care of aging family members, definite demographic factors work against the use of three-generation families.

An additional factor working against elderly persons residing full-time with immediate family is the preferences of the aging themselves. According to Sussman (1976), older persons generally value "intimacy at a distance" rather than shared living arrangements. The two main reasons for this preference are uncertainty about their welcome and a genuine desire for independence.

Despite the substantial constraints, public policies could be modified to increase the likelihood that family support systems will not erode further in the coming years. One step would be to eliminate penalties for spouses who try to provide extensive support. Medicaid rules too often discourage a spouse from continuing to care for the more impaired member of a marriage, since social services may be covered less completely than nursing home care. A few recent proposals also have involved requirements for support either financially or through shared living arrangements on the part of adult children with mid-level or high personal incomes. Historically, more than half of the states at some point attempted this approach with laws seeking some support from financially able adult children. These programs proved difficult to administer and were highly unpopular. It also seems doubtful that a very caring environment can be created for an older person when the financial support or living arrangement is provided on the basis of threatened financial penalties. A more promising approach is the use of tax incentives for those willing to provide family care for the frail elderly (Newman 1979). This has the disadvantage of adding an additional dimension of complexity to the tax system, and such an approach would need to be designed carefully. Nonetheless, a system of tax credits and payments, plus the elimination of present penalties against family care, would constitute an appropriate step in the effort to strengthen family support systems.

If family supports are to be used more extensively, the level of social services being provided may need to increase. Social services are often essential when the younger son or daughter providing support is age 60 or even older. How is a daughter age 62, for example, going to provide the bathing care needed for an 85-year-old mother? Getting a frail older person in and out of a bathtub can be difficult for a person with a strong back, let alone for a person whose own health is deteriorating. In a variety of situations, a policy of enhancing family support systems actually may call for more social services rather than less. In short, family support policies are important, but they cannot be viewed as a substitute for social services.

The Dependency Issue. Questions of social services policy also raise the basic issue of whether some of the present services, and those being promoted by advocates, really help the recipients. The primary concern of some critics surrounds the possibility that governmental provision of social services will undermine the use of family, community, and private sector action. For others, the key problem is the tendency to produce unnecessary dependency on the part of the older person.

In the early 1970s, the planning activities undertaken in the aging services' network often contained an unrealistic attempt to elaborate a wide range of needs which presumably had to be met with various service programs. Yet in fairness to those early planners, it should be emphasized that the language of the Older Americans Act encouraged some of those rather ponderous planning efforts. Fortunately, recent amendments to the Older Americans Act have reduced the emphasis on extensive planning.

Estes (1979, 221-247) has presented an extensive critique of existing policies and advocated greater emphasis on income maintenance. She argues that defining the aging as a distinct group in American society and then emphasizing their need for separate services is an inappropriate approach to the problem. Some policies, she argues, begin to develop a self-perpetuating demand for those services. Often the result is unwieldy and easily fragmented policy initiatives. For Estes, an important change in America's approach to the aging thus would be attitudinal. She also urges greater emphasis on income oriented policies such as Supplemental Security Income (SSI) and Food Stamps and an integration of existing social services programs.

In evaluating the appropriateness of different levels of commitment to social services programs and the underlying question of potential dependency, several additional factors need to be considered. First, present expenditures are very strongly oriented toward income maintenance programs rather than social services. Kahn (1979, 33) estimates that as of 1976 social services for Americans of all ages were costing between $10 and $15 billion per year. A sum in the neighborhood of $2 to $3 billion is now being spent on social services for the aging exclusive of such specialized efforts as those being undertaken by the Veterans Administration (Ross 1980; U.S. House Select Committee on Aging 1981). The issue of dependency on services often seems to be more appropriate for a situation in which substantially higher social services expenditures are taking place.

The argument for an income policy as distinct from a services policy raises the question of the extent to which services can be made available through shared financial arrangements and by private sector providers. The problems of financial abuse and improper care that occurred with the rapid expansion of privately owned nursing homes in the late 1960s suggest the importance of caution in the manner in which private services are developed. Whether publicly provided services promote dependency or not, the costs of those services point to the importance of developing policies that include shared contributions from the recipients of those services.

Taking a different perspective on the dependency issue, Kane and Kane (1981a) argue that many current policies seek to maximize the safety of individuals but not their independence. Where services become a basis for avoidance of nursing home residency, they can be defended as a device for reducing, rather than increasing, the dependency of the older person. The proper mix of overall policy commitments should be thoroughly debated along with different strategies for improving the delivery of those services. It nonetheless seems difficult to escape the necessity of a substantial commitment to social services. One underlying issue continues to be the level of support for social services in relationship to the commitment to, and allocations for, nursing home use.

185

Social Services and Nursing Home Use. Since the early 1970s, the use of social services as an alternative to long-term care facilities has been debated extensively. The aging themselves often have been among the advocates of increased social services commitments since the prospect of entering a traditional nursing home is seldom viewed with enthusiasm. According to some studies, 50 to 76 percent of the individuals entering nursing homes are assigned unnecessarily (Weissert 1980a, 2). Although estimates of inappropriate admission vary, it is clear that far too many individuals are being institutionalized.

From the standpoint of the preferences of the aging for a maximum amount of personal independence, what are the alternatives to confinement to a nursing home? In New York there have been important experiments with nursing homes without walls. These facilities are responsible for an individual's health, but full-time residence is not a requirement. Similarly, the growth of adult day care centers with their health service orientation constitutes an important use of extensive services in an effort to avoid institutionalization.

Unfortunately, some of the proposed programs are not less expensive on an individual basis and do not necessarily contribute to a less costly overall set of policy responses. In fairness, some of the experiments with adult day care centers undoubtedly face initial costs that would not be totally replicated in a more extensive program. In addition, some of the best day care centers give individuals more extensive care than they would receive in some nursing homes. Nonetheless, the cost comparisons carried out at the U.S. National Center for Health Services Research by Weissert (as well as the ones he summarizes) are disappointing regarding the view that alternatives to institutionalization save costs. On a daily basis, day care costs are in some instances actually higher than costs in nursing homes. This becomes understandable when one considers the greater availability in day care centers of some services and the fact that most states reimburse nursing homes at a rate of only about $25 to $30 per day.

Day care services often turn out to be additional services and not an actual alternative to institutionalization. In a careful study of 1,871 patients in six day care centers and a control group covered by traditional services, Weissert (1980b, 3) concludes:

> The results of this experiment were disappointing. Day care had no statistically significant effect on nursing home entry or length of stay in nursing homes. Moreover, the rate of use of nursing homes was so low

in the control group that it showed that even if day care had been effective, it could not have prevented much use because only 21 percent of control group patients used a nursing home and their average length of stay was 1.3 months. . . . Most patients (79 percent) used day care as an add-on to existing services rather than as a substitute for nursing homes.

In a companion study, the results for home care programs were also disappointing although there were some indications of improvement in the health of those with home care programs vis-à-vis the control group. The problems inherent in research efforts in this area point to the importance of caution in considering initial studies. Sample sizes are often too small, and the development of appropriate control groups can be difficult.

In short, social services programs are not necessarily cheaper than nursing homes. Their primary advantage is not financial but personal; it has long been established that the nation's aging prefer noninstitutionalized care. As Weissert (1980b, 7-8) notes:

> . . . the fact that some of the alternatives to institutionalization do not seem to accomplish the initially suggested goals of reducing costs and rates of institutionalization does not mean that these strategies should be ignored. Rather, social service policies need to be approached with a realization that they are often helpful, but are not likely to be a cost-saving step.

A system of social services designed to reduce nursing home use is not apt to reduce overall costs without a more thorough "gatekeeping" role for those services than we have had in the past (Vladeck 1980). The difficult problem from a policy standpoint is that many individuals may opt for additional services who would otherwise not enter a nursing home. While these services may be desirable and helpful, they may not be feasible financially.

Case Management. To develop more adequate social services, improvements in the organizational methods of dealing with individual needs are essential. Other necessary steps are coordinating the delivery of those services and applying cost-sharing formulas for individual users who have moderate to high incomes. While it would be nice to be able to say "let's provide those services free," the potential cost and overuse of marginally necessary services make that strategy unwise.

There have been a variety of experiments in service delivery for the aging in recent years. In Connecticut, Triage was formed to develop a range of homemaker, nutrition, and chore services for a select group of clients. Rather than dealing with multiple agencies and often rigid federal requirements, individuals in this experiment were able to gain needed services through a single agency. The experiment has been a financial success and also has reduced hospital and nursing home utilization. In their review of social services programs, Gottesman et al. (1979) emphasize the opportunities for real progress. Steinberg (1978, 1) is also optimistic:

> Human services professionals are in the midst of a new wave of efforts to forge our patchwork of agencies, programs and categorical funding patterns into a planned continuum of care or a holistic approach to people in trouble. The so-called bottom line of this reawakened interest in a century old idea is usually known as case management or case integration.

The case management approach involves two basic ideas. First, there should be an organizational capacity to respond to special groups of clients in terms of the whole person. Second, there should be a capacity for obtaining the entire range of services that may be needed by people with multiple problems. Individuals need a central agency they can turn to which will be able to evaluate their needs and assist them in finding suppliers of specific services.

A wide variety of organizations have sought to develop case management skills in recent years. In Pennsylvania and Washington, the lead has been taken by State Administrations on Aging. In other states, separate agencies have been created that do not have any direct program management function. Sometimes the case management role has been assigned to an information and referral agency within a larger local government organization. While finding no single preferable manner for managing cases, Steinberg and Carter (1983) see a need for multiple organization-building strategies. Expanded case management capacities should be an important reform objective in the coming years. Greater attention also needs to be given to the development of a comprehensive gatekeeping role for social services.

Gatekeeping Roles. As discussed by Vladeck (1980, 234-237), the gatekeeping role becomes more extensive than case management approaches in several respects. The concept of a gatekeeping agency is similar to case management in its emphasis on assessments of those seeking services followed by referrals. Vladeck argues, however, that two additional functions should be filled by the key agency. First, funds for services should be pooled to increase overall administrative efficiency. Second, broad-based financing formulas for clients who are able to pay for some services should be created to facilitate the development of coherent cost-sharing approaches.

The development of an expanded gatekeeping role is an essential element in the evolution of social services because it would reduce public expenses through expanded sharing of costs. There is also an important opportunity for controlling the use of services with marginal value. If social services are to play a larger role in the avoidance of nursing home use, then it is essential that the gatekeeping role be strengthened. Because of the differing political traditions and mores throughout the nation, a single approach is unlikely to emerge as the most effective (Steinberg and Carter 1983). Rather, a number of experiments need to be pursued by state and local governments.

In sum, the provision of social services is an essential component of policies for the aging. Yet to meet the demands of the 1980s and future decades, major advances must occur in the manner in which those services are provided.

HOUSING POLICIES

The availability of suitable living arrangements is closely related to questions involving social services, family support systems, and nursing home use. Housing policies are also important for another reason: in today's housing market there is a shortage of affordable homes for young persons. A young potential home buyer might well ask, "Why don't all those elderly widows get out of their big, three bedroom houses and let younger people buy them?" One answer is that many older persons have few suitable options. From the perspective of the young and the old, housing policies and politics are likely to receive increasing attention in the 1980s.

Present Conditions

More than 60 percent of the aging population today own their own homes, and about 70 percent live in homes owned either by themselves or by others. The difficulty experienced by young couples in the 1970s in getting into the housing market has important policy implications for the future, since a continuation of that housing shortage would make housing and retirement income planning increasingly difficult for the aging in the years ahead. In the 1980s, while the needs of the low-income elderly and the elderly without homes present the most acute problems, housing policy questions also must include issues involving older persons in a wide variety of circumstances.

Housing conditions have improved for major segments of the aging population. To a considerable extent, the aging have enjoyed the overall improvement that has occurred in the nation's housing quality since the 1940s. Rabushka and Jacobs (1980) surveyed homeowners from different geographic areas, community sizes, and income levels throughout the country. They found that the attitudes of the aging themselves toward housing conditions are strikingly positive. Only 5 percent were dissatisfied with their housing, and less than 10 percent were interested in moving to condominiums, mobile homes, or multistory apartments. About 75 percent concluded that the size of their present housing was about right. This finding is interesting in light of some observers' beliefs that the aging tend to have too much housing space in relationship to their needs or economic means. In addition, respondents reported high levels of satisfaction with existing neighborhoods, while displaying an emphasis on the importance of community ties.

A number of more disquieting aspects of the present housing picture also must be recognized. The high incidence of mortgage-free homes is a key factor in keeping housing costs low for the more than six million individuals who own their homes without a mortgage. The aging spend an average of only 23 percent of their income on housing. Yet in 1976, some 2.3 million elderly persons spent more than 35 percent of their total income on housing (Struyk and Soldo, 1980, 2-3). Second, inflation and a national housing shortage have intensified problems for those who must rent. Third, because the aging tend to occupy old homes (many of them in northern cities), they are apt to face the high heating costs associated with buildings that are poorly insulated and badly designed. Finally, while attitudes and assessments by experts differ, it is clear that a segment of the older population lives in homes that are substandard. Of the 1.2 million households headed by an older black in 1976, 162,000 of them lacked complete plumbing facilities, and approximately one million units occupied by older individuals or families had at least one of six major housing deficiencies. Thus while the evolution of home ownership and its level of satisfaction for older residents is encouraging, it is premature to conclude that major housing questions have been effectively resolved.

Housing Politics

In the United States, housing policies, like social services policies, have received less public sector commitment than in some other countries. Great Britain and the Netherlands, for example, have developed public housing for substantial segments of the aging (and significant proportions of the nonaging) population. Great Britain provides publicly owned housing for one-third of its elderly population, and one-fourth of the elderly population in the Netherlands live in some form of special purpose housing (Rubenstein 1979). In the United States in 1980, the number of public housing units available for all age groups was only 1.2 million units, with the aging occupying slightly more than 40 percent of those units (Lowy 1980, 137).

Public attitudes have worked both for and against the development of public housing for the aging in the United States. Housing policies clearly have been influenced by the general American preference for individual home ownership in all age groups. Far more than in Europe, home ownership has been both an aspiration and an achievement for a majority of the U.S. population. In nations in which apartment living is more prevalent, promoting public housing is undoubtedly easier.

The aging frequently have benefited from public housing more than other groups. In the evolution of public housing projects, the emphasis during the depression on housing for workers with limited incomes gave way by the 1950s to greater use by urban minorities as well as the aging. In both filling existing projects and planning new ones, occupancy by senior citizens was often seen as preferable to occupancy by minorities. The presence of seniors did not raise local fears of crime by the young or racial tensions in schools. In community controversies, these problems sometimes were attributed to minority-dominated housing projects. Friedman (1966) emphasizes the tendency for local communities to prefer older tenants over other groups of poor persons. While prevailing attitudes did not produce a groundswell of support for expanding public housing for seniors, the use of available public housing units for the aging did increase in the 1950s. In that process in terms of underlying racial issues, some 35 percent of older persons being assisted were black — a figure higher than their percentage in the aging population but lower than their percentage in the category of individuals eligible for public housing.

An intense lobby effort by various interests associated with the housing industry also has had a major impact on policy development. During the 1950s, builders and real estate dealers lobbied hard to reduce or even eliminate the nation's commitment to public housing (Freedman 1969; Friedman 1968; and Wolman 1971). In the 1960s, with public housing appropriations producing few new projects, the building industry underwent a change in leadership that produced a greater willingness to endorse programs that expanded opportunities for home ownership through governmental assistance. Top leaders within the National Association of Home Builders worked closely with President Johnson in promoting general domestic programs such as Model Cities and also programs of mortgage assistance and rent supplements (Lilley 1971). In recent years there has been a continuing interest among home construction groups in policies that create additional demands for new housing construction. The real estate lobby, however, has continued to oppose several of those initiatives. Unfortunately, none of the major lobby groups involved with the production and financing of housing has been particularly interested in rehabilitation policies — a fact which has undoubtedly contributed to the limited efforts to improve housing for that substantial majority of the aging who are living in their own homes.

Major Housing Policies

This section examines a wide range of housing initiatives including financing new facilities and assisting the elderly in meeting their housing costs. Federal and state programs and basic issues pertaining to the creation of expanded housing options also are discussed.

Public Housing. The first major step in federal housing was taken in 1937 with the efforts to develop publicly financed and publicly owned rental units for low-income families. That legislation provided federal assistance to communities that would establish local housing authorities to operate local public housing projects meeting the various eligibility criteria set by the federal government. The local agencies, in turn, have been responsible for the actual construction and the subsequent operation of those projects. In a few communities, often in older industrial sections of the nation, public housing has evolved to constitute a significant housing program for the elderly. Nationally, however, the total magnitude of that program has remained small in relationship to its initial goals, with approximately 1.2 million units and a recent pattern of slow growth. About 500,000 older persons (or approximately 2 percent of the aging population) live in traditional public housing units. The continuing enthusiasm for public housing among the aging has been demonstrated in the surveys by Winiecke (1973). The lengthy waiting lists for public housing in most cities also testify to this interest and demand.

Mortgage and Construction Assistance. During the late 1950s, several programs were developed to provide assistance with the financing of housing designed for low-income and elderly individuals. These programs, administered by the Department of Housing and Urban Development, included several forms of mortgage guarantees to developers which served to reduce the interest rates that the banks would offer on a loan. Some programs were available for both profit and nonprofit organizations. A popular one directly targeted for the aging was the direct loan program, known as "Section 202" in the 1959 Housing Act. In this program loans were made directly at a 3 percent rate for nonprofit sponsors of elderly housing. The major funding occurred in the 1960s; some 45,000 units were constructed in 330 projects.

Rent Supplements. A major innovation in the nation's approach to the housing needs of low-income families and individuals has occurred in the past decade as a result of the shift to rent supplements. This program often is referred to as "Section 8" in the Housing and Community Development Act of 1974. The fundamental shift occurred with a movement away from the emphasis on direct financial support of new construction and toward a more flexible program of assistance to local communities in developing adequate, affordable housing.

Under Section 8, local housing agencies enter into lease agreements with those willing to enter the program through either their own construction of new units or the rehabilitation of existing structures to meet federal standards. As projects are occupied, the local authority then pays the project owners a subsidy that makes up the difference between a fair monthly rental and the payment made by the renter. Until 1981, the renter's maximum payment was 25 percent of income, thus making the subsidy more substantial for those with low monthly incomes. Cuts in housing program support in 1981 increased the renter's maximum contribution to 30 percent. Eligibility for the program is based upon total personal income, which in the case of a one-person elderly household cannot exceed 56 percent of the family medial income in a given geographic area. Because the monthly incomes of the elderly are often quite low, they have comprised an important segment of the rent supplement clientele. In 1977, the aging occupied 50 percent of the 357,774 units then in the program. Because of the flexibility that is given local communities in this program, Struyk and Soldo (1980) have seen rent supplements as an important new policy development.

Special Programs. Efforts in the 1970s and early 1980s to provide more adequate housing for the aging also have included programs directed toward rural housing needs and programs funded through federal revenue sharing. The most important rural assistance program has been operated by the Department of Agriculture through its Farmers Home Administration. This assistance was expanded in 1978 to include experiments with rehabilitation assistance as well as the more conventional assistance with housing construction. Other programs, generally focused in urban areas, have included housing assistance efforts through the Community Development Block Grants. Block grant programs provide more flexibility in the use of federal funds being targeted for fairly broad areas of social need. This has involved, in particular, an attempt in recent years to assist with rehabilitation loans as part of a general concern with neighborhood preservation. The future of the Community Development Block Grant Program and several other housing programs became increasingly uncertain during the Reagan administration. The housing programs (in contrast with Social Security benefits) were subject to reduction by direct appropriation changes and were thus a major target for domestic budget-cutting efforts.

Energy Cost Assistance. In the face of rapidly increasing energy costs, greater efforts have been made to assist low-income individuals with their energy bills. Federal expenditures grew from $200 million in 1977 to $1.85 billion in 1981, aided in part by the agreements worked out at the time of the natural gas deregulation decision in 1978. In 1982, assistance dropped to approximately $1.4 billion. While it is uncertain just how many of the recipients of aid are elderly, the aging comprise a major segment of the target clientele and are given emphasis in the legislation. In the face of substantial regional pressures in Congress, the aid formula for the distribution of federal funds has included needs for assistance with air conditioning costs as well as heating bills. As reviewed by the Senate Special Committee on Aging (1981), the state responses showed substantial variation in the determination of eligibility, the manner of payment, and the maximum benefit which was allowed.

In 1981, Congress followed the recommendations of the Reagan administration in changing the existing program into a more flexible block grant approach. This response was taken in the wake of substantial criticism over the existing procedures, which were fairly complex. By giving the states greater flexibility, it was hoped that they could more efficiently target assistance to those with the greatest needs and reduce some of the administrative confusion which had surrounded the initial program (U.S. Senate, Committee on Labor and Human Resources 1981).

Energy assistance programs have been criticized and commended. Greene (1982) argues that the programs constitute a cumbersome way to approach the underlying issue — inadequate income. Other critics claim that without a strong conservation strategy (which some states, such as Minnesota, have been emphasizing), the programs perpetuate a meager economic existence in housing that should be either weatherized or vacated by their present occupants.

Program supporters defend heating and cooling assistance for the elderly on the basis of their susceptibility to health problems when confronted with extreme temperatures (U.S. Senate, Special Committee on Aging 1981, 2). Proponents also argue that energy assistance is a justifiable means of relating to a specific need. The poor elderly spend a large portion of their income on heating costs. In 1980, the poor in all age groups spent between 20 and 35 percent of their income on household energy. The Senate Special Committee on Aging (1981, 3-4) showed even higher percentages for those who live in the worst climates and have incomes near the poverty level. Energy assistance programs are more likely to win public support than income maintenance programs, others point out in defense. Ultimately, weatherization programs would seem to constitute an appropriate category for increased emphasis in the overall energy cost assistance policies of many states.

Rehabilitation Programs. The quality of housing for the aging will be influenced very substantially by the extent to which existing homes are effectively maintained. Despite the growing popularity of migration on the part of the aging, they actually move less often than other segments of the population, and a larger percentage live in the same home for a long time. Consequently, efforts to help the elderly maintain their homes and provide insulation and other energy-saving features are an important part of the contemporary policy response (Struyk and Soldo 1980). Unfortunately, the fragmentation and poor funding of present programs have reduced their effectiveness. Potentially, existing legislation providing low-income families with energy cost assistance could be used to develop more effective programs. A greater financial commitment to some of the other programs also could provide very helpful improvements in the housing of the nation's elderly population and at far less cost than such policies as public housing.

Property Tax Relief. Since the mid-1960s, state programs of property tax relief for the aging have become highly popular. Although some assistance had been legislated prior to the 1960s, those laws did not involve substantial savings for the taxpayer. As of 1979, all of the states provided some form of tax relief for elderly homeowners, and in an increasing number of states the magnitude of relief for older homeowners was quite substantial. Reviews of these developments have been conducted by Abt Associates (1974) and Gold (1979).

The most significant development in the design of property tax relief began in 1964 in Wisconsin's establishment of a "circuit breaker" provision for property taxes. By 1979, circuit breakers had been adopted by 28 states and the District of Columbia. Eight of those programs included individuals of all ages and renters as well as homeowners. Conceptually, the circuit breaker programs take into consideration both income and property tax payments. The name is based upon the analogy of an electrical overload in a home and the need for a circuit breaker to prevent dangerous situations. With the use of sliding scales, individuals with low incomes may be exempted from property taxes above a stipulated percent of their total income. In Vermont, for example, individuals with an annual income of less than $4,000 were not required to pay a property tax in excess of 4 percent of that income.

Proponents of the circuit breaker approach point to one obvious advantage: circuit breakers allocate financial assistance directly in relationship to financial need. Gold joins those who see the circuit breakers as a useful tool for focusing financial assistance and disputes the position taken by Aaron (1975) which emphasized the greater opportunity available for wealthier individuals to profit from circuit breaker legislation. The major questions regarding circuit breakers have been twofold. First, is it appropriate to single out the aging for assistance since only a few state programs include low-income groups of all ages? Second, where the aging are living in concentrated geographic areas, there is a question as to whether this may have a negative impact on the capacity for local governments to raise needed revenues. Both of these issues require careful consideration in the evolution of property tax policies.

Tax relief also takes other forms. The most widespread is simply a homestead exemption that exempts a specified amount of a home's assessed value. For example, if a home is assessed at $30,000, an exemption of $3,000 simply means that the tax is based upon an assessed valuation of $27,000. In turn, tax credit provisions simply subtract a stipulated amount from an individual's tax bill. As used in a few states, tax freezes have provided an alternative form of relief in which individuals older than a given age are given legal assurance that their taxes will not be increased. This can be an important incentive to the aging to undertake home improvements which they might otherwise avoid due to fears of property tax increases.

Ten states in 1979 had programs of renter credit available to all age groups. Assistance was made available through state income tax forms. Minnesota's renter credit of $120 led the nation in the level of assistance provided. In evaluating this and other tax alternatives, it is important to consider such issues as ease of administration, the impact of the tax loss on particular programs and communities, and the degree of equity achieved among deserving groups in a state's population.

Reverse Mortgages. The close relationship between housing and income problems for many older persons has produced interest in policies that capitalize on the money many individuals have tied up in their homes. These policies, called reverse annual mortgage agreements (RAMs), allow banks to buy homes back from owners by paying a monthly payment. Struyk and Soldo (1980, 288-293) discuss the variety of derivations of this basic approach that are being considered. The obvious advantage of the RAM approach is that it allows individuals to capitalize on their otherwise nonliquid home assets without having to move. With more than six million persons owning their homes, the potential for generating income in this manner is quite substantial.

RAMs have disadvantages as well as advantages. In a period of high interest rates, entering such an agreement can be unwise. Not surprisingly, the surge in interest rates between 1979 and 1981 reduced interest in RAMs even in states that had provided initial authorizing legislation. There is the related problem, as well, of having individuals live longer than their contract and then find themselves in a difficult situation. Interestingly, the French have approached this problem by allowing individuals to sell their homes but stay in them as long as they live. In the United States one alternative might be for the government, perhaps the Department of Housing and Urban Development, to agree to underwrite policies when an individual outlives the time covered by a RAM. A potentially helpful innovation, RAMs are worth pursuing, but because of the problems inherent in this approach new initiatives should be undertaken cautiously.

Issues and Options. Housing practices and policies have continued to evolve in recent years as the aging and policy makers have sought to confront the problems resulting from higher housing costs. Options which in some cases began some years ago have received additional attention, including retirement communities, mobile parks, congregate housing, and shared living arrangements. Several of these options involve a shift toward greater use of age-segregated housing, an issue we will consider before discussing specific reforms.

Several of the housing options being promoted for the elderly will have the result of creating increasingly large concentrations of older persons in age-segregated environments. This process of segregation by age has some advantages. The elderly living in age-segregated communities are more apt to develop close friendships than are those living in non-age-segregated neighborhoods (Rosow 1967). This has been particularly evident in the extensive rounds of social activity in many retirement communities. In addition, some elderly persons' concerns for personal safety make them prefer to live in communities without youngsters.

Yet others take a different view of age-segregated environments. Some seniors — and scholars — believe contact with individuals of differing ages is a definite stimulus. Lowy (1980) argues that age-diverse communities provide needed opportunities for intergenerational contact and may help reduce the stereotypes that often impede this contact. Some fear that age segregation leads to selfishness on the part of older persons. Others believe a high degree of age segregation may make it more difficult to improve voluntary support systems for the frail elderly. For example, it is often hard for a church congregation drawn from an older neighborhood to develop a strong visitation program for the most frail members of its congregation.

Age-segregated environments have pros and cons. Undoubtedly, the personal preferences of the elderly will continue to vary. As they make their choices, it is essential that they have a variety of housing options from which to choose.

Retirement Communities. Separate retirement communities began to emerge in the 1960s and 1970s as a housing option for a small but significant segment of the older population. By the 1980s it was not difficult to find entire books, such as the work by Dickinson (1981), devoting major sections to surveys of southern and western retirement communities and their strengths and weaknesses. Because of the increasing cost of land acquisition in a period of inflation, however, construction of retirement communities began to decline beginning in the late 1970s. Nonetheless, retirement communities continue to be the preferred housing option for an increasing number of elderly persons. Each cold northern winter brings prospective buyers to such places as Sun City in Arizona and Leisure World in California.

It has not been difficult to find critics of retirement communities among either housing specialists or the aging themselves (Jacobs 1974). All of the issues noted regarding age-segregation obviously apply, and perhaps with more intensity than in any other housing option because of the closed nature of these communities. Yet for some, retirement communities have been an attractive alternative — an opportunity for active retirement living, often amidst many new friends, and without some of the concerns of life in their former neighborhoods. Here, just as in so many other areas of policy development for the aging, it is essential to make available a wide variety of choices.

Mobile Homes. Mobile home parks have become an increasingly popular form of housing, particularly in the Southwest, for older persons with moderate to low incomes. Mobile home use has been particularly attractive for older persons with lower middle class backgrounds for whom mobile home parks are seen as an opportunity for living on a modest income (Johnson 1971). In 1980, almost 7 million Americans lived in three million mobile homes, and a significant number of them were older persons. Because some of the mobile homeowners are quite nomadic, they can create problems for local officials seeking to plan for a given number of older persons in a particular urban area or county. There are also important consumer problems that need to be confronted. Mobile home park owners have engaged too often in such questionable practices as refusing to prorate utility company discounts among park residents and arbitrarily setting park rules. Some observers have argued that mobile homes are a poor solution because of their rapid depreciation, especially if homes are moved with any frequency. Nonetheless, fairly supportive communities can emerge within the mobile home parks, and they constitute one option that seems likely to continue to attract a significant clientele.

Congregate Housing. Congregate housing represents an important policy option. Vladeck (1980) sees congregate homes as a major alternative to present levels of nursing home use. Congregate housing, in simple terms, involves low-cost housing in which some or all dwelling units have no kitchens and in which there is a central dining facility. Efforts in this area have been largely experimental in the past decade, but the results are encouraging and some advocate expanding this form of housing. (See the papers published by the International Center for Social Gerontology, 1977.) By providing opportunities for nutritious meals and a supportive environment, congregate housing can help individuals preserve a measure of independence impossible in other living arrangements. Social services coordination must be an important part of the future development of congregate housing. Carp (1977) concludes that with proper planning and development there would be a substantial demand for such facilities.

Shared Living Arrangements. Improvements in living arrangements may occur without extensive (and expensive) formal public policies. The development of cooperative social networks in apartment buildings where many elderly persons reside is a positive step in some urban areas. As an interesting response to the high cost of housing in recent years, there also have been more extensive efforts to allow seniors to double up in their living arrangements. This can save on financial costs and also reduce the isolation associated with living alone. Local agencies in Santa Monica, California, and Seattle, Washington, have engaged recently in interesting experiments along these lines. It can be difficult to find people who enjoy the new associations, and in present inflationary times it can be difficult to find the person who wants to sell a home to live in the residence of another person. Nonetheless, shared living arrangements constitute an obvious step worth pursuing in an age of increasing costs and shortages in the nation's housing supply.

Individual Planning. One of the encouraging developments in recent years has been the increasing attention the aging are giving to their own housing options. The growing number of preretirement programs, higher education levels among the aging, and the availability of more information about new housing options have contributed to improved individual planning by the elderly. Planning for future housing arrangements is not always easy, since it is impossible to know in advance when illness or death may strike. Nonetheless, the sharply increased interest in retirement planning is an encouraging indication that a large segment of the aging population in the coming years will be planning more carefully for their own futures.

CONCLUSION

Housing and social services policies have proven to be politically vulnerable in the 1980s. The level of financial support often has been quite low, and the evolution of program development has produced substantial fragmentation. In addition, housing and social services do not have the protection of the statutory funding base that exists for Social Security and Medicare. As Hartman (1982) points out, this makes housing and social services programs easier budget-cutting targets.

Despite the problems surrounding the array of housing and social services policies we have discussed, there have been important experiments and new developments worth continued nurturing. This list would include such initiatives as case management and gatekeeping strategies for social services, congregate housing projects, and rent supplements. Ultimately, the development of more adequate support systems and living arrangements for the aging requires the development of public programs *and* the effective use of communities and families. It is hoped that improving economic conditions for major segments of the aging population also will increase the ability of the elderly to contribute to the financing of new housing arrangements and social services. These prospects become an essential part of the issue agenda for the 1980s.

IX

POLICY AGENDA FOR THE 1980s

The White House Conference on Aging in early December 1981, which was attended by more than 2,000 delegates, dramatized the growing number of aging issues that are likely to compete for attention in the 1980s. The dominant thrust of the 1961 conference was health care, the 1971 conference income maintenance. The conference in 1981, however, did not produce a single dominant theme but underscored the diversity of aging-related issues. Fourteen committees issued reports in major areas, including economic well-being, Social Security and employment, health and long-term care, community participation, educational opportunities, family supports, governmental organization, housing, older women, private sector roles, and research needs. Most domestic areas of federal government activity and many state programs were discussed, along with possible private sector changes ranging from greater employment of older workers to the provision of private insurance covering the costs of long-term care.

The policy agenda for the 1980s is being shaped by several factors, among them the changing characteristics of the aging population itself, the nation's economic performance, and the political climate, which in 1982 was not conducive to increased public sector commitments. This chapter reviews a number of issues that seem likely to gain increasing attention in this decade and discusses future directions in public policies for the aging.

FEDERAL AND STATE ROLES

Since World War II, policy efforts for the aging at both the federal and state level have increased. Federal government efforts have expanded most dramatically in the areas of Social Security benefits and health assistance through Medicare and Medicaid. Commitments at the state level, which did not expand as rapidly as federal commitments, also grew. The states have been active in a wide range of areas including Medicaid, nursing home reimbursement and regulation, social services, tax assistance, and generic drug reform. (For a general review of growth patterns in the federal government and in state governments, see Hale and Palley, 1981.)

In 1981 and 1982, President Ronald Reagan proposed major changes in federal-state relations, changes that would greatly affect public policies for the aging. The 1981 proposals, which were not adopted in the largest expenditure areas, emphasized the use of block grants to increase state discretion in policy development. The block grants were to be less specific regarding the expenditure of funds for social services; states were to be given more opportunities for choice between aging recipients and other clientele groups. In 1982, the specifics of the Reagan administration's proposals changed (Peterson 1982). The president proposed a major program switch with the states: the federal government would assume the financial responsibility for Medicaid, and the states would provide all of the financing for Aid to Families with Dependent Children (AFDC) and Food Stamps. These proposals raised key issues surrounding the division of responsibility between the federal government and the states. The level of federal financial assistance for state programs was a major concern.

An important case can be made for an enhanced state role in several of the policy areas affecting the aging. Some of the more populous states have large numbers of older persons as residents (see Table 1-2, pp. 16-17), and these states should be able to generate important expertise and specialization for aging policy development. Moreover, some of the problems cited as examples of state administrative inefficiencies may be the result primarily of complicated federal eligibility requirements. The difficulties the Social Security Administration experienced in administering aspects of the Supplemental Security Income (SSI) program after the federal role was expanded in 1974 caused some observers to reassess the supposed advantages of federal rather than state level administration (Grimaldi 1980).

The states also have shown useful capacities for policy innovation (Sharkansky 1972). Various federal government responses, from regulation of long-term care facilities to development of in-home services, have followed heightened interest in these areas at the state level. The states also have acted more forcefully than the federal government in trying to control Medicaid costs (Feder, Holohan, and Marmor 1980, 45-56). On various policies affecting the aging, New York, Pennsylvania, Wisconsin, Minnesota, Washington, California, and a number of other states deserve credit for significant innovative efforts.

As we have seen, the states have made, and can make, an important contribution to aging policy development. Yet a central question remains. Will the changes in federal-state relations proposed by the Reagan administration and the cuts in government spending lead to more effective policies? Several points should be recognized. First, the states may be less willing than the federal government to focus assistance on those who are the least well off (Hudson 1981, 21). Second, national standards can bring the states with the most limited efforts up to some minimum standard. Third, while tax capacity has been equalized somewhat in the past three decades (as a result of the decreased industrialization of the South and the slower growth in the Midwest and Northeast), some states have less tax revenue and thus, if left to their own resources, invariably will experience a severe budgetary crunch. Furthermore, states whose resources are growing have not shown a strong political willingness to use those resources for new programs (Klingman 1982). Finally, it is often more feasible to change regulatory policies by passing federal legislation rather than by working for change in 50 different state legislatures.

Questions concerning the overall level of spending were more pressing in the early 1980s than questions concerning state versus federal roles. The budget cuts achieved by the Reagan administration in 1981 greatly reduced federal aid to state and local governments. Of the $35 billion cut from the initial 1981 budget, over half came from aid to subnational governments (Stanfield 1981). Second, many governors in 1982 felt that President Reagan's proposals to shift program responsibility to the states would cost the states too much. It was feared that the additional financial responsibilities would exceed the new revenues being suggested by the administration. State governors thus were faced with a difficult choice. While many had criticized the rigidity of federal requirements in the past, they became increasingly concerned that the new flexibility given the states would increase their financial burdens. Thus a number of governors, including several Republicans, became outspoken critics of the Reagan administration's approach to federal-state relations.

Despite the limitations of the initial proposals by the Reagan administration, three points need to be emphasized in considering future state roles. First, state capacities for innovative policy development should be maintained and, if possible, enhanced. Second, national standards should not necessarily be viewed as maximum standards. These standards should bring states with poor performances up to a minimum level, but they should not squash the initiatives of the more innovative states. Third, states with a large aging population should be able to develop major capacities for program development and implementation.

Clearly, a significant contribution can be made by the states. Yet the Reagan administration's proposals had the likely consequence of reduced total spending by the states and the federal government. In the short run, questions concerning the extent of public spending tended to overshadow issues of federal-state relations.

PROGRAM IMPLEMENTATION:
THE PROS AND CONS OF SEPARATE PROGRAMS

The emphasis on separateness in program advocacy and implementation for the aging has been more pronounced in the United States than in any other major western nation. (For a review on social services, see Kahn, 1979.) Income maintenance policies, Medicare, the planning and administration of social services through the Older Americans Act of 1965, and many housing programs have focused specifically on the aging. The 1981 White House Conference on Aging produced strong resolutions favoring the continued operation of separate programs through state and local Administrations on Aging.

The case for separatism includes several components. Certain policies do affect the older population either exclusively or predominantly. Income maintenance policies are the most obvious example, but the aging are also the major users of long-term care facilities and home care assistance. It is thus argued that policy implementation should focus on the dominant clientele group.

Issues surrounding adverse perceptions of welfare programs also are involved. For many elderly people, the distinction between earned benefits and benefits based upon need is extremely important. Although there is some indication that resistance to welfare-based programs is declining (Binstock 1979, 1,714), some individuals nonetheless refuse to apply for SSI benefits for which they are eligible because they feel that the SSI program is synonymous with "welfare." To move rapidly toward more integrated programs thus raises the question of a lack of enthusiasm, and possibly a lack of participation, among some of the aging.

Benefits for the aging, developed separately, can constitute a first step in the development of needed services for other groups, some argue. Such an argument, it should be recalled, was used to justify the separation of the aging as the first target group for national health insurance in the wake of the defeat of President Harry S Truman's proposals for a universal program. The evolution of Medicaid and Medicare in 1965 did give a measure of support for the "first step" view, since the establishment of Medicaid (and its provisions for assistance to impoverished individuals of all ages) followed legislation providing health care for the aging. Indeed, even the ordering of the statutory provisions, with Medicaid following Medicare, suggests the ranking of legislative interest. These initiatives in 1965, however, have not led to significant improvements in health care assistance for other segments of the American population.

Finally, advocates of separatism claim that there is sometimes greater chances for success if the relative popularity of the aging is emphasized rather than the more general areas of need within the population as a whole. Saddling program development for the aging with multiple concerns may make coalition politics difficult because spokesmen for each prospective clientele group may vie with each other for advantage. Some state interest group leaders thus have concluded that it is difficult to maintain an effective focus for lobby efforts that cover a broad range of issues.

The Gray Panthers, led by Maggie Kuhn, urge less separatism in program advocacy and implementation. In Kuhn's writings and in various statements from the Panther organization, it has been argued that separatism reduces the effectiveness of policy responses and heightens intergenerational conflicts (Hessel 1977). Fundamental to the Gray Panther orientation is the belief that many of the problems of the aging only can be resolved in the context of fundamental changes in American politics. Other critics of separatism have focused on the resulting tendency toward fragmentation in service delivery. The frequent difficulties experienced by small, "demonstration" programs constitutes one of the major concerns (Estes 1979). At its worst, separation has led to programs that are inefficient and inadequate. Efforts to establish separate transportation services, for example, are often questionable on cost-effectiveness grounds.

Some reduction in the emphasis on separation is appropriate in the 1980s. Reform in a number of policy areas, involving in particular the health care system, is apt to require broad changes. Health policies must confront such key issues as cost control and the scope of public coverage. Strong coalition efforts will be essential. Separate structures and programs such as those created by the Older Americans Act nonetheless do serve several functions. Those organizations have helped state and local governments focus on aging interests, and in at least some situations they have promoted interest in services for the aging by other departments carrying out major policy activities. Selective rather than wholesale change in program implementation is in order.

PROGRAM ELIGIBILITY:
MEANS TESTS—GOOD OR BAD?

Closely related to the question of separate programs for the aging is the issue of whether program eligibility should be based upon personal financial resources. In the past two decades, income and assets (or personal wealth) tests have been increasingly used in a variety of programs serving the general population, including housing subsidies, Food Stamps, school lunch programs, and Medicaid (Lampman 1977). The incomes and assets which segments of the older population will possess in the coming years, coupled with the financial problems confronting the Social Security system in particular and federal government operations in general, present a logical basis for reexamining eligibility questions.

In confronting the means test issue, it is important to bear in mind these basic aspects of the financial position of the aging. First, a tiny segment of the older population is extremely wealthy, constituting a major segment of the stock and bond holdings in the country. Second, home equities have been giving a majority of the aging a new economic resource, but relatively few older persons enjoy the equities being created by the most rapidly increasing housing prices. The small town and older central city homes owned by many older persons have not appreciated in value as much as many other homes. Third, while the assets of segments of the older population are apt to be substantially higher than the meager levels that occurred in the past, wise personal financial management must include concern for uncovered hospital and long-term care facility costs. Fourth, the assets held by the aging are greatly affected by the level and form of state and federal inheritance taxes. So far this is an area that has not been sufficiently addressed from the perspective of gerontology policy.

Means test issues occur in many areas and involve widely differing practices. Under present long-term care policies, persons who have had moderate incomes throughout their working lives can find that they do not qualify for Medicaid and yet are under severe financial strain to meet the cost of a nursing home. (This is a particularly acute problem when a spouse is trying to maintain the family home.) Nonetheless, some question whether the aging need property tax relief. The tax freeze enacted in Minnesota caused some observers to wonder why certain individuals, such as the heirs to the fortunes built at Daytons and Minnesota Mining and Manufacturing, needed to have their property taxes frozen. Regarding social services programs, it has been debated whether there should be a fee for those who can afford to pay for a meal or a social outing. Finally, and most fundamentally, the Social Security system raises the question of the extent to which benefits should be based upon financial need regardless of previous levels of contribution.

The case for sensitivity to incomes and assets can be made on a cost effectiveness basis. Since social services, housing, and income support programs often are stretched to a point of ineffectiveness with an emphasis on universal coverage, the question becomes: why not focus on those in greatest need? A comparison of social security systems in other countries suggests that a flat grant approach coupled with some contribution-based assistance is a fairly common compromise (Kaim-Caudle 1973). A concern with more targeted assistance recently has been expressed by Binstock (1979, 1,713) in his advocacy of a guaranteed minimum income for the aging. As a variant of this argument, some suggest that the nation's top priority should be helping those in economic need regardless of age.

The proposals for expanded use of means tests for various forms of assistance present sobering questions. First, some suspect, quite possible correctly, that programs based upon need would lose, over time, popularity and political support. Conceivably, these programs might yield lower results for the poor than programs with a broader base of support. As some in the war on poverty in the 1960s sadly observed, programs for the poor too often turn out to be poor programs. Second, the use of income and assets tests, unless accompanied by changes in health care policies, could increase the number of individuals denied benefits because of their financial position and yet unable to meet the costs of a major illness or extended nursing home care.

Different approaches deserve consideration in different policy areas. Social services policy issues have been resolved successfully in some instances by the use of voluntary contributions. This reduces cumbersome paperwork which can surround efforts to determine income eligibility for a given program. Relatively simple changes also could increase the income sensitivity of other programs. For example, it makes a major difference in tax laws whether the federal government grants tax exemptions, as it now does, or tax credits for those age 65 and over. More than half of the benefit from that tax exemption in the early 1970s went to a small proportion of older persons with annual incomes exceeding $10,000 (Rabushka and Jacobs 1980). Since tax exemptions are more valuable to those in the upper tax brackets, a shift to tax credits would distribute the financial advantage in equal amounts to all income groups within the older population.

In the new few years the primary issue regarding Social Security seems likely to be the extent to which benefits are tilted toward low-income families and individuals. Because of the increased politicization of Social Security issues in the 1980s, those seeking to improve the position of the elderly at or below the poverty level face a difficult fight on such policies as the minimum benefit.

Policies focusing specifically on assets are logically (although not always politically) related to the question of inheritance and gift taxes. In farm states, the following question often arises: should a son be able to receive the family farm as a gift or inheritance while the state pays for his mother's nursing home costs because she was eligible for Medicaid? Relative responsibility laws were never popular, and inheritance taxes are often intensely opposed by the aging themselves. Yet the importance of the inheritance tax issue is reflected in the amount of money involved.

In 1981, as part of President Reagan's tax proposals, Congress reduced federal inheritance and gift taxes, cutting prospective revenues in 1985 from $10.4 billion to $7.8 billion. After 1987, no federal estate taxes must be paid on estates valued below $600,000. Had that better than $2 billion annual revenue base been preserved, it would have funded almost a fourfold increase in the total budget of the Administration on Aging. As states began developing larger exemptions from similar taxes, there was a potential further loss of about $2 billion. Changes in tax laws in California alone were projected to cause at least one-fourth of that annual loss in revenues.

In some states, widows or widowers find themselves unable to pay an estate tax on a family business unless they sell it. In agricultural states, inheritance taxes sometimes have disrupted farming and ranching, which throws into question the wisdom of such a tax policy. (For the federal tax, this problem was substantially reduced in 1976, and it was virtually eliminated with the sharp reduction in 1981 of the number of persons who must pay an inheritance tax.) Cases involving widows (and not those involving families with the largest assets and the most to gain) have been the easiest to promote by advocates of reductions in the nation's inheritance tax laws.

Assets and inheritance policies deserve increased attention. As Samuelson (1981) has observed, inheritance tax reform often occurs with a very quiet handling of important policy issues. Assets tests and inheritance taxes often have been strongly opposed by the aging themselves, as reflected in their unwillingness in many cases to engage in tax deferral plans that may burden their children. Yet some support for tighter Medicaid eligibility requirements has come from within the older population and from relatively conservative proponents. In Iowa, for example, a sense of fairness and a concern for costs made advocates of legislators representing prosperous Republican farm areas. In the quest for policies linking inheritance taxes and programs for the aging, the question of increased voluntary contributions also deserves greater attention. Opportunities for contribution to social services, for example, could be much more visible. While it is important not to overstate the possible role of voluntary contributions, skilled fund-raising efforts can have a significant impact. It also might be feasible to reduce the elderly's discontent with inheritance taxes by earmarking the tax revenues for the Social Security Trust Fund. This would constitute a very direct way to transfer financial resources from the well off in the older population to the less fortunate.

America's performance on income and wealth questions suggests that such issues are apt to be confronted indirectly. In the past, complicated formulas or tax laws that were not well understood helped make it possible to skirt basic social class issues. Cost consciousness, however, may lead to more open and direct initiatives in the coming years. Within that overall debate, a variety of income-test, assets-test, and inheritance tax issues should be pursued.

SPECIFIC ISSUES

The Problems of Older Women

Women substantially outnumber men in the aging population. Especially among the very elderly, there are far more women than men. Because they tend to outlive their spouses, women are more apt to live alone and become nursing home residents. The income levels of elderly women are far below elderly men's as a result of existing Social Security policies and the frequency of low lifetime earnings among women.

The lives of today's older women are affected by several major policies. For the many women living alone and in nursing homes, basic policy issues are similar to those for all individuals in those situations. Concern with the "frail elderly" pertains disproportionately to older women. The recommendations of the Federal Council on Aging (1978) are thus highly relevant. The council proposed targeting social services to those who are the most likely to be institutionalized, and it emphasized the importance of developing suitable living arrangements for the aging. Current issues surrounding SSI benefit levels and the minimum benefit under Social Security also disproportionately affect older women. The combination of longer lives and lower benefits produces a situation in which a clear majority of the recipients of SSI benefits are women.

A broad range of policy alternatives can be pursued regarding the economic status of older women. Because of the rapid increase in female labor force participation since World War II, issues relating to income levels prior to retirement are becoming increasingly critical. Despite existing legislative efforts, the average income levels for women have continued to lag behind those for men. In 1980, the average weekly wages for women were only 63 percent of those received by men. The extent to which women's economic status is affected by sex discrimination, differences in career choices, and more discontinuous work careers

212

has been the subject of varying interpretations (U.S. Department of Labor 1976). It is becoming increasingly clear, however, that serious problems exist in the allocation of Social Security benefits to women.

Robertson (1981) and Treas (1982) discuss the impact of Social Security policies on the income of present and future female recipients. Women have received lower levels of Social Security benefits than their male counterparts as a result of current policies and the traditionally lower earning levels for women. According to a 1975 analysis of sex differences in the monthly Primary Benefit Amount, men received an average of $190.06 and women an average of $144.34 (Treas 1982). These figures paint a somewhat misleading picture, however. The progressively designed lower proportions of the Social Security benefits levels are based upon limited contributions. This fact and the greater longevity of women than men makes the relationship between Social Security contributions and earnings often quite favorable for women — and more favorable than for many men. More than directly discriminating, the Social Security system, as analyzed by Robertson (1981, 145-152), simply has become less adequate in meeting the needs of women in a changing society.

One major issue is the extent to which women should be given credit toward Social Security benefits on the basis of years spent raising children. The National Commission on Social Security (1981, 234-238) has suggested a system of partial credit which they concluded would help resolve the existing problem and not add unduly to overall system costs.

A second issue has surrounded the handling of earnings by married women. For many couples in which both husband and wife work, the existing rules do not "count" the Social Security tax contributions from the second income as substantially as if each person were single and working. When applying for benefits, couples technically are entitled to the larger of either the husband's benefits plus the spousal allowance to which they are automatically entitled *or* the husband's benefits plus the wife's benefits derived from her covered earnings. While the wife is increasingly finding that this is higher than the spousal benefit (Treas 1982), at least some portion of her own coverage merely duplicates the spousal benefits.

Why not combine spousal benefits and the wife's earnings? This seemingly obvious question raises issues that reflect the multiple and sometimes contradictory goals of the Social Security system. If the goal is

213

individual equity, then the larger, combined payment would make sense. Yet at least two objections are obvious. First, this approach would discriminate against single workers, since they would be contributing to a system in which future benefits for married couples would be increasingly large in relationship to their prospective benefits. Second, if the goal is adequacy of retirement income (which was the basis for the spousal benefit initially), then this reform would be quite costly, with a significant proportion of the future funds going to families in which two sets of lifetime earnings had allowed for other retirement planning and perhaps the development of fairly substantial assets. Policy choices ultimately must reflect compromises between equity considerations based upon past earnings and an emphasis on adequacy of income for female recipients now and in the future.

A third major issue concerns rights to Social Security benefits (either present rights or future rights) when marriage ends in divorce. Recently, benefits for women who have been married for 10 years, rather than at least 20, have been expanded. Important issues nonetheless remain. First, if a husband dies, the wife is entitled to survivors' benefits if they have been married for at least a year; yet, with divorce, eligibility is only for the spousal benefit (and not the total benefit based upon the husband's previous earnings), and that spousal benefit was designed as a supplement and not as an adequate minimum system. If an adequate retirement income without other sources than Social Security benefits is considered to be the basic goal, this policy has serious limitations.

The problems of older women deserve serious attention. For the present population of older women and for those about to reach retirement age, the manner in which minimum income policies are pursued will continue to be important. For those who are presently in younger age brackets, actions that increase annual incomes from employment (and thus future benefit levels) and some modifications in existing policy are in order. Changes relating to credit for homemaker roles and modifications in the handling of benefits for divorcees deserve particularly serious consideration.

The Hospice Movement

Hospices are becoming an increasingly popular alternative to traditional hospital care for the terminally ill. DuBois (1980) and Zimmerman (1981) are among the scholars who have analyzed the growing hospice movement. A report by the General Accounting Office (1979, 1) thus explains hospice care:

It is generally agreed that the hospice concept in the United States is a program of care in which an organized interdisciplinary team systematically provides palliative care (relief of pain) and supportive services to patients dying from terminal illness. The team also assists the patient's family in making the necessary adjustments to the patient's illness and death. The program's objective is to make the patient's remaining days as comfortable and meaningful as possible and to help the family cope with the stress.

The modern day hospice program is generally attributed to the pioneering work of Cicely Saunders in the development of St. Christopher's Hospice in Syndenham, England, in 1967 (DuBois 1980, 69-84). In the United States, the first hospice was begun in 1971 in New Haven, Connecticut. Yale University provided important leadership. By the end of the decade, 59 hospices were in operation and more than 20 were being developed (Cohen 1979).

The importance of hospice care as an alternative to more traditional approaches can be seen from several perspectives. Hospice care is particularly important for people who have cancer. Cancer patients constitute the majority of hospice patients. Unfortunately, the need to provide care for individuals with cancer is a major undertaking. According to the General Accounting Office (1979, 18), 387,430 individuals died of cancer in 1977; 60 percent of them were 65 years of age or older. Of course, some individuals and families are unable to admit the terminal nature of an illness and thus would not be candidates for hospice care. Nonetheless, a significant proportion of older persons in nursing homes or acute care hospitals are potential candidates for hospice care.

The high cost of lengthy stays in acute care hospitals also has increased interest in hospice care. Hospital and/or nursing home care for older persons in their last days or months of life constitutes a substantial portion of all health costs for the aging. Hospice care thus offers one way to reduce health care costs. It should be recognized, however, that actual costs vary substantially from hospice to hospice and the degree of cost saving is dependent upon capital construction costs (GAO 1979, 20-22).

The greater attention being given to the emotional needs of the terminally ill and their families also has increased public interest in hospice care. Being able to relate to a person trained in talking with dying persons may be far more important to a patient than having all the latest

215

equipment near by. Too often in acute care hospitals, no staff person has the time, training, or inclination to help the terminally ill prepare for death.

The development of more extensive capacities for delivering hospice care will require a variety of actions. The recruitment and training of personnel is extremely important for this very emotionally demanding form of work. The problems surrounding the rapid expansion of the nursing home industry in the late 1960s are indicative of the difficulties that arise when an area of care grows rapidly. Regulatory provisions need to be considered carefully, including organizational accountability in the development of new facilities. Financial issues regarding the form of public support also must be confronted. The initial steps taken toward the inclusion of hospice care under Medicare in August 1982, while commendable, require careful monitoring.

Hospice care obviously cannot become a substitute for other health policies such as home care for individuals without terminal illnesses. Nonetheless, recent initiatives in this area should be encouraged. Clearly, care for the terminally ill can be improved, and in that process lessons also may be learned regarding care for other segments of the elderly population.

Crime

One of the most tragic aspects of life for all too many older persons is the constant fear of crime. A 1975 Harris Poll showed crime to be the foremost concern among older Americans. When all forms of crime are considered, the aging are statistically less apt to be victims than are individuals in younger age groups. When one focuses on crimes against households, however, the aging are much more apt to be victims than the younger segments of the population (Malinchak 1980, 14-15).

The aging are easy criminal targets for several reasons. First, they tend to live alone. Second, they often are unable to physically resist an assailant. Third, vulnerability is increased because the aging tend to live in older neighborhoods in which crime rates are apt to be disproportionately high. Fourth, the distribution of Social Security checks on a regular basis and the regularity of many elderly person's banking habits makes them likely targets of crime at particular times of the month.

A solution to the problem of crime against the elderly ultimately involves the difficult task of ameliorating a condition affecting all age groups. Nonetheless, there are a few specific steps that can be taken. Unfortunately, crime prevention programs geared toward the aging often generate a state of fear, and the heightened fears that are created sometimes outweigh the positive accomplishments of the program. Malinchak (1980, 170) favors improved educational programs. He recommends much wider dissemination of information on such questions as when criminals are more likely to commit crimes, ways to make homes less penetrable, tips on preventing purse snatching, and strategies for avoiding swindling techniques. It also has been common for campaigns seeking tougher penalties and swifter punishment for criminals to include an emphasis on the problems of the aged as victims as a justification for the harsher measures. These programs raise a variety of difficult issues surrounding the ultimate effectiveness of those approaches.

Less widely discussed approaches also deserve attention. Following the lead of California, New York, and Hawaii in the mid-1960s, close to half of the states now have programs providing some compensation to the victims of crime. These programs are particularly important for the aging because so many older victims have difficulty in replacing the lost money or household goods. Another approach to the crime problem involves increased use of the aging as volunteers. Because of their greater free time and the personal importance to them of crime prevention, the elderly are often useful volunteers in such varying roles as helping with information dissemination and participating in neighborhood watch programs.

The question of crime prevention is related to the issue of housing alternatives. For example, for the older woman now residing in a high crime neighborhood of a central city, the most direct way to reduce her fear of crime might be to move. Yet changing location for many individuals is contingent upon the development of additional housing options that are affordable and located in less crime-prone areas.

Con artists with their various ruses to trick the elderly present a difficult crime problem for the aging. Far too many elderly persons living alone are enticed into collaborating in a seemingly legitimate quick profit scheme. For example, a con artist may leave on the front walk of an elderly person an envelope of money, perhaps with a note indicating that it has been won at a race track (and thus is not hard-earned money). Counting on the victim's trusting view of new acquaintances, the con man will then offer his services to handle the processing of the newly found money. Too often the unwitting individual is led into a devastating loss of personal savings when funds are requested for legal fees. While other forms of crime are more commonly noticed, the use of confidence games to lure money from unsuspecting older persons is a continuing problem.

There is no simple way of preventing or reducing crimes against the aging. However, the magnitude of the concern and the direct financial loss — and physical harm — which is being afflicted on the nation's older population makes increased efforts in this area extremely important.

The Aging as Consumers

Improving opportunities for the aging as consumers involves protection against inadequate and unfair marketing and the development of products that more adequately meet personal needs. Because of their growing numbers in the population and the enhanced economic position of many older persons, the availability of more satisfactory items in the marketplace is of major importance. There must be better answers for the exasperated daughter who returns from a shopping trip with her elderly mother and remarks, "It was awful; there are simply not any shoes that are safe for her to walk in which she is willing to wear; in her eyes the safe ones all look like Army shoes!" Indeed, for the economy as a whole, manufacturers have just begun to sense that the aging as consumers constitute a market with major growth potential.

Several attempts have been made to protect the often limited purchasing power of the aging. Hearing aid legislation provides one good example. The 650,000 individuals who bought hearing aids annually in the mid-1970s confronted an industry in which most state laws provided very limited protection against overly aggressive sales approaches, faulty equipment, and inadequate (if not actually dishonest) testing. (See the 1973 report of the Public Citizen's Retired Professional Action Group, a Ralph Nader organization.) Since approximately 30 percent of the nation's older population has been estimated to suffer from hearing impairments, and a substantial proportion of those individuals are seen as potentially profiting from some form of hearing assistance, the issue presented by a poorly regulated industry has substantial implications. In the eyes of the Federal Trade Commission's Consumer Protection Bureau (1978a), there is a major need for such reforms as required trial periods, improvements in the training of those giving examinations, and prohibitions against faulty advertising. Two other consumer areas — prescription drugs and funeral industry practices — presented similar issues with even larger financial stakes.

Generic Drugs. The price of prescription drugs is an especially important issue for the aging because they use medication on a regular basis much more than other age groups. In 1976, Americans of all ages spent more than $60 per person each year on prescription drugs. By the late 1970s, drug expenditures constituted more than 1 percent of the Gross National Product.

Savings to the consumer on generic drugs could be quite substantial. Wholesale prices for generic drugs run less than 10 percent of the price of comparable brand-name drugs (Silverman and Lee 1974, 334). Since about three-fourths of the drugs presently on the market are sold under patent, however, major savings are not possible for some products. Yet for many of the medications used by elderly patients, equivalents have emerged with dramatic price-saving consequences.

The movement toward increased use of generic drugs has involved state legislative efforts. In 1972, Kentucky became the first state to broaden its law with a hotly contested statute that allowed pharmacists to substitute generic drugs if they were included on a list of generics approved by a state drug formulary council. By 1979, 45 states had enacted some legislation allowing the use of generic drugs (Lammers and Klingman 1981a).

The development of more widespread use of generic drugs is destined to be a difficult issue. Historically, U.S. drug firms have been among the most profitable enterprises in the country, and they have lobbied actively against greater use of generic drugs. One Kentucky legislator observed, in the wake of the drug controversy in his state, that a bomb blast in the state capitol would wipe out half of the pharmaceutical vice-presidents in the country (Silverman and Lee 1974, 166). Besides the legislative struggles, the effectiveness of generic drug laws also will hinge upon administrative implementation and the extent to which physicians are willing to help their patients save money.

Funeral Industry Practices. Interest in funeral industry practices among spokesmen for the aging has grown in recent years. The sheer size of the industry, coupled with the predominance of the aging as those most in need of services, makes that concern appropriate. According to the Federal Trade Commission's Consumer Protection Bureau (1978b), as of the late 1970s some $2.35 billion was spent on funerals directly, another $1.75 billion on cemetery charges, and at least $1.3 billion on related expenses, for an impressive total of almost $6.5 billion. The funeral industry's efforts to protect its profits, strongly condemned by Mitford (1963), involved the actions of more than 20,000 funeral home owners and the active political participation of several major associations. Although regulation has been primarily a state responsibility, the Federal Trade Commission in the late 1970s made several attempts to establish federal regulation.

At the state and federal level, interest in funeral industry reform has focused on a few basic issues. Reformers have pursued requirements allowing customers to consider their specific needs in light of a range of potential services, the availability of price information, and the removal of restricture provisions against organizations promoting the use of cremation. (In some states embalming is required even when a body is to be cremated.) Despite a decade of record interest, the states by 1978 had enacted only 5 percent of the requirements proposed by the Federal Trade Commission concerning funeral industry regulation.

The antiregulatory climate of the early 1980s increasingly thwarted reformers efforts in Washington, and they again began to focus attention at the state level. Strong industry opposition often made reform difficult, yet the potential gains in protecting the scarce dollars of elderly consumers made the issue worthy of aggressive pursuit. Scrutiny of funeral industry practices should continue in this decade.

The Aging and Inflation

The declining inflation rate in the early 1980s reduced public interest in inflation issues but not their underlying significance. A 5 to 7 percent inflation rate was clearly less traumatic than a 10 to 12 percent rate. Nonetheless, at 7 percent the cost of living doubles every 10 years. Significant but incomplete progress has been made in protecting the aging from the brunt of inflation. The indexing of Social Security benefits, SSI payments, and most government pensions has helped the aging protect their annual incomes at least as effectively as other age groups in the past 10 years. In contrast to their situation in earlier

inflationary periods, the aging have not been unique victims of inflation in their annual incomes (Case 1981, 17-21). Many individuals,
however, have been badly hurt, particularly if they retired on pensions
that were not indexed. Some companies have voluntarily raised pension
levels, but the overall process of adjustment has been sporadic and often
inadequate.

The impact on the assets of the aging in some instances has been more
adverse than the impact on annual income. For those with investments,
overall stock values have not kept pace with inflation in the past two decades. Home ownership presented an important opportunity for expanding total assets in the 1970s, but it was less clear that this would be the
case in the next decade. Furthermore, home ownership sometimes tied
individuals to inappropriate living arrangements.

Treasury bills, while offering high rates of interest, also produced
surprise and even anger as some older investors suddenly found themselves with unexpectedly large income taxes. The question of how to
preserve assets thus has become an extremely important issue for many
older persons. Extensive hospital and/or nursing home care can eliminate
their savings quickly, and this awesome possibility is a spectre facing
many today.

One recently discussed approach to protecting investments is the
indexing of government bonds to give a small return (perhaps 3 percent)
above the rate of inflation. This would allow investors to protect their assets against erosion through inflation. While indexing has been criticized
by some analysts as a factor contributing to inflation, and the costs to the
government would be significant, this plan has some merits. It is
straightforward and addresses a specific problem facing older persons
seeking to preserve their assets (Schulz 1980, 80-81). The 1981 tax reform
provisions for All Savers Certificates accomplish the same objective but
with an important difference: these provisions were primarily beneficial
to those with large personal assets.

Ultimately, the one sure way to protect against the loss of assets and
purchasing power through inflation is to reduce the rate of inflation itself.
Indexing procedures can help, but it is difficult for all areas affecting the
aging to be indexed, and this means that there will be some who are not
effectively protected. In protecting against inflation, as in so many other
policy areas, the solution of problems for the aging is closely linked to the
solution of problems affecting Americans of all ages.

OPPORTUNITIES FOR THE AGING

The aging population in the 1980s is likely to include more individuals interested in furthering their education or becoming involved in volunteer work than in the past. While the future aging population (persons over 65) will include many frail elderly whose activities are fairly restricted, growing numbers will be able to avail themselves of a wide range of opportunities.

Educational Opportunities

The importance of educational opportunities for the aging has been recognized somewhat belatedly by educators in the United States. The expansion of interest that has taken place recently was prompted perhaps by a realization that the 18 to 21 year-old population was declining, thus reducing the demand for traditional services. State universities and colleges and many community colleges now have begun to offer and promote courses targeted to older students. Free tuition has been used in a number of states, along with such strategies as arrangement of courses in easy-to-reach settings.

One innovative approach has been Elderhostels. In these programs, individuals, usually over the age of 65, spend a week on a college campus while enrolled in special, intensive courses. Planners have found segments of the older population to be keenly interested in rigorous basic educational classes as well as in lighter, topical issues. The week spent on college campuses (housing is generally provided in one of the dormitories) also has been an enjoyable social experience for many. Because of the decentralized manner in which adult education traditionally has developed, there is room for considerable expansion in this approach.

Volunteerism

The aging population constitutes an invaluable community resource. Older persons who are healthy and financially able to forgo paid employment often find volunteer roles rewarding. To better utilize the potential for community volunteers, various programs need to be pursued ranging from foster grandparent programs to crime prevention efforts.

One interesting experiment involves the efforts by large corporations to mobilize their retired workers as community volunteers. By making a small investment, it is possible for corporations to provide a valuable service, enhance their reputation in the community, and also help their retirees. In Minneapolis, for example, Honeywell developed a very successful program with the large group of retirees continuing to reside in the area. Even calculated at the minimum wage, several million dollars of services were being generated each year in the late 1970s, and the retired workers were able to engage in a variety of new roles. Interestingly, there is a tendency in these corporate programs for individuals to reverse roles, with former executives gaining satisfaction from driving a bus and retired accountants helping shut-ins with home repairs. Past skills can be utilized, but often "doing something new" is appealing and rewarding for the participant.

A particularly important dimension of volunteerism in the future will be the manner in which the more fortunate segments of the aging population are mobilized to assist those in their ranks who are less fortunate. A variety of programs are now available, from the nationally organized Meals on Wheels (which provides one hot meal a day to persons in their homes) to various local church activities. These programs large and small could be strengthened. An important policy question in the next years will surround the best ways to enhance opportunities for volunteer work. Among the concerns that will be addressed are ways to improve recruitment and organizational structures and such practical problems as legal liability for automobile use. Despite the impediments which too often slow volunteer operations, there is a substantial opportunity for expanded volunteer activity.

CHANGING STEREOTYPES OF THE AGING

Opportunities also can be expanded by greater attention to the manner in which attitudes toward the aging process are developed in all segments of American society. For the elderly themselves, activities can be broadened by a greater emphasis on the diversity of appropriate behavior. We often define expected roles too narrowly. In the early post-World War II period, too much emphasis was given to the "normalcy" of withdrawing from activities in one's senior years. A recent counter emphasis has stressed active and independent lives. While serving as a useful correction to earlier views, the new orientation also can create problems. Some may not want to be "Super Gram," and too much emphasis on independence may cause a lack of sensitivity to the natural interdependence which life entails for individuals of all ages.

The reduction of stereotypes can affect many aspects of life for the aging. We are beginning to sense that older persons can work effectively in a variety of employment settings. Fortunately, desires for new educational opportunities are now being seen as a logical activity in the later years of the life cycle. In the organization of nursing homes, it also should not come as a surprise to discover that the desire for intimacy and sexual relations does not disappear with age. Passive behavior and declining levels of activity are not necessarily the normal approach to the last phases of the life cycle.

Many stereotypes regarding what life "ought to be like" at different ages need to be changed. One step in the right direction would be better education concerning aspects of the aging process itself. More generally, the manner in which older persons are depicted in movies and on television will continue to have a strong impact. In recent years the number and variety of roles played by elderly persons in the movies has improved somewhat. Henry Fonda, Helen Hayes, and Kathryn Hepburn are among the stars who have contributed to this development.

The depiction of the aging on television also has improved, but the networks continue to cast actors portraying older persons in stereotypical or very limited roles (Arnoff 1974; Gerbner et al. 1980). In relationship to their numbers in the population, older men and older women are still grossly underrepresented on TV. The selection of roles raises troubling questions. Older women, for example, tend to disappear from romantic roles, with older men generally cast with younger women. At the same time, in television dramas older men are more likely to play evil characters than any other age group.

Perhaps the most important innovation in television's approach to the aging has been the national public broadcasting series called "Over Easy," first aired in November 1977 and hosted by Hugh Downs. The objectives of "Over Easy" have been threefold: 1) to inform viewers about services available, possible work projects, and the experiences of older persons in coping with their problems, 2) to encourage positive attitudes about aging, both on an individual and a societal level, and 3) to improve interaction among the generations. Specific program content varies from show to show. Segments have included interviews with prominent older persons, suggestions of new approaches to nutritional needs, and discussions of policy issues. Evaluations of "Over Easy" generally have been quite favorable, as reflected in the extensive survey by the Office of

Communication Research of the Corporation for Public Broadcasting (1980). Given the importance of television in shaping all age groups' attitudes about aging, the projection of a more informative and less stereotyped view of the elderly is an essential dimension in the pursuit of expanded opportunities for older Americans.

THE POLICY AGENDA

As we have seen, numerous issues affecting the aging have emerged in the 1980s, among them the hospice movement, crime prevention programs geared toward the elderly, generic drug and funeral industry reforms, and improved opportuniites for education and volunteer work for the aging. The likely issues involving the aging in the next years suggest several basic conclusions and provide the basis for final recommendations.

First, the diversity and change that is occurring within the older population will continue to require adaptive policy responses. Second, many of the problems affecting the aging affect all segments of the population. Thus it is often difficult to solve the problems of older persons without addressing broader policy issues. Third, just as in the past, policy responses will reflect not only underlying economic and social conditions but also the manner in which issues and potential solutions are defined by proponents of reform.

Before turning in the final chapter to potential sources of change in future policy, it is in order to summarize the actual policies that one might hope would be pursued. This observer recommends:

- Income maintenance policies that increase benefits for the poor elderly and are built around an expansion in SSI and special minimum benefits in Social Security.

- Modifications in Social Security laws to more adequately provide for retirement income for the future population of older women.

- Expanded opportunities for individuals to participate in the development of their retirement income sources through strengthened private sector pension plans and the use of individual retirement accounts (IRAs).

- Expanded work opportunities, job sharing plans, and increased incentives designed to reverse the trend toward early retirement.

- A gradual increase in the age of eligibility for full Social Security benefits coupled with an expansion in disability coverage.

● Renewed efforts to control the costs of health care for all Americans.

● Less emphasis on the "medical model" in long-term care programs, including an expanded development of hospice care.

● Expanded development of social services, including the targeting of public funds for the frail elderly, shared individual and government financing for those with larger incomes, and an improvement in gatekeeping functions and case management roles by local agencies.

● A sharp increase in the range of available housing options, including congregate care facilities, with the goal of reducing the extensiveness of nursing home use.

● Expanded use of the aging as community volunteers and more educational, recreational, and intergenerational activity.

These policy positions are similar in several respects to the "basic eight" developed by the aging-based interest groups prior to the 1981 White House Conference on Aging. The most pronounced differences surround the groups' views on changing Social Security eligibility requirements and reforms in the nation's health care system. Previous chapters already have emphasized the importance of some of the above recommendations, such as the need for targeting, gatekeeping, and case management roles for social services and congregate housing as an alternative to nursing home use. Because a continuation of present policies is likely to lead to major demands in the late 1980s for increased construction of traditional nursing home facilities, action should be taken without delay.

The reluctant endorsement of gradual increases in the age of complete eligibility for Social Security benefits is based upon the importance of planning for the retirement of the baby boom generation in the next century. It is hoped that some of the resulting savings can be used to support other policy changes. An emphasis on reallocating some of the savings to other programs for the aging might indeed be used as a specific bargaining position by spokesmen for the aging. Ideally, voluntary actions in the wake of improved work opportunities would make this step unnecessary. For the long-run stability of Social Security financing and the opportunity to expand funding of other forms of assistance, however, the increase in the age of eligibility for Social Security is a defensible policy step. With these reform proposals in mind, it is essential to consider what combination of forces is likely to influence aging policy in the next years and what political roles may — and should — emerge.

X

POLITICS, POLICY, AND THE FUTURE

The aging in America today have more opportunities to lead rewarding lives than their predecessors had in previous decades. They are healthier, better educated, and more likely to be active in their communities. Not only have volunteer roles expanded in recent years, but the aging are likely to become an increasingly valuable segment of the nation's labor force.

A brighter future for America's older population is by no means inevitable, however. Changes in economic conditions, in societal attitudes, and in specific policies affecting the aging will determine their status in the years ahead. Undoubtedly, the growing numbers of individuals over 75 and the expected increases in the numbers of frail elderly will present a continuing challenge.

To understand what might occur in the development of aging policy in the future, it is helpful to review some of the forces that have shaped policy in the past. In this chapter the formation of aging policy for the aging will be discussed along the lines of the developmental framework presented in Figure 2-1 on page 27. Key issues surrounding changing interest group roles then will be explored.

POLICY FORMATION RECONSIDERED

Particular attention has been paid in previous chapters to the forces that have produced a wide variety of legislation affecting the aging, including 1) the Social Security Act in 1935, 2) Medicare and Medicaid in 1965, 3) social services bills and the Older Americans Act in 1965, 4) the federalization of Supplemental Security Income (SSI) in 1972, 5) the Employee Retirement Income Security Act (ERISA) in 1974, 6) expanded Social Security benefits in the 1970s, and 7) legislation in 1978

227

prohibiting mandatory retirement prior to age 70. Socioeconomic and political influences affected each of these developments.

Systemic Factors

Size of the Aging Population. The size of the aging population (persons 65 or older) has affected policy development but usually indirectly and belatedly. The greatest percentage increases in the aging population occurred prior to the 1970s; yet it was in that decade that many substantial expansions in policy commitments were enacted. During the late 1960s, in the wake of the health care and social services legislation, action on aging-related matters was surprisingly limited even though the numbers of elderly persons were increasing rapidly.

The lower percentage of aging persons in the U.S. population, in comparison with the aging population in other countries, may have been one reason for this country's slow responses in the areas of income maintenance and health. It is interesting to note, however, that other nations with low old age populations (Canada in particular) took action well before similar income maintenance and health care policies were enacted in the United States. (On Canadian responses see Bryden 1974; Taylor 1978; Guest 1980; and Pratt 1981.)

Specific Needs of the Aging. Economic and health needs of the aging have contributed to policy responses but usually after the fact and only once they became part of the "need case" presented by advocates. In the 1920s, reduced family support and a sharp decline in veterans' benefits greatly increased the financial problems of the aging, but no federal action occurred in response (Sanders 1980). In the 1950s, a large proportion of the elderly were not covered by private health plans. It was a decade later that Medicare was passed. Although the health care issues received major discussion in the 1950s, it was only years later and with the help of extensive political action that policies were developed.

In short, economic and health needs of the aging may contribute to policy responses but not immediately and not without additional steps involving issue-raising activity and the building of support for new policy alternatives.

Economic Conditions. High unemployment may have contributed to the passage of the Social Security Act in 1935, and reduced unemployment levels and improvements in other economic indicators following the recession of 1974 appears to have contributed to passage of nonmandatory retirement legislation in 1978. Historically, policy changes altering labor force participation levels have been easier to achieve when they were congruent with the general employment needs of the nation.

Overall economic conditions and the resulting impact on projected government revenues are an underlying factor in some policy changes. The 1965 decisions on health care and the passage of the Older Americans Act came at a time when the economy was expanding, and revenue increases were expected. The declining costs of the Vietnam War in the early 1970s also contributed to a willingness to expand Social Security benefits and many domestic programs. The establishment of other programs in our case studies, however, produced fewer indications of a direct economic relationship. Although the economy was improving in 1935, it was still in considerable trouble, thus contributing to the selection that year of a fairly limited Social Security plan.

Regulatory policy enactments such as pension reform do not suggest a major relationship to economic conditions. Nonetheless, where programs are perceived as costly, a growing economy — and the resulting optimism concerning future growth in government revenues — can be an important factor in the evolution of new policy commitments.

Private Sector Efforts. What has been the relationship between private sector programs and initiatives in the public sector? During the 1930s, the absence in the United States of private sector pension schemes comparable to those in Europe seems to have worked against the development of public programs because the whole concept of pensions was new to Americans (Rimlinger 1971). In the development of Medicare, the limited coverage of older persons in private plans appears to have been a factor in prompting public sector action. Regarding social services, there is not a pattern, as Soderstrom (1978) describes for Canada, in which the services provided by the Victorian Order of Nurses constituted a major substitute for public programs.

Is the relationship between public and private programs more competitive or complementary? This question clearly deserves additional analysis. It may be that the common pattern is actually the one observed in the 1950s, when Social Security benefit levels and private pension coverage both expanded rapidly. Interest in an issue may affect both sectors simultaneously. In some instances, private sector lobbying against public sector programs has resulted in heightened interest in private as well as public forms of assistance and a general desire for new services. In sum, it seems fairly clear that the existence of large private sector programs has not been a major factor in shaping American policy responses.

Societal Attitudes and Values. In the development of basic policies and in the choice of specific policy approaches, societal attitudes and values have been important. Americans' emphasis on individualism was seen by many analysts as an important factor in the development, albeit belatedly, of a social security system in this country. Similarly, underlying public uncertainty about "welfare" was a factor influencing the choice of a system of earned benefits through contributions rather than a system of universal benefits or a system based upon a means test. This skepticism about welfare policy roles has been reflected in varying degrees in subsequent decisions.

The expansion of SSI as a means-tested program (which might seem to contradict an opposition to assistance based solely on economic need) was, comparatively, a rather belated response and is still more limited than the means-tested programs found in some western nations. Similarly, while Medicaid benefit levels have increased sharply, many state legislators have provided these increases grudgingly.

Reluctance to accept the concept of assistance as a matter of right has been accompanied by a unique American emphasis on programs designed specifically for the aging. This separateness in program implementation was manifested most clearly following the fight over health care in the administration of President Harry S. Truman. The aging were chosen as the logical clientele group to receive assistance with health care costs. Thus the United States became the only industrial nation to introduce national health insurance with the aging as the initial beneficiaries.

Decisions involving service delivery through the Older Americans Act also reflected the continuing emphasis on the appropriateness of the aging as a distinct clientele group for government programs. The reluctance to accept welfare approaches and a willingness to view the aging as a specific target group have been persistent influences in American policy development.

Political Roles and Structures

It is difficult to distinguish the influence of individual or institutional action on policy formation for the aging from the influence of economic conditions and public attitudes. Nonetheless, political participants clearly have had an important impact on aging policy development. Roles played by political actors include 1) generating interest in an issue, 2) formulating policy designs, 3) building political support for a specific proposal, 4) influencing the bargaining processes that determine the final policy response, and 5) implementing programs and then overseeing them.

Elections. Newly elected executives and legislators may come to office with strong desires to change past policies. Incumbents' actions in office then are often shaped by their desire for reelection. Expansions in Social Security benefits, the establishment of SSI in 1972, and the indexing decision and benefit increase in 1972 have been seen as part of the tendency for elected officials to look toward the next election in responding to policy interests of the aging.

The establishment of Medicare and Medicaid in 1965, while attributable to multiple factors, was strongly influenced by the election to the presidency of Lyndon B. Johnson in 1964. Passage of the Older Americans Act might be similarly explained. Thus among the seven policy cases listed on page 227, only pension reform and nonmandatory retirement do not appear to have had a fairly immediate relationship to the electoral process.

Presidents. Neither the increased presidential attentiveness to the aging in recent years nor President Franklin D. Roosevelt's influential and highly popularized actions on their behalf in 1934 and 1935 should obscure this fact: presidents have not been predominant figures in policy development for the aging.

Presidential action in the 1960s included President John F. Kennedy's efforts to increase public interest in health care issues and Johnson's assistance in making Medicare a top priority in Congress in 1965. While significant, these actions were accompanied by important initiatives by legislators and interest groups. Johnson's whirlwind approach to the domestic agenda aided passage of the Older Americans Act. The president, however, was not personally active on this issue and should not be considered a significant participant.

The 1970s produced a mixed record of presidential influence and involvement. President Richard M. Nixon's interest in welfare reform in 1969 produced a legislative initiative (the Family Assistance Plan) which ultimately resulted in the legislative interest in SSI in 1972, and Nixon's endorsement of the bill was one reason for its easy passage. However, the choice of the specific policy design and the nature of the bargaining process were influenced more by legislative action than presidential action.

Similarly, the shift to indexing in 1972 and the establishment of pension reform and nonmandatory retirement legislation were not predominantly presidential policy moves. Nixon supported indexing, but the bargaining process was primarily in key congressional committees. In the 10-year evolution of ERISA, presidents were important as issue raisers, and some of the policy ideas in the 1960s emanated from the presidency. In terms of adding weights to the political forces at play in 1974 or in altering the bargaining process, however, a president preoccupied with Watergate — and weakened by that scandal's impact — simply was not in a position to have an extensive role. Finally, on nonmandatory retirement, President Jimmy Carter's primary contribution was not in policy design or in legislative bargaining. He was largely responsible, however, for limiting the issue to nonmandatory retirement questions rather than letting it expand to include a possible extension in the age of eligibility for Social Security benefits.

Obviously, advocates of aging-related policy changes may be helped if the occupant of the Oval Office is sympathetic to their policy objectives. This is particularly true if the president is willing to personally promote their objectives, focus public attention on them, and expend valuable bargaining chips to convince key members of Congress to back him up. This happens infrequently, however. Most of the cases we have considered indicate that presidents tend to share policy development roles with other political participants. The periodic display of publicly visible but relatively insignificant activity by presidents — such as endorsing bills after congressional passage is assured or hosting elaborate bill-signing ceremonies at the White House — should not lead to an overemphasis on their credit for policy development.

Administrators. The key administrative role in aging policy formation has been to influence or even largely determine the selection of a specific policy design. For example, administrators were important in the selection of the aging as the clientele group for health care assistance. (It is important to recall, however, that the ultimate program design in 1965 was developed by House Ways and Means Chairman Wilbur Mills (D-

Ark.). This design then was accepted by a rather startled group of officials in the Department of Health, Education and Welfare.)

The Social Security Administration, while very important in the design of programs in the 1950s, had a mixed role in the cases we have examined. Furthermore, the increasingly intense controversies surrounding the Social Security system appear to have reduced the Social Security Administration's influence in designing new policies. In evaluating administrative roles, interdepartmental rivalries, as manifested in the struggle between Treasury and Labor over ERISA, also can be a significant factor in the evolution of political supports behind different policy choices.

Congress and Its Members. The legislative arena has had considerable influence in determining specific policies for the aging. Individual legislators often have been important as issue raisers, particularly concerning the problems of their constituents with the delivery of health services or treatment at long-term care facilities.

In the 1970s, the House and Senate committees on aging and the publicity generated in particular by Rep. Claude Pepper (D-Fla.) were important in focusing attention on aging issues. The choice of policy design also has been influenced by members of Congress. The 1965 Medicare legislation is one example. More important, however, have been the legislative bargaining roles in the movement toward specific policy choices. With an eye toward reelection, legislators sometimes take initiatives not strongly promoted elsewhere. Frequently their actions alter the proposals that issue from the White House or federal agencies.

Interest Groups. Aging-based interest groups and groups with a wider focus that provide services to the aging (pharmaceutical, medical, housing and other kinds of services) have influenced aging policy development to varying degrees.

Aging-based interest groups have played an important role as issue raisers on a wide variety of legislation including the Social Security Act of 1935 and subsequent amendments expanding benefits as well as pension reform and nonmandatory retirement legislation. In the area of policy design, however, they have been less influential. Roosevelt rejected many of the approaches they advocated in the early 1930s. The final choice of the aging as the clientele group for health insurance came at a time in the 1950s when aging-based interest groups were relatively ineffectual.

Medicare and Medicaid policy design decisions were shaped more by state legislators, members of Congress, presidents, and federal administrators than by aging-based interest groups.

The weight of available evidence tends to give these groups a fairly modest role in generating the support necessary for passage of the Social Security Act in 1935. Medicare's passage in 1965, while aided by their lobby efforts, was primarily the result of the favorable political climate after the 1964 presidential election. Social Security benefit expansion in the 1970s again produced lobby activity by aging-based interest groups, but on the indexing question in 1972 these groups were divided. While they attracted increasing attention in the halls of Congress in the 1970s, they rarely convinced legislators to switch their votes on benefit increases. Perhaps not surprisingly, the two bills for which aging-based interest groups have been most extensively credited with building necessary political support involved relatively minor direct costs — the Older Americans Act in 1965 and the nonmandatory retirement legislation in 1978.

Ultimately, the level of influence behind desired policy alternatives achieved by aging-based interest groups must be considered in relationship to the strength of opposing groups. If both sides on an issue improve in numbers and political skill, the result may be a stand-off for the aging-based interest groups. The actions of business groups, while differing from those of the aging-based interests, often have been very effective. Frequently, efforts have been made to prevent policy questions from receiving visible attention within Congress and state legislatures. When issues have arisen, strenuous efforts have been made to pass legislation that minimizes public control over private sector activities. Thus the insurance lobby pushed for a strong private system prior to 1935, and the medical lobby pushed for a minimal disruption of private patient practices and rate-setting activities in the controversies leading to the establishment of Medicare.

In the case studies we have considered, there have been few instances in which business lobbies encountered severe defeats. The insurance lobby felt defeated in 1935, yet the initial program did not jeopardize its position. In 1965, the medical profession (in particular the American Medical Association) felt that it had lost a tremendous battle. Yet in retrospect, while there is no indication that the medical profession was keenly aware of the potential at the time, Medicare — with its lack of cost control provisions — proved to be a major boon to the pocketbooks of the nation's doctors.

It is clear that the private sector felt threatened by the implications of the 1977 expansion in Social Security benefit levels and that a campaign was mounted to increase the attention being given to private planning for retirement. Companies operating private pensions were not enthusiastic about ERISA, but they significantly influenced the final compromises that emerged. On nonmandatory retirement, major spokesmen for business interests were neither entirely united in their opposition, nor did they feel that the stakes were particularly large — in part because the number of persons who would take advantage of the new provisions was projected to be extremely small. Finally, in terms of consumer protection issues, the record of limited state action in such areas as funeral home regulation and generic drug law reform again underscores the often strong position of business lobby groups on aging-related issues.

In the face of that opposition, aging-based interest groups have improved their capacity for issue raising in recent years. They can be credited with more successes than in earlier decades. Nevertheless, it is important not to overstate their ability to match the political strength of other major interest groups. The political battles emerging in the 1980s promise important new tests of interest group strength.

Policy Characteristics

The importance of involvement in developing specific policy approaches becomes apparent as we turn our focus to the consequences of policy design along with general program and structural characteristics. In several instances, initial "technical" decisions have had a strong subsequent impact.

Policy Design. In evaluating Social Security benefits, it seems clear that the scope of that policy response was influenced by the separate trust fund approach and the indexing of benefits. The use of separate taxes for the Social Security system (and the inclusion of a listing of half of the total tax on each employee's paycheck) definitely helped those seeking to expand the system. Social Security seemed like a good deal to many, and at points surpluses actually existed in the trust funds — an obvious invitation to expand the program. Indexing, in turn, has been important in the benefit expansion of the late 1970s. Ironically, that step was most strongly supported by those who wanted to curtail the expansion of benefits — a strong indication that a policy design (chosen before the inflationary impacts of the 1970s were recognized) was a major factor in subsequent expansion.

Program Cost, Impact, and Visibility. As Lowi (1969) and Ripley and Franklin (1976) have argued, policy responses will differ substantially depending upon their size and their impact on major groups in American society. Policies sometimes labeled as redistributive will involve major costs and can be seen as redistributing benefits and costs among different groups and classes in American society. As a result, redistributive policy responses generally will include a wide range of interest groups and political leadership roles and will take a long time to resolve.

Medicaid is a clear example of a redistributive policy and was so classified by Marmor (1970, 95-123). The passage of ERISA following a lengthy period of debate, despite the limited direct governmental costs of the legislation, also manifested major characteristics of a redistributive issue. Nonmandatory retirement, on the other hand, never evolved to a comparable status and was passed more quickly. Similarly, passage of the Older Americans Act in 1965 was of primary interest to its cadre of supporters and did not produce substantial opposition.

From the perspective of program size and impact, the various decisions on the Social Security system have interesting implications. Clearly, passage in 1935 and many of the important steps preceding passage involved a wide variety of major interest groups. This is characteristic of a redistributive issue. However, some of the expansionary decisions, even though they did in fact redistribute benefits and costs in a significant manner among various segments of the population, were not as intensely contested as one might have expected. The choice of policy design, including the efforts to minimize discussions of the tradeoffs between groups in the population, contributed to the fairly limited controversy over the expansionary decisions taken in 1972. Significantly, by 1977 the level of controversy had risen sharply suggesting that Social Security issues increasingly may resemble other redistributive policy controversies.

While it is often difficult to categorize specific policies in a rigid typology, existing studies do suggest a basic relationship. Program size and/or perceived impact, when substantial, will lead to greater controversy, more extensive interest group activity, wider involvement by a range of political leaders, and — barring a disruptive economic or social change — a slower shift to new policy commitments than often occurs on more peripheral issues.

Summary

In our reconsideration in this chapter of aging policy formation, systemic factors, political participants, and policy characteristics have been examined. One other potential influence on the development of aging policy in the United States deserves attention, namely, the political system itself. The lack of concentrated authority in the federal government frequently has been cited as a source contributing to the slow start in this country of policies for the aging.

In the seven policy cases presented, Medicare represents the clearest indication of structures contributing to delay. The veto process in Congress through the strong roles of committee chairmen was a definite factor in slowing the evolution of Medicare legislation in the early 1960s. In the development of the Social Security Act, on the other hand, Congress was not a stumbling block. Actually, there was significant congressional support for new proposals before President Roosevelt began to take action in 1934 and 1935.

Obviously, it is difficult to speculate whether certain policy interests would have emerged earlier if authority for making final decisions was concentrated rather than disbursed in our political system. Nonetheless, given the actions which did occur, it is reasonable to conclude that the lack of centralized authority in national politics, while important on some occasions, has not been a particularly decisive factor in American policy responses for the aging.

What factors then have been decisive? The impact of basic influences can be summarized as follows:

● Characteristics of the aging population and specific needs of the elderly do not translate very directly into policy responses.

● Economic conditions and projections of future tax revenues have a major impact on policy responses; they affect the position of the aging in the labor force and decisions concerning the funding of new policy commitments.

● Americans have been reluctant to develop programs based upon universal eligibility or means tests, and they generally have viewed the aging as a clientele group more deserving of assistance than other groups. American values thus have influenced policy responses.

237

- Presidents may contribute to the mobilizing of support for aging-related issues or help determine the choice of a policy design, but they usually play a fairly secondary role in the final evolution of basic policy responses.

- Bureaucratic leaders have been influential through their ability to shape the design of specific policies.

- Legislators have been of major importance in aging-related policy development both as issue raisers and as developers of specific policy designs.

- Aging-based groups have been most effective as issue raisers on nonredistributive issues.

- Private businesses affected by policy choices for the aging have had substantial success in defending their positions.

A central message thus emerges from the range of factors that have influenced policy development for the aging. The future of aging-related policies in this country will be greatly affected by the overall evolution of American society and, in particular, by the state of the economy. If either stagflation or high unemployment predominates in the coming years, financing for needed programs will become even more difficult. The difficulties involved in the development of aging policies in the early 1980s dramatically underscored the impact of economic conditions.

THE FUTURE POLITICS OF AGING

Political roles, which are often shaped by social and economic factors, will influence policy developments to a great extent. For those with specific interests in policies affecting the aging, the question of future political roles often focuses on the likely — and appropriate — actions of aging-based interest groups. How should these groups be evaluated, and what strategies should they pursue?

Aging-based Interest Groups

The importance of expanded interest group activity often is taken as an article of faith among those who seek improved public policy for the aging. As Estes (1979) has emphasized, the pervasiveness of interest group activity in all areas of American politics has led to a strong affirmation of the role of interest groups among promoters of new policies for the aging. It is necessary, however, to consider both the pros and cons, the strengths and limits, of expanded interest group behavior.

Proponents of expanded interest group activity commend the issue-raising role aging-based interest groups have played in the case studies we have considered. Indeed, interest groups have helped focus public attention on nursing home reform, home health care programs, and retirement issues, to name a few. Interest groups also are defended on the basis of their ability to help administrators, social workers, and elected officials recognize the specific concerns of elderly persons, concerns that might otherwise have been overlooked. The establishment of advisory councils for state and local units on aging under the Older Americans Act reflects that desire to let the aging speak for themselves. In a broader sense, this strategy is part of the orientation in American politics that stresses the importance of extensive individual participation (Bachrach 1980).

The case for enhanced interest group activity also involves a definite view of patterns of political influence on major issues. Many argue that because the political process in the United States is dominated too often by special interests, aging-based interest groups must improve their organizational capacities and political skills so they can compete success-fully with other groups.

Limitations with interest group roles also need to be considered. The policy preferences of aging-based interest groups at points have been called into question (Putnam 1970). Too often policy preferences unduly reflected the personal preferences of group leaders. Research by Dobson and Karns (1979), however, points to improvements in this area. Cooperation between leaders and members of interest groups has improved in recent years.

An additional problem is the tendency for some issues to be poorly promoted by aging-based interest groups simply because they are not particularly popular with older persons. For example, drug rehabilitation programs in some states have received little attention among aging-based groups even though health studies have indicated that chemical dependency is a significant problem for many elderly persons. The paradox for the interest groups, of course, is that the goal of improving the public image of the elderly may conflict with policy approaches that focus attention on their problems.

Interest groups sometimes are viewed as overly concerned with short-run — and publicly visible — policy goals. Like legislators, interest group leaders can become overly interested in gaining tangible policy outcomes to describe in the next newsletter. It also should be noted that several of the major aging-based interest groups have been chosen to administer housing and special jobs programs. The resulting involvement with established policies may limit the range of new policy alternatives that they will want to address.

Finally, and perhaps most importantly, skeptics of aging-based interest group activity often question the effectiveness of these groups in addressing the problems of the most needy elderly. Can middle- and upper middle-class retirees identify sufficiently with the problems of the poor and the frail elderly to embrace programs that are geared toward those in greatest need of assistance? If not, will expanded interest group activity on the part of some segments of the aging population focus upon policy goals which are questionable in terms of the distribution of policy benefits among the aging themselves and among the aging and other deserving groups in American society?

Promoters of aging-based interest groups can point to instances in which those who were better off physically and financially favored expansion of Supplemental Security Income benefits and nursing home reform. The coalition efforts among the aging groups that have occurred in the last several years have found all major groups endorsing SSI increases, for example. In state politics, organizations with a substanstantial middle-class following sometimes have pursued diverse goals. Washington's Senior Lobby, for example, had a useful role in nursing home policy development, and the Minnesota Senior Federation has worked for benefits helping the poorest segment of its membership. But what actions will interest groups with a predominantly middle-class membership pursue when budgetary pressures worsen and feasible program choices are even more limited than they are today? This is a central question affecting the aging policy agenda in the 1980s.

Given the fairly modest political influence aging-based interest groups have had on very costly and controversial issues, fears that their actions suddenly will produce inappropriate policies are unwarranted. Both as issue raisers and as mobilizers of political strength, aging-based interest groups perform a necessary and defensible role. Yet there is a danger that their focus may become overly narrow. Broad policy interests for the aging and for public policy generally need to be encouraged.

A Final Perspective

If the quality of life for the aging is to improve, political coalitions must be strengthened, creative approaches must be encouraged, and human values must be emphasized.

First, to achieve maximum success, groups must work together. Those seeking to improve policies affecting the aging serve neither their own interests nor those of the nation as a whole by taking an overly narrow view of the problems they confront or the potential scope of shared political action. Coalitions are particularly essential in the area of health care. Medicare, after all, was itself the result of coalition politics. Cost containment for health care and improved organization of social services may well require similar coalition-based action.

The changing characteristics of the aging also point to important prospects for creativity in policy development. Examples are numerous. Community specialists are helping to locate older persons who wish to share living quarters. Retired workers from major industries are increasingly being used as community volunteers. Part-time-work options are expanding. All of these creative initiatives began when an individual, a group, or company simply tried out a new idea. A variety of innovative policies and actions need to be explored.

But effective political strategies and creative policy developments alone cannot ensure enhanced life situations for the aging in America. They must be accompanied by a heightened sense of personal concern. Although declining family and community ties may have reduced some of the necessary motivations, the frequence and importance of that "helping hand" can be seen in many actions for and by the aging. The mutual benefits of contacts within and between generations constitute an essential value for Americans of all ages to pursue.

241

GLOSSARY

Age Discrimination in Employment Act (ADEA). Federal legislation enacted in 1967 to combat age discrimination in employment and amended in 1978 to prevent termination of most employees under age 70 solely on the basis of their age.

American Association of Retired Persons (AARP). The largest aging-based interest group in the United States, with approximately 13 million members. Prior to 1982 the organization was known as the National Association of Retired Teachers — American Association of Retired Persons (NRTA-AARP).

Area Administrations on Aging (AAAs). Local organizations established by the 1973 amendments to the Older Americans Act in an effort to expand local services planning and delivery for the elderly.

Birth cohort. Persons born in a given time period, such as the 1920s or the period of the "baby boom" between 1945 and 1962.

Congregate housing. Shared housing arrangements for groups of older persons. Some meals and social services programs usually are provided.

Dependency ratio. The ratio of the nonworking age population to those between age 18 and 65.

Elderhostels. Intensive educational programs for the aging often held on college campuses during the summer for one to two weeks.

Employee Retirement Income Security Act (ERISA). Federal legislation enacted in 1974 to provide standards for vesting of private pensions and to standardize reporting and minimum funding requirements for future pension obligations.

Federal Insurance Contributions Act (FICA). The portion of the Internal Revenue Code that authorizes employers to deduct Social

Security payments from covered employees and to submit those funds to the Internal Revenue Service for transmittal to the Social Security trust funds.

General Revenue. All tax revenues that are placed into the general account of the federal government. Payments to the Social Security trust funds are received and administered separately from general revenue funds.

Hospice Care. A program of care for the terminally ill that emphasizes the patient's comfort rather than all forms of medical technology. Hospice care, while sometimes given at home, is usually provided in a separate facility.

Individual Retirement Account (IRA). Federal tax code provisions expanded in 1981 to give incentives to individuals who want to save for their retirement. Individuals can save $2,000 annually without paying taxes on that income until it is spent during retirement.

Long-term Care Facility. The term used in federal legislation to refer to facilities traditionally known as nursing homes. Long-term care facilities are either skilled nursing facilities (SNFs) or intermediate care facilities (ICFs), depending on the extent of nursing and related medical care provided.

Means Tests. Eligibility requirements for government programs. Income tests are means tests based solely upon income; assets tests are means tests based solely on personal assets.

Medicaid. The program of federal and state medical assistance for the aging and other groups of persons who are eligible on the basis of requirements which include a means test. Medicaid, established in 1965, constitutes the main source of public assistance for nursing home costs.

Medicare. The federal program established in 1965 to assist older persons with health costs. Part A, known as hospital insurance (HI), covers hospital costs; Part B, known as Supplemental Medical Insurance (SMI), covers physician services.

National Council of Senior Citizens (NCSC). The second largest aging-based interest group, with approximately three million members. NCSC was formed in 1961 with assistance from organized labor.

Older Americans Act (OAA). Federal legislation enacted in 1965 to promote and coordinate programs for the aging. The act established the Administration on Aging and State Units on Aging (SUAs).

Replacement rate. A standard measure of retirement income as a percentage of prior earnings. If a worker solely dependent upon Social Security benefits earned $500 a month prior to retirement and now receives $350 in monthly benefits, the replacement ratio would be 70 percent.

State Units on Aging (SUAs). The organizations established in each state to promote policies for the aging and administer programs under the Older Americans Act.

Social Security Act. Federal legislation enacted in 1935. Major Social Security benefit increases were enacted in 1972 and 1977. The act provides for payments to the aging, the disabled, and survivors. Trust funds for the aging and survivors — Old Age and Survivors Insurance (OASI) — and for the disabled — Disabled Insurance (DI) — are maintained separately, along with separate funds for Part A and Part B of Medicare.

Supplemental Security Income (SSI). In 1972 this assistance replaced Old Age Assistance (OAA), which had been provided under the Social Security Act of 1935. Payments are made to aged, blind, and disabled individuals on the basis of a means test. Most states supplement the federal payments.

Title XX programs. Social services programs for the aging and other needy groups that were funded until 1981 under Title XX of the Social Security Act. These programs have been converted to more general block grants.

Vesting. Provisions in private pension plans granting participants the right to benefits after contributing for a certain number of years. Once the contributions have been made for the required period (which is often ten years), individuals are entitled to pension payments when they reach a stipulated age even if they have not been recent contributors to that retirement plan.

REFERENCES

Aaron, Henry J. 1975. *Who Pays the Property Tax?* Washington, D.C.: The Brookings Institution.

ABT Associates. 1974. *Property Tax Relief Programs for the Elderly: A Compendium Report.* Washington, D.C.: U.S. Department of Housing and Urban Development.

Altmeyer, Arthur J. 1968. *The Formative Years of Social Security.* Madison, Wis.: University of Wisconsin Press.

Arnoff, C. 1974. "Old Age in Prime Time." *Journal of Communication* 24: 86-87.

Bachrach, Peter. 1980. *The Theory of Democratic Elitism: A Critique.* Washington, D.C.: University Press of America.

Ball, Robert M. 1978. *Social Security: Today and Tomorrow.* New York: Columbia University Press.

Barfield, Richard E., and James N. Morgan. 1974. *Early Retirement: The Decision and the Experience and a Second Look.* Ann Arbor, Mich.: University of Michigan's Survey Research Center.

Barone, Michael, and Grant Ujifusa. 1982. *The Almanac of American Politics.* Washington, D.C.: Barone & Co.

Barro, Robert J. 1977. "Social Security and Private Saving: Evidence from the U.S. Time Series." Rochester, N.Y.: University of Rochester.

Binstock, Robert H. 1972. "Interest Group Liberalism and the Politics of Aging." *The Gerontologist* 12 (Autumn): 265-280.

———. 1978. "Federal Policy Toward the Aging: Its Inadequacies and Its Politics." *National Journal* 10 (November 11): 1838-1845.

———. 1979. "A Policy Agenda on Aging for the 1980s." *National Journal* 41 (October 13): 1711-1717.

Boskin, Michael J. 1977. "Social Security and Retirement Decisions." *Economic Inquiry* 15 (January): 1-25.

Bowler, M. Kenneth. 1974. *The Nixon Guaranteed Income Proposal: Substance and Process in Policy Change.* Philadelphia: Ballinger Publishing Co.

Brody, Elaine M. 1981. "Women in the Middle and Family Help in Older People." *The Gerontologist* 21: 471-480.

Bruner, Charles H. 1978. *Representation by Surrogate: The Politics of Aging in a State Legislative Setting.* Ph.D. diss., Stanford University, Stanford, Calif.

Bryden, Kenneth. 1974. *Old Age Pensions and Policy-Making in Canada.* Montreal: McGill-Queens University Press.

Buchanan, Robert J. 1981. *Health-Care Finance.* Lexington, Mass.: Lexington Books.

Burke, Vincent J. 1974. *Nixon's Good Deed: Welfare Reform.* New York: Columbia University Press.

Caldwell, Janice M., and Marshall B. Kapp. 1981. "The Rights of Nursing Home Patients: Possibilities and Limitations of Federal Regulation." *Journal of Health Politics, Policy and Law* 6 (Spring).

Campbell, Colin. 1979. *Financing Social Security.* Washington, D.C.: American Enterprise Institute for Public Policy Research.

Campbell, John Creighton, and John Strate. 1980. "Are Old People Conservative? How Much?" Paper presented at the Annual Convention of The Gerontological Society, San Diego, Calif., November 19.

Carp, Francis M. 1976. "The Impact of Environment on Old People." In *Aging in America: Readings in Social Gerontology,* by Cary S. Kart and Barbara Manard. Port Washington: N.Y.: Alfred Publishing Co.

Case, John. 1981. *Understanding Inflation.* New York: William Morrow & Co.

Chambers, Clarke. 1963. *Seedtime of Reform: American Social Service and Social Action, 1918-1933.* Minneapolis: University of Minnesota Press.

Clark, Robert L., and David T. Barker. 1981. *Reversing the Trend Toward Early Retirement.* Washington, D.C.: American Enterprise Institute for Public Policy Research.

Cobb, Roger W., and Charles D. Elder. 1972. *Participation in American Politics: The Dynamics of Agenda-Building.* Boston: Allyn & Bacon.

Coberly, Sally. 1980. "Extending the Worklife of the Older Worker: Part-time Work Options." Testimony before the House Subcommittee on Oversight, Committee on Ways and Means, September 10.

Cohen, K. P. 1979. *Hospice: Prescription for Terminal Care.* Germantown, Md.: Aspen Press.

Congressional Budget Office. 1977. *Long-Term Care for the Elderly and Disabled.* Washington, D.C.: U.S. Government Printing Office.

Congressional Quarterly. 1977. "Social Security Amendments." *Almanac 1977.* Washington, D.C.: Congressional Quarterly, 161-172.

———. 1981. *Congressional Quarterly Weekly Report,* Jan. 10, 119-121; Nov. 28, 2329-2346.

———. 1982. *Budgeting for America: Politics and Process of Federal Spending.* Washington, D.C.: Congressional Quarterly.

Cornwell, Elmer E. 1966. *Presidential Leadership of Public Opinion.* Bloomington, Ind.: Indiana University Press.

Cowgill, Donald Olen, and Lowell D. Holmes, eds. *Aging and Modernization.* New York: Appleton-Century-Crofts.

Crimmins, Eileen M. 1981. "The Changing Pattern of American Mortality Decline, 1940-1977, and Its Implications for the Future." *Population and Development Review* 7 (June): 229-254.

Crittenden, John A. 1962. "Aging and Party Affiliation." *Public Opinion Quarterly* 26 (Winter): 648-657.

Cronin, Thomas E. 1980. *The State of the Presidency.* Boston: Little, Brown & Co.

Cutler, Neal E. 1969. "Generation, Maturation, and Party Affiliation: A Cohort Analysis." *Public Opinion Quarterly* 33: 583-588.

———. 1977. "Demographic, Socio-Psychological, and Political Factors in the Politics of Aging: A Foundation for Research in 'Political Gerontology.' " *American Political Science Review* 71 (March): 1011-1025.

Cutler, Neal E., and Vern L. Bengtson. 1974. "Aging and Political Alienation: Maturation, Generation and Period Effects." *The Annals of the American Academy of Political and Social Science* 415 (September): 160-175.

Davidson, Stephen M. 1980. *Medicaid Decisions: A Systematic Analysis of the Cost Problem.* Cambridge, Mass.: Ballinger Publishing Co.

Davidson, Stephen M., and Theodore Marmor. 1980. *The Cost of Living Longer: National Health Insurance and the Elderly.* Lexington, Mass.: Lexington Books.

Decker, Jane Elizabeth, and Robert K. Whelan. 1982. "The Older Americans Act: A Case Study in Intergovernmental Relations and the Process of Policy Development and Implementation." Paper presented at the Annual Meeting of the American Political Science, Association, Denver, Colo., Sept. 2-5.

Deming, Mary, and Neal Cutler. 1983. "Demography." In *Aging: Scientific Perspectives and Social Issues.* 2d ed. Edited by Diana Woodruff and James Birren. Monterey, Calif.: Brooks/Cole Publishing Co.

Demkovich, Linda E. 1979. "The 'Maximum Reimbursement' Game: Hospitals May Face New Rules." *National Journal* 11 (November 18): 1940-1942.

Department of Social and Health Services. Bureau of Aging. 1979. *Washington State's Approach to Senior Advocacy.* Olympia, Wash.: State of Washington.

Derthick, Martha. 1975. *Uncontrollable Spending for Social Services.* Washington, D.C.: The Brookings Institution.

———. 1979. *Policymaking for Social Security.* Washington, D.C.: The Brookings Institution.

Dickinson, Peter A. 1980. *Sunbelt Retirement.* New York: E. P. Dutton.

Dobson, Douglas, and David A. Karns. 1979. *Public Policy and Senior Citizens: Policy Formation in the American States.* Final Report to the Administration on Aging. No. 90-A1005. DeKalb, Ill.: Northern Illinois University.

Drucker, Peter F. 1976. *The Unseen Revolution: How Pension Fund Socialism Came to America.* New York: Harper & Row.

DuBois, Paul M. 1980. *The Hospice Way of Death.* Port Washington, N.Y.: Human Sciences Press.

Dunlop, Burton D. 1979. *The Growth of Nursing Home Care.* Lexington, Mass.: Lexington Books.

Dye, Thomas R. 1966. *Politics, Economics, and the Public.* Chicago: Rand McNally & Co.

Dye, Thomas R., and Virginia Gray. 1980. *The Determinants of Public Policy.* Lexington, Mass.: Lexington Books.

Easterlin, Richard A. 1976. "The Conflict Between Aspirations and Resources." *Population and Development Review* 2 (September): 417-426.

_____. 1978. "What Will 1984 Be Like? Socioeconomic Implications of Recent Twists in Age Structure." *Demography* 15 (November): 397-432.

_____. 1980. *Birth and Fortune: The Impact of Numbers on Personal Welfare.* New York: Basic Books.

Estes, Carroll L. 1979. *The Aging Enterprise.* San Francisco: Jossey-Bass.

Feder, Judith, John Holahan, and Theodore Marmor. 1980. *National Health Insurance: Conflicting Goals and Policy Choices.* Washington, D.C.: The Urban Institute.

Federal Council on Aging. 1978. *Public Policy and the Frail Elderly.* Washington, D.C.: U.S. Department of Health, Education and Welfare.

Federal Trade Commission. Bureau of Consumer Protection. 1978a. *Hearing Aid Industry.* Final Report to the Federal Trade Commission and Proposed Trade Regulation Rule. Washington, D.C.: U.S. Government Printing Office.

_____. 1978b. *Funeral Industry Practices.* Final Report and Proposed Trade Regulation Rule. Washington, D.C.: U.S. Government Printing Office.

Feingold, Eugene. 1966. *Medicare: Policy and Politics (A Case Study and Policy Analysis).* San Francisco: Chandler & Sharp Publishers.

Feldstein, Martin S. 1976. "Social Security and Saving: The Extended Life Cycle Theory." *American Economic Review* 66 (May): 77-86.

Feldstein, Paul J. 1977. *Health Associations and the Demand for Legislation: The Political Economy of Health.* Cambridge, Mass.: Ballinger Publishing Co.

Fenno, Richard F., Jr. 1978. *Home Style: House Members and Their Districts.* Boston: Little, Brown & Co.

Fischer, David H. 1978. *Growing Old in America.* New York: Oxford University Press.

Foner, Anne. 1972. "The Polity." In *Aging and Society.* Vol. 3. Edited by M. H. White et al. New York: Russell Sage Foundation.

Freedman, Leonard. 1969. *Public Housing: The Politics of Poverty.* New York: Holt, Rinehart & Winston.

Friedman, Joseph, and Jane Sjogren. 1981. "Assets of the Elderly as They Retire." *Social Security Bulletin* 44 (January): 16-31.

Friedman, Lawrence. 1966. "Public Housing and the Poor: An Overview." *California Law Review* 54 (May): 642-669.

_____. 1968. *Government and Slum Housing: A Century of Frustration.* Chicago: Rand McNally & Co.

Fries, James. 1980. "Aging, Natural Death and the Compression of Morbidity." *New England Journal of Medicine* 303 (July 17): 130-135.

General Accounting Office. 1977. *Home Health: The Need for a National Policy to Better Provide for the Elderly.* Washington, D.C.: Comptroller General of the United States.

———. 1979. *Hospice Care: A Growing Concept in the United States.* Washington, D.C.: Comptroller General of the United States.

———. 1982. "Preliminary Findings on Patient Characteristics and State Medicaid Expenditures for Nursing Home Care." Washington, D.C.: Comptroller General of the United States.

Gerbner, George, Larry Gross, and Nancy Signorielli. 1980. "Prime Time and the Aging." *Journal of Communication* 30 (Winter): 37-47.

Gibson, Robert M., and Dwight R. Waldo. 1982. "National Health Expenditures, 1981." *Health Care Financing Review* 4 (September): 1-35.

Gilbert, Neil, and Harry Specht. 1982. "A 'Fair Share' for the Aged: Title XX Allocation Patterns, 1976-1980." *Research on Aging* 4 (March): 71-86.

Gillaspy, R. Thomas. 1980. "Labor Force Participation of the Older Population." In *Work and Retirement: Policy Issues.* Edited by Pauline K. Ragan. Los Angeles: University of Southern California Press.

Givens, Harrison, Jr. 1978. "An Evaluation of Mandatory Retirement." *The Annals* 438 (July): 51-58.

Glenn, Norval D. 1974. "Aging and Conservatism." *The Annals* 415 (September): 176-186.

Gold, Steven David. 1979. *Property Tax Relief.* Lexington, Mass.: Lexington Books.

Gottesman, Leonard E., et al. 1979. "Service Management Plan and Concept in Pennsylvania." *The Gerontologist* 19 (August): 379-385.

Greene, Leonard M. 1982. *Free Enterprise Without Poverty.* New York: W. W. Norton & Co.

Greenough, William C., and Francis P. King. 1976. *Pension Plans and Public Policy.* New York: Columbia University Press.

Grimaldi, Paul L. 1980. *Supplemental Security Income: The New Federal Program for the Aged, Blind and Disabled.* Washington, D.C.: American Enterprise Institute for Public Policy Research.

Guest, Dennis. 1980. *The Emergence of Social Security in Canada.* Vancouver: University of British Columbia Press.

Gwirtzman, Milton. 1982. Remarks made on television by the chairman of the National Commission on Social Security, which were reported in the *Los Angeles Times*, December 6, 1982, pt. 1, p. 16.

Hale, George E., and Marian Lief Palley. 1981. *The Politics of Federal Grants.* Washington, D.C.: CQ Press.

Harbert, Anita S. 1976. *Federal Grants in Aid: Maximizing Benefits to the States.* New York: Praeger Publishers.

Harris, Louis. 1975. *The Myth and Reality of Aging in America.* Washington, D.C.: National Council on the Aging.

Harris, Richard. 1969. *A Sacred Trust*. Baltimore, Md.: Penguin Books.

Hart, Peter D. 1980. *A National Survey of Attitudes Toward Social Security*. Washington, D.C.: National Commission on Social Security.

Hartman, Chester. 1982. "Housing." In *What Reagan is Doing to Us*. Edited by Alan Gartner, Colin Greer, and Frank Riessman. New York: Harper & Row.

Heclo, Hugh. 1974. *Modern Social Politics in Britain and Sweden*. New Haven: Yale University Press.

———. 1977. *Study the Presidency*. New York: The Ford Foundation.

Hessel, Dicter. 1977. *Maggie Kuhn on Aging*. Philadelphia: Westminster Press.

Hofferbert, Richard I. 1974. *The Study of Public Policy*. Indianapolis, Ind.: The Bobbs-Merrill Co.

Holtzman, Abraham. 1963. *The Townsend Movement*. New York: Bookman Associates.

Horn, Linda, and Elma Griesel. 1977. *Nursing Homes: A Citizen's Action Guide*. Boston: Beacon Press.

Hsiao, William C. 1979. "An Optional Indexing Method for Social Security." In *Financing Social Security*. Edited by Colin D. Campbell. Washington, D.C.: American Enterprise Institute for Public Policy Research.

Hudson, Robert B. 1974. "Rational Planning and Organizational Imperatives: Prospects for Area Planning in Aging." *The Annals* 415 (September): 41-54.

———. 1978. "The 'Graying' of the Federal Budget and Its Consequences for Old-age Policy." *The Gerontologist* 18: 428-440.

———. 1981. "A Grant to the States for Long Term Care." *Journal of Health Politics, Policy and Law* 6 (Spring): 9-28.

International Center for Social Gerontology. 1977. *Congregate Housing for Older People*. Washington, D.C.: U.S. Department of Health, Education, and Welfare.

Jacobs, Jerry. 1974. "An Ethnographic Study of a Retirement Setting." *The Gerontologist* 14: 483-487.

Jacobson, Beverly. 1980. *Younger Programs for Older Workers: Case Studies in Progressive Personnel Policies*. New York: Van Nostrand Reinhold Co.

Johnson, Sheila K. 1971. *Idle Haven*. Berkeley, Calif.: University of California Press.

Kahn, Alfred J. 1979. *Social Policy and Social Services*. New York: Random House.

Kahn, Alfred J., and Sheila B. Kamerman. 1977. *Not for the Poor Alone: European Social Services*. Philadelphia: Temple University Press.

Kaim-Caudle, P. R. 1973. *Comparative Social Policy and Social Security: A Ten Nation Study*. Port Washington, N.Y.: Kennikat Press Corp.

Kane, Robert L., and Rosalie A. Kane. 1981a. "The Extent and Nature of Public Responsibility for Long Term Care." In *Policy Options in Long Term Care*. Edited by Judith Meltzer, Frank Farrow, and Harold Richman. Chicago: University of Chicago Press, 78-117.

____. 1981b. *Symposium: The Canadian Experience with a Universal Health System.* Annual Convention of the Gerontological Society, Toronto, Canada, November 9.

Kaplan, Robert S. 1979. "A Comparison of Rates of Return to Social Security Retirees under Wage and Price Indexing." In *Financing Social Security.* Edited by Colin D. Campbell. Washington, D.C.: American Enterprise Institute for Public Policy Research.

Kart, Cary S., and Barbara B. Manard. 1976. *Aging in America: Readings in Social Gerontology.* Port Washington, N.Y.: Alfred Publishers.

Klingman, David. 1982. "The Impact of Changing Intergovernmental Relations on State and Local Expenditures and Revenues." Paper presented at the Annual Convention of the American Political Science Association, Denver, Colo., Sept. 2-5.

Klingman, David, and William W. Lammers. 1980. "Age Discrimination and Retirement Policies in the States: Sources of Changing Innovation Patterns." Paper presented at the Annual Convention of the American Political Science Association, Washington, D.C., Aug. 28-31.

Ladd, Everett Carll, Jr. 1977. "The Unmaking of the Republican Party." *Fortune* 96 (September): 91-105.

Lammers, William W. 1980. "The Congressional Role in Pension and Retirement Policy." In *Work and Retirement: Policy Issues.* Edited by Pauline K. Ragan. Los Angeles: University of Southern California Press.

____. 1981. "Presidents and the Aging: Symbolism or Policy Leadership." Paper presented at the Western Social Science Association Convention, San Diego, Calif., April 23-25.

____. 1982. "Governors as Policy Leaders: A Quantitative Assessment." Paper presented at the Annual Convention of the American Political Science Association, Denver, Colo., Sept. 2-5.

Lammers, William W., and David Klingman. 1981a. "Consumer Protection and the Aging: Sources of State Regulatory Policy." Paper presented at the Western Political Science Association Convention, Denver, Colo., March 26-28.

____. 1981b. "Sources of Changing State Medicaid Policies for the Aging." Paper presented at the Annual Convention of the Gerontological Society, Toronto, Canada, November 5-8.

____. 1982. "Sources of Changing State Policy Efforts for the Aging." Final Report to the National Institute on Aging. Grant No. 5 RO 1 AG01408. Los Angeles: Andrus Gerontology Center.

Lammers, William W., and Joseph L. Nyomarkay. 1980. "The Disappearing Senior Leaders: Cabinet Member Age Structures in Western Nations, 1868-1978." *Research on Aging* 2 (September): 329-349.

Lampman, Robert J. 1977. *Ends and Means of Reducing Income Poverty.* Madison, Wis.: Institute for Research on Poverty.

LaPorte, Valerie, and Jeffrey Rubin. 1979. *Reform and Regulation of Long Term Care.* New York: Praeger Publishers.

Laurie, William F. 1981. *Need for Meals: A National Perspective*. Washington, D.C.: U.S. General Accounting Office.

Leaf, Alexander. 1982. "Long-lived Populations and Extreme Old Age." *American Geriatrics Society* 30 (August): 485-487.

Leuchtenberg, William E. 1963. *Franklin D. Roosevelt and the New Deal*. New York: Harper & Row.

Levin, Arthur. 1980. *Regulating Health Care*. New York: The Academy of Political Science.

Lilley, William, III. 1971. "Home Builder's Lobbying Skills Result in Success, 'Good-guy' Image." *National Journal* 2 (February 27): 431-435.

Lowi, Theodore J. 1964. "American Business, Public Policy, Case Studies, and Political Theory." *World Politics*, 16: 677-715.

———. 1969. *The End of Liberalism*. New York: W. W. Norton & Co.

Lowy, Louis. 1980. *Social Policies and Programs on Aging*. Lexington, Mass.: Lexington Books.

Lyell, Ruth Granetz, ed. 1980. *Middle Age, Old Age*. New York: Harcourt Brace Jovanovich.

McConnell, Stephen. 1980. "Alternative Work Patterns for an Aging Labor Force." In *Work and Retirement: Policy Issues*. Edited by Pauline K. Ragan. Los Angeles: University of Southern California Press.

McGill, Daniel M. 1975. *Fundamentals of Private Pensions*. 3d ed., 4th ed. Homewood, Ill.: Richard D. Irwin.

Malinchak, Alan. 1980. *Crime and Gerontology*. Englewood Cliffs, N.J.: Prentice-Hall.

Manard, Barbara B., et al. 1976. *Old Age Institutions*. Lexington, Mass.: Lexington Books.

———. 1977. *Better Homes for the Old*. Lexington, Mass.: Lexington Books.

Marmor, Theodore R. 1970. *The Politics of Medicare*. Chicago: Aldine Publishing Co.

Matura, Raymond C. 1981. "Self Advocacy by the Elderly: A Case Study." Paper presented at the Annual Convention of the Gerontological Society, Toronto, Canada, November 11.

Mendelson, Mary Adelaide. 1974. *Tender Loving Greed*. New York: Alfred A. Knopf.

Minnesota State Planning Agency. 1980. *Housing for the Elderly*. St. Paul, Minn.: The State of Minnesota.

Moss, Frank E., and Val J. Halamandaris. 1977. *Too Old, Too Sick, Too Bad*. Corte Madera, Calif.: Anthelion Press.

Moynihan, Daniel P. 1973. *The Politics of a Guaranteed Income*. New York: Vintage Books.

Munnell, Alicia. 1974. "The Impact of Social Security on Personal Savings." *National Tax Journal* 27 (December): 553-567.

———. 1977. *The Future of Social Security*. Washington, D.C.: The Brookings Institution.

References

Nader, Ralph, and Kate Blackwell. 1973. *You and Your Pension.* New York: Grossman Publishers.

National Center for Health Statistics. 1976. 1978. *Data from the National Health Survey.* Washington, D.C.: U.S. Department of Health, Education and Welfare.

National Commission on Social Security. 1981. *Social Security in America's Future.* Washington, D.C.: National Commission on Social Security.

Newman, Sandra J. 1980. "Government Policy and the Relationship Between Adult Children and Their Aging Parents: Filial Support, Medicare, and Medicaid." Paper presented at the Annual Convention of the Gerontological Society, San Diego, Calif., Nov. 23.

Office of Communication Research. 1980. *An Evaluation of Over Easy.* Washington, D.C.: Corporation for Public Broadcasting.

Oktay, Julian S., and Howard Palley. 1982. "Home Health and In-Home Service Programs for the Chronically-Limited Elderly: Some Equity and Adequacy Considerations." *Home Health Care Services Quarterly* 3 (Spring): 5-28.

Olson, Mancor, Jr. 1970. *The Logic of Collective Action: Public Goods and the Theory of Groups.* New York: Schocken Books.

Peterson, David A., Chuck Powell, and Laurie Robertson. 1976. "Aging in America: Toward the Year 2000." *The Gerontologist* 16: 264-270.

Peterson, George E. 1982. "The State and Local Sector." In *The Reagan Experiment.* Edited by John L. Palmer and Isabel V. Sawhill, 157-218. Washington, D.C.: The Urban Institute.

Poen, Monte M. 1979. *Harry S. Truman Versus the Medical Lobby: The Genesis of Medicare.* Columbia: University of Missouri Press.

Pollack, William. 1980. "Long Term Care." In *National Health Insurance: Conflicting Goals and Policy Choices.* Edited by Judith Feder et al. Washington, D.C.: The Urban Institute.

Posner, Barbara Millen. 1979. *Nutrition and the Elderly.* Lexington, Mass.: D. C. Heath & Co.

Pratt, Henry J. 1974. "Old Age Associations in National Politics." *The Annals* 415 (September): 106-119.

____. 1976. *The Gray Lobby.* Chicago: University of Chicago Press.

____. 1980. "Consolidation or Cooptation: Dilemmas of Mass-Based Associations." Paper presented at the Annual Convention of the Gerontological Society, San Diego, Calif., November 22.

President's Commission on Pension Policy. 1980. *Employment of Older Workers: Disincentives and Incentives.* Washington, D.C.: President's Commission on Pension Policy.

Price, Daniel N., and Andrea Novotny. 1977. "Federal Civil-Service Annuitants and Social Security." *Social Security Bulletin* (November): 6.

Public Citizen's Retired Professional Action Group. 1973. *Paying Through the Ear: A Report on Hearing Health Care Problems.* Washington, D.C.: Public Citizens.

Putnam, Jackson K. 1970. *Old-Age Politics in California: From Richardson to Reagan*. Stanford, Calif.: Stanford University Press.

Rabushka, Alvin, and Bruce Jacobs. 1980. *Old Folks at Home*. New York: The Free Press.

Rifkin, Jeremy, and Randy Barber. 1978. *The North Will Rise Again: Pensions, Politics and Power in the 1980s*. Boston: Beacon Press.

Riker, William H. 1964. *Federalism: Origin, Operation, Significance*. Boston: Little, Brown & Co.

Rimlinger, Gaston V. 1971. *Welfare Policy and Industrialization in Europe, America, and Russia*. New York: John Wiley & Sons.

Ripley, Randall B., and Grace A. Franklin. 1976. *Congress, the Bureaucracy, and Public Policy*. Homewood, Ill.: Dorsey Press.

Robertson, A. Haeworth. 1981. *The Coming Revolution in Social Security*. Reston, Va.: Reston Publishing Co.

Rosenbaum, Walter A. 1981. *Energy, Politics and Public Policy*. Washington, D.C.: CQ Press.

Rosenfeld, Albert. 1976. *Prolongevity*. New York: Alfred A. Knopf.

Rosow, Irving. 1967. *Social Integration of the Aged*. New York: The Free Press.

Ross, Stanford G. 1980. "Income Security: A Framework for Reform." *National Journal* (October 10): 1772-1777.

Rubenstein, James M. 1979. "Housing Policy Issues in Three European Countries." Paper delivered at the Annual Convention of the Gerontological Society, Washington, D.C., November 28.

Salisbury, Robert. 1970. *Interest Group Politics in America*. New York: Harper & Row.

Samuelson, Robert J. 1978. "Busting the U.S. Budget: The Costs of Aging in America." *National Journal* 10 (February 18): 256-260.

———. 1981. "Death and Taxes." *National Journal* 13 (July 4): 1992-1996.

———. 1982. "Misbehaving Budget." *National Journal* 14 (March 20): 516.

Sanders, Heywood T. 1980. "Paying for the 'Bloody Shirt': The Politics of Civil War Pensions." In *Political Benefits*. Edited by Barry S. Rundquist. Lexington, Mass.: Lexington Books.

Schiltz, Michael. 1970. *Public Attitudes Toward Social Security, 1935-1965*. Social Security Administration. Office of Research and Statistics. Research Report No. 33. Washington, D.C.: U.S. Department of Health, Education, and Welfare.

Schottland, Charles I. 1970. *The Social Security Program in the United States*. 2d. ed. Englewood Cliffs, N.J.: Prentice-Hall.

Schulz, James H. 1980. *The Economics of Aging*. Belmont, Calif.: Wadsworth Publishing Co.

Sharkansky, Ira. 1968. *Spending in the American States*. Chicago: Rand McNally & Co.

———. 1972. *The Maligned States: Policy Accomplishments, Problems, and Opportunities*. New York: McGraw-Hill.

Sheppard, Harold L., and Sara E. Rix. 1977. *The Graying of Working America: The Coming Crisis in Retirement-Age Policy.* New York: The Free Press.

Silverman, Milton, and Philip R. Lee. 1974. *Pills, Profits and Politics.* Berkeley: University of California Press.

Smith, David Barton. 1981. *Long Term Care in Transition: The Regulation of Nursing Homes.* Washington, D.C.: AUPHA Press.

Soderstrom, Lee. 1978. *The Canadian Health System.* London: Croom Helm.

Stanfield, Rochelle L. 1981. "Ready for 'New Federalism,' Phase II?" *National Journal* 13 (August 22): 1492-1497.

Stein, Bruno. 1980. *Social Security and Pensions in Transition: Understanding the American Retirement System.* New York: The Free Press.

Steinberg, Raymond M. 1978. "Case Coordination: Lessons From the Past for Future Program Models." Paper presented at the National Conference on Social Welfare, Los Angeles, Calif., May 24.

Steinberg, Raymond M., and Genevieve W. Carter. 1983. *Designing Case Management: A Handbook for Development, Implementation, and Evaluation of Case Coordination Programs for the Elderly.* Lexington, Mass.: Lexington Books.

Stevens, Robert, and Ruth Stevens. 1974. *Welfare Medicine in America: A Case Study of Medicaid.* New York: Free Press.

Stoddard, Sandol. 1978. *The Hospice Movement: A Better Way of Caring for the Dying.* New York: Stein & Day.

Strehler, Bernard. 1974. "Implications of Aging Research for Society." vol 34. no. 1. Proceedings of the Annual Meeting of the Federation of American Societies for Experimental Biology.

Struyk, Raymond J., and Beth J. Soldo. 1980. *Improving the Elderly's Housing.* Cambridge, Mass.: Ballinger Publishing Co.

Sundquist, James L. 1968. *Politics and Policy: The Eisenhower, Kennedy and Johnson Years.* Washington, D.C.: The Brookings Institution.

Sussman, Marvin B. 1976. "The Family Life of Old People." In *The Handbook of Aging and the Social Sciences.* Edited by Robert H. Binstock and Ethel Shanas. New York: Van Nostrand Reinhold Co.

Taylor, Malcolm G. 1978. *Health Insurance and Canadian Public Policy.* Montreal: McGill-Queens University Press.

Tilove, Robert. 1976. *Public Employee Pension Funds.* New York: Columbia University Press.

Treas, Judith. 1982. "Women's Employment and Its Implications for the Status of the Elderly of the Future." In *The Elderly of the Future.* Edited by James G. March. New York: Academic Press.

Tufte, Edward R. 1978. *Political Control of the Economy.* Princeton, N.J.: Princeton University Press.

U.S. Department of Commerce. Bureau of the Census. 1980. *Annual Survey of Housing.* Washington, D.C.: U.S. Government Printing Office.

___. Bureau of the Census. 1981. *Statistical Abstract of the United States.* Washington, D.C.: U.S. Government Printing Office.

U.S. Department of Labor. 1976. *The Earnings Gap Between Men and Women.* Washington, D.C.: U.S. Government Printing Office.

U.S. House. Select Committee on Aging. 1981. "Analysis of the Fiscal Impact of the Proposed Fiscal Year Budget Cuts on the Elderly." Washington, D.C.: U.S. Government Printing Office.

U.S. Senate. Special Committee on Aging. 1979. *The Proposed Fiscal 1980 Budget: What it Means for Older Americans.* Washington, D.C.: U.S. Government Printing Office.

——. Special Committee on Aging. 1981. *Energy and the Aged.* Washington, D.C.: U.S. Government Printing Office.

——. Subcommittee on Aging, Family and Human Services. Committee on Labor and Human Services. 1981. Hearing on Low-Income Energy Assistance. March 24. Washington, D.C.: U.S. Government Printing Office.

Uslaner, Eric M., and Ronald E. Weber. 1977. *Patterns of Decision Making in State Legislatures.* New York: Praeger Publishers.

Verba, Sidney, and Norman H. Nie. 1972. *Participation in America.* New York: Harper & Row.

Viscusi, W. Kip. 1979. *Welfare of the Elderly: An Economic Analysis and Policy Prescription.* New York: John Wiley & Sons.

Vladeck, Bruce C. 1980. *Unloving Care: The Nursing Home Tragedy.* New York: Basic Books.

Walker, James W., and Harriet L. Lazer. 1978. *The End of Mandatory Retirement: Implications for Management.* New York: John Wiley & Sons.

Weiler, Philip, and Eloise Rathbone-McCuan. 1978. *Adult Day Care: Community Work with the Elderly.* N.Y., N.Y.: Springer Publishing Co.

Weissert, William G. 1980. "Toward a Continuum of Care for the Elderly: A Note of Caution." Paper presented at the Annual Meeting of the American Public Health Association, Detroit, Mich., October 19-23.

Weissert, William G. et al. 1980. "Effects and Costs of Day-Care Services for the Chronically Ill." *Medical Care* 18 (June): 567-583.

White House Conference on Aging. 1981. Summary Reports of the Chairmen.

Wilensky, Harold L. 1975. *The Welfare State and Equality.* Berkeley, Calif.: University of California Press.

Williamson, John B.; Linda Evans; and Lawrence Powell. 1982. *The Politics of Aging: Power and Policy.* Springfield, Ill.: Charles C. Thomas, Publisher.

Winiecke, Linda. 1973. "The Appeal of Age Segregated Housing to the Elderly Poor." *International Journal of Aging and Human Development* 4: 293-306.

Wiseman, Robert F. 1979. "Regional Patterns of Elderly Concentration and Migration." In *Location and Environment of Elderly Population.* Edited by Stephen M. Golant, 21-36. Washington, D.C.: V. H. Winston & Sons.

Witte, Edwin. 1962. *The Development of the Social Security Act.* Madison, Wis.: University of Wisconsin Press.

Zimmerman, Jack M. 1981. *Hospice: Complete Care for the Terminally Ill.* Baltimore-Munich: Urban Schwarzenberg.

SUGGESTIONS FOR FURTHER STUDY

The preceding list of references that appear in the text should be useful to readers who want to examine specific topics in more detail. Included in these suggestions for further study are particularly helpful source materials, works with extensive bibliographies, and recent compilations.

For background on general characteristics of the aging, see Robert H. Binstock and Ethel Shanas, *Handbook of Aging and the Social Sciences* (New York: Van Nostrand Reinhold Co., 1976); Richard H. Davis, ed., *Aging: Prospects and Issues*, 3rd rev. ed. (Lexington, Mass.: Lexington Books, 1981); Cary S. Kart and Barbara B. Manard, *Aging in America: Readings in Social Gerontology* (Port Washington, N.Y.: Alfred Publishing Co., 1976); David J. Mangen and Warren A. Peterson, *Research Instruments in Social Gerontology: Social Roles and Social Participation*, vol. 2 (Minneapolis, Minn.: University of Minnesota Press, 1982); and Diana S. Woodruff and James E. Birren, *Aging: Scientific Perspectives and Social Issues*, 2nd ed. (Monterey, Calif.: Brooks/Cole Publishing Co., 1983).

For political interpretations of aging issues, see Martha Derthick, *Policymaking for Social Security* (Washington, D.C.: The Brookings Institution, 1979); Robert B. Hudson, ed., *Aging in Politics: Process and Policy* (Springfield, Ill.: Charles C. Thomas, 1981); Theodore R. Marmor, *The Politics of Medicare* (Chicago: Aldine Publishing Co., 1970); and Henry J. Pratt, *The Gray Lobby* (Chicago: University of Chicago Press, 1976).

Helpful analyses of the Social Security system include Robert M. Ball, *Social Security: Today and Tomorrow* (New York: Columbia University Press, 1978); James H. Schulz, *The Economics of Aging* (Belmont, Calif.: Wadsworth Publishing Co., 1980); and Bruno Stein, *Social Security and Pensions in Transition: Understanding the American Retirement Sys-*

tem (New York: The Free Press, 1980). Scholarly works on retirement policy include Robert L. Clark and David T. Barker, *Reversing the Trend Toward Early Retirement* (Washington, D.C.: American Enterprise Institute for Public Policy Research, 1981) and Harold L. Sheppard and Sara E. Rix, *The Graying of Working America: The Coming Crisis in Retirement Age Policy* (New York: The Free Press, 1977).

On health policy issues, see Judith Feder, John Holahan, and Theodore R. Marmor, *National Health Insurance: Conflicting Goals and Policy Choices* (Washington, D.C.: The Urban Institute, 1980) and Bruce C. Vladeck, *Unloving Care: The Nursing Home Tragedy* (New York: Basic Books, 1980). Social services have been reviewed and evaluated in Carroll L. Estes, *The Aging Enterprise* (San Francisco, Calif.: Jossey-Bass, 1979) and Louis Lowy, *Social Policies and Programs on Aging*. For discussions of housing policies, see Jon Pynoos, John Schafer, and Robert Hartman, eds., *Housing Urban America* and Raymond J. Struyk and Beth J. Soldo, *Improving the Elderly's Housing: A Key to Preserving the Nation's Housing Stock and Neighborhoods* (Cambridge, Mass.: Ballinger Publishing Co., 1980).

Several government publications also are extremely useful. Commission reports on the Social Security system released in 1981 and 1983 contain extensive analyses. For annual trends, see *Developments in Aging*, published by the U.S. Senate Special Committee on Aging. For expenditure data on specific programs, see the *Statistical Abstract of the United States*, published annually by the Census Bureau and the *Special Analyses of the U.S. Budget*, published annually by the Office of Management and Budget.

INDEX